# *One* COSMOS *under* GOD

# OMEGA BOOKS

The OMEGA BOOKS series from Paragon House is dedicated to classic and contemporary works about human development and the nature of ultimate reality, encompassing the fields of mysticism and spirituality, psychic research and paranormal phenomena, the evolution of consciousness, and the human potential for self-directed growth in body, mind, and spirit.

John White, M.A.T., Series Editor of OMEGA BOOKS, is an internationally known author and educator in the fields of consciousness research and higher human development.

**MORE TITLES IN OMEGA BOOKS**

BEYOND THE HUMAN SPECIES: The Life and Work of Sri Aurobindo and the Mother, *Georges van Vrekhem*

THE GHOSTS OF CONSCIOUSNESS
*Herbert Demin, Ph.D.*

KUNDALINI: EMPOWERING HUMAN EVOLUTION
Selected Writings of Gopi Krishna, *edited by Gene Kieffer*

KUNDALINI EVOLUTION AND ENLIGHTENMENT
*Edited by John White*

LIFECYCLES: Reincarnation and the Web of Life
*Christopher M. Bache*

THE MEETING OF SCIENCE AND SPIRIT
Guidelines for a New Age, *John White*

ONENESS PERCEIVED: A Window Into Enlightenment
*Jeffrey Eisen, Ph.D.*

THE RADIANCE OF BEING: Understanding the Grand Integral Vision; Living the Integral Life
*Allan Combs, Foreword by Ken Wilber*

THE SACRED MIRROR: Nondual Wisdom and Psychotherapy
*John J. Prendergast, Peter Fenner, and Shiela Krystal*

# *One* COSMOS *Under* GOD

*The Unification of Matter, Life, Mind & Spirit*

ROBERT W. GODWIN

PARAGON HOUSE
St. Paul, Minnesota

Published in the United States by
Paragon House
2285 University Avenue West
St. Paul, Minnesota 55114



The Omega Books series from Paragon House is dedicated to classic and contemporary works about human development and the nature of ultimate reality.

**Library of Congress Cataloging-in-Publication Data**

Godwin, Robert W., 1955-
One cosmos under God : the unification of matter, life, mind & spirit / Robert Godwin.-- 1st ed.
p. cm.
Includes bibliographical references.
ISBN 1-55778-836-7 (pbk. : alk. paper)
1. Creation. I. Title.

BL325.C7G63 2004
213--dc22
2004009455

Illustrations by Gusave Dore (1861–1868), for Dante's Divine Comedy.

Manufactured in the United States of America

The paper used in this publication meets the minimum requirements of American National Standard for Information Sciences—Permanence of Paper for Printed Library Materials, ANSIZ39.48-1984.

10 9 8 7 6 5 4 3 2 1

For current information about all releases from Paragon House, visit the web site at www.paragonhouse.com

The modernistic searcher after meaning may be likened to a man furiously beating the earth and imagining that the finer he pulverizes it, the nearer he will get to the riddle of existence. But no synthesizing truths lie in that direction. It is in the opposite direction that the path must be followed....

—Richard Weaver, *Visions of Order*

The misfortune that has overtaken the spiritual outlook of man is that as his universe expanded his conception of the deity did not expand with it.

—F. Wood Jones, *Design and Purpose*

All time is one body, Space a single book.

—Sri Aurobindo, *Savitri*

FOR LESLIE.

*In loving memory of*

KT MORRIS SAMUELS

*and to two left in her Wake,*

STEVE AND AIDEN.

*May the circle be unbroken.*

# CONTENTS

## Book Three
## Psychogenesis: The Presence of Mind . . . 91



## Book Four
## Cosmotheosis: It's a Onederful Life . . . 185

# APOLOGIA *&* JOYCETIFICATION

"What was that all about, then?" Anticipating the bewildered reaction of the unwary reader, perhaps a few words are in order in regard to the brief *tour de farce* that opens (and closes and reopens) this absurcular book. Those familiar with James Joyce's famously obscure masterpiece, *Finnegans Wake,* will undoubtedly recognize the inspiration, if not the rationale, behind the seemingly abstruse "preramble" that follows. *Finnegans Wake,* in order to achieve its purpose of composing a universal human history in the form of one long dream in the mind of a single sleeping individual, playfully disintegrates and recombines words from more than a dozen languages, and has a circular design, beginning and ending in the middle of the same sentence.

Why circular? When asked, Joyce replied that he was endeavoring in *Finnegans Wake* to bore "into a mountain from two sides. The question is how to meet in the middle."[1] In his case, he was specifically attempting to enter the collective dream world of mankind through the only two shafts of light available to him: our "fall" into sleep and the "wake" out of it.[2] Finnegans Wake begins and ends in "the suspended tick of time between a [sleep] cycle just passed and one about to begin,"[3] enunciating all of the themes that Joyce elaborated and expanded upon throughout the remainder of the book.

The mountain this book attempts to "bore through" is the very cosmos, the whole of creation, the totality of interacting objects, events, forces, and laws. Science, as we have come to understand it, bores through the cosmic mountain from one side, the side of *quantities,* of objects interacting with one another. As such, the scientific "book of

1. Quoted in Bishop, 1986, p. 20.

2. Ibid.

3. Campbell & Robinson, 1980, p. 15.

nature" is necessarily linear and ends in genuine absurdity, since it can never explain or "meet up" with the one doing the boring: the irreducibly *qualitative* human subject. Idealist philosophies bore through the mountain from the opposite direction, but also fail to meet in the middle, as they either dismiss the material world as illusory, or neglect to ground our subjectivity in something more fundamental. In effect, both sides climb into a metaphysical hole and try to pull the whole in after them, which makes an unholy mess of metaphysics.

The aim of this book is to bore through the cosmic mountain from both sides: from the *inside out,* where science explores a world of diverse material objects and forces to which we are subject, and from the *outside in,* where the teeming multiplicity of the world is synthesized in the transcendental human subject. Is there a center where these two shafts could possibly meet? Without jumping too far ahead (or behind), let us stipulate that the brief creation myth that follows is a playgiarized "telogram" pieced together from a host of rumors, fragments, and tidings that have been making the metaphysical rounds for the past 2500 years or so. Borrowing freely from Christian, Greek, Jewish, Hindu, Taoist and other sources, the creation to which it refers did not happen just "once upon a time" some 13.7 billion years ago, but occurs continuously, in the timeless ground anterior to each moment. Er, how's that? Put it this way: neither the cosmos nor this book have a proper "beginning," but both have a *center,* a center that starts where science ends and must therefore be described in mythological terms. The purpose of myth is to help us re-collect what we have forgotten about our timeless source, our eternal nature, and our ultimate destiny. The metamyth that follows is no different, as it attempts to lift the veil and peer back "before" creation—it is a Word from our *eternal* Sponsor, and should not be evaluated from the standpoint of *time.*

Nor should it come as any surprise that grammatical lawlessness breaks out at the infra-linguistic and ultra-semantic frontiers of this book, where Subject and Object no longer exist as a basis for rational, "wideawake and cutandry" language. After all, we are attempting to venture where language cannot go, to eff the ineffable, unscrew the inscrutable, and English the unglishable.[4] As Eliot put it, "Words strain, crack and sometimes break" under such a burden. While I make no claim to be a poet, it is probably best to first read my cracked and broken "punnish antic" in a rhythmic, incantatory, mantric fashion, without eagerly grasping at the meaning or peeking at the fine print (the exblarnetory footnotes which translate the blarney into plain English).[5] Every word of it makes *perfect* nonsense, and couldn't really have been conveyed in a more unigmatic manner. However, if for any reason the reader finds this brief prologue to be more of an unspeakable overchore, I ask you to please forgive my syntax and "bore with me," as we soon restore order to the language, pitch our tense in a familiar locution, and set our course for the heart of the magic mountain that lies before, behind, ahead and, most importantly, inside of us.

---

4. I believe Alan Watts is responsible for "unscrew the inscrutable," but I'm not sure about "eff the ineffable," although it is not original to me. "Wideawake and cutandry" is from *Finnegans Wake.*

5. The footnotes may also provide a helpful glossary for when some of the same words and concepts are used later.

# COSMONAUGHT:
## *Before The Beginning*

Imagine a state of being prior to the manifestation of the universe—prior to the Big Bang, if you prefer it—in which there is no differentiation between subject and object; it is a universally diffused blend of subjectivity and objectivity. There is no focus of awareness to which anything could appear as an object. So there is no I and no It, no here and no there, no now and no then. It is uniform, all over at once. Mystics describe it as nothingness, or as being-consciousness-bliss.

—Sri Madhava Ashish, *Relating to Reality*

Or say that the end precedes the beginning,
And the end and beginning were always there
Before the beginning and after the end.
And all is always now. Words strain,
Crack and sometimes break, under the burden...

—T. S. Eliot, *Four Quartets*

There was something formless and perfect
before the universe was born.
It is serene. Empty.
Solitary. Unchanging.
Infinite. Eternally present.
It is the Mother of the universe....

—Stephen Mitchell [Tr.], *Tao Te Ching*

1. This black whole is not a blank page, but a page full of nothing, as "There is something in the soul which is above the soul, divine, simple, an absolute nothing; rather unnamed than named; unknown than known.... higher than knowledge, higher than love, higher than grace, for in all these there is still a distinction." Meister Eckardt, quoted in Radhakrishnan Vol 2, p. 485.

# .... nothing,

*pure emptiness, a formless void without mind or life, a shadow spinning before the beginning over a silent static sea, unlit altar of eternity, fathomless vortex of the Infinite Zero.*[2] *Darkest night, dreamless sleep:*[3] *Outside in. Spacetimematterenergy. No beforeafter, nobodaddy, no mamafestation, nothing but neti.*[4] *One brahman deathless breathing breathless, darkness visible the boundless all. Unknown origin prior to time and space, fount of all being, unborn thus undying, beginning and end of all impossibility, empty plenum and inexhaustible void. Who is? I AM. A wake. A lone. Hallow, noumena!*[5]

---

2. "What is eternal cannot have a beginning, and whatever has a beginning is not eternal." Shankara. "The **Void** is beginning and end itself," the "Final Reality," the "All Peaceful," " the state of perfect enlightenment." Leary, et al, p. 117. "The divine nature is like a **sea** of essence, indeterminate and without bounds, which spreads far and wide beyond all notion of time or of nature." Lossky, 2002, p. 36. "The highest superontological principle, symbolized by **zero**, is designated as the Infinite, that is, what is limited by nothing, by no specific nature or essence, and which therefore encompasses everything and knows no contradiction." Borella, in Faivre, 1995, p. 342. "Primordial unity is in fact nothing other than the affirmation of Zero." Guenon, 181, p. 57.

3. "... in the relative world the nearest approach to the peace and desirelessness of Brahman is the experience of deep **[dreamless] sleep**." Nikhilananda, Vol 1, p. 94. "I dreamt that I... was pregnant and full with Nothingness... And that out of this Nothingness God was born." Eckhart, 1982, in Fox [tr], p. 71.

4. ***Neti neti***, meaning "It is not this, It is not that." There is no positive conception by which we can name, limit, or define it. Ultimately we can only say what it is not.

5. **Noumena**: the unknowable ultimate reality behind appearances.

**In The Beginning** was the weird, and the weird was with God, and the weird was God. But it was not good that this Godhead, the Most High, should be allone, so He expired with a big bong and said "let there be higher physics," and it was zo.[6] "Zohar zo good," zedamon to himzeus.[7] And nothing He made was it made without being made of the weird light with which everything was made from the Word (lo)go.[8] And after about nine billion years the weird became flesh, and eventually began asking questions. And the weird light shines in the dark, but the dorks don't comprehend it.[9] For truly, the weirdness was spread all through the world, and yet, the world basically kept behaving as if this were just your ordinary, standard-issue cosmos.[10]

---

6. "Breathing is a microcosmic representation of the macro-cosmic process." Woodroffe, 2001, p. 49. "The Breath carries the Word and enables it to find utterance; the Word makes the silence of the Breath heard..." Clement, 1993, p. 64. **"Expired"** can also be taken in another sense, in that the universe is "God's sacrifice" of His unlimited potential (non-being) through manifestation (being). "That there should be **physics** is a miracle." Nobel laureate physicist James Cronin, quoted in Kass, 2003, p. 38. "Nature is supernatural," wrote the poet Browning.

7. The ***Zohar*** is a mystical Jewish text of esoteric speculations on the origin of the universe and the nature of the Godhead.

8. The weird, uncreated light of the ***logos*** "is identical with the Pneuma, the Breath or Holy Spirit..." Pryse, 1965, p. 10. It is both the divine intelligence manifest in creation and the intelligibility of creation manifest in the human mind.

9. "Nothing comes into existence unless the divine spark of consciousness, no matter how faint or dim, lies at its center." Smoley, 2002, p. 135. "Sparks of holiness are imprisoned in the stuff of creation. They yearn to be set free, united with their Source... " Kushner, 1998, p. 113.

10. "The universe is not only queerer than we suppose, it is queerer than we can suppose." J.B.S. Haldane. Terence McKenna elaborated on this in a lecture, adding

In etherworlds: Once upon a timaeus, One's upin a timeless without a second to spore and noplace to bang anyway.[11] The abbasolute first day, before eve or any other middling relativities.[12] Only himsoph with nowhere to bewrong, hovering over the waters without a kenosis.[13] Vishnu were here, but just His lux, God only knows only God, and frankly, ishvara monotheotonous--no one beside Him, no nous, same old shunyada yada yada.[14] Jewsus, allah you'd be sikh of siddhing Oround all naught playing soliptaire too![15] Ah, this old ombody's so philled with jehoviality, can't He create anamour?[16] 'Elo, him, what

---

that, since the world is stranger than we can suppose, we might as well suppose that it is as strange as we can suppose, because that still won't be strange enough. This is my best shot.

11. **Ether,** ethereal: referring to the immaterial, unworldly, upper regions beyond the earth. The ***Timaeus,*** of course, was Plato's dialogue on the origins of the cosmos. Ultimate reality is **One without a second.**

12. In ultimate reality all **relativities** are dissolved. At this level of pure metaphysics, "everything belonging to the individual order is truly nonexistent,... being entirely detached from all relativities..." Guenon, 1981, p. 14.

13. ***Kenosis*** in Orthodox Christianity is "the self-emptying or self-surrender of the Godhead whereby he both creates the world and becomes incarnate in the Son of Man." Watts, 1994, p. 60.

14. In Hinduism ***Ishvara*** is God with attributes, as opposed to the impersonal Brahman that is beyond attributes. "The first emanation of the original essence is **Nous....** The indivisible unity of the Nous is the archetype of the whole visible world." Radhakrishnan, 1939, pp. 209, 210. ***Shunyata:*** the void, the Nothing which is the non-dual ground and source of all.

15. ***Siddhi*** refers to spiritual powers.

16. ***Om*** "May be compared to the Word in Christianity... or the Greek Logos, from which the creative process began." Adiswarananda, 2003, p. 106. **Phil**led: "... there is no greater love than that of the sacrifice of eternity for the limitations of existence in the transient moment." Tomberg, 1992, p. 45. An**amor**: Love "first emanates from God to humans and then from humans to God." Markides, 2001, p. 46.

samadhi you?[17] Stop deidreaming and gita life, bodhi![18] Make sefiromthing of yoursaleph![19]

Olaf! What a punnish ontic![20] Is the author of this cacography an ainsoferable gnosis all or just an inrisible mythmatician?[21] Don't kid the keter, telos what happyns next in this holy babel of eccluesiastical scraptures.[22] Seelambs! Is a prophet without honor in his own homily? Lesson! My yokes are easy, my words enlight.[23] Beholied! A divine desire to reveil and find Itself, unnarcissary yet inevitable, conceived in d'light immaculate (every lila son of adwaita is born of a voidgin) and now swelling in the night-filled womb of unmanifest being, the radiant urizon of an insindiary Dawn approaches.[24] Brahma, when puru-

---

17. ***Elohim:*** one of the Hebrew names for God. ***Samadhi:*** total absorption of consciousness in the godhead.

18. A ***bodhisattva*** is one who renounces the eternal peace of ***nirvana*** and pledges to incarnate until all sentient beings have achieved the same.

19. The ***Sefiroth*** or Sefirotic tree is the key to the Kabbalistic system of cosmogenesis, forming the prototype of both man and the created universe. Along with the Torah and Talmud, the Kabbalah "may be called God's dream of the existence of the world and the existence of man." Steinsaltz, 1980, p. 89. **"Aleph,"** the first letter of the Hebrew alphabet, is related to the Greek alpha, which also refers to the "beginning." "I am the beginning, the middle and the end in creation.... In the alphabet, I am A." Bhagavad Gita (Isherwood), p. 110.

20. The **Upanishads** embody the highest esoteric wisdom of Vedanta (Hindu) philosophy, and consist of meditations on the nature of ultimate reality, called *brahman,* and how to attain it. **Ontic:** relating to or having real being.

21. The ***ain sof*** of Kabbalistic thought refers to the ultimate, unknowable, limitless and infinite Godhead, similar to the Hindu *brahman.* ***Gnosis*** is higher spiritual knowledge.

22. The ***keter*** is the crown of the Kabbalistic *sefirot* and first emanation of the *ain sof.* It is analogous to the dimensionless point that contained everything prior to "exploding into manifestation with the Big Bang." Smoley & Kinney, 1999, p. 79. The ***telos*** is the spiritual end toward which the cosmos is striving (I hope).

sha comes to shiva with an unmentionable demiurge (the unspoken Word), how Lo can He go?[25] How about all the way inside-out and upside down, a vidy long descent

---

23. "A prophet is not without honor" except in his own family, house and country. *Mark* 6:4. "My yoke is easy and my burden is light." *Matthew* 11:30.

24. "[T]he play of the Self is to lose itself and to find itself in a game of hide-and-seek without beginning or end. In losing itself it is dismembered: it forgets that it is the one and only reality, and plays that it is the vast multitude of beings and things which make up this world." Watts, 1968, p. 96. **Reveiled:** "when the divine plenty is manifested in its complete fullness there is no room for the existence of anything else. A world can exist only as a result of the concealment of its Creator." Steinsaltz, 1980, p. 20. **Unnarcissary:** "The act of creation.... is the spontaneous overflow of God's nature.... Out of the fulness of his joy, God scatters abroad life and power." Radhakrishnan, Vol 2, p. 551. "God's motive in creation is his love.... Creation is not an act so much of his free will as of his free love. Ware, 1979, p. 44. "The universe is created in **Delight** and for Delight." Sri Aurobindo, 1970, p.7 "Advaita" is pronounced ***"adwoita"*** (read: "a daughter" with a sort of modified Brooklyn accent), meaning non-dual knowledge of ultimate reality. In Hindu cosmology the entire universe is ***"lila,"*** or God's play. In a cosmic sense we are all born of a **"voidgin"** or "virgin," for "the Father ceaselessly begets his Son and, what is more, he begets me as his son--the selfsame Son!" Meister Eckhart, quoted in Smoley, 2002, p. 26. *Brahman* comes from the root *brih,* "to expand" or "**swell,**" implying also a "force which unfolds" (von Bruck,1991, p. 22). "The original unity is pregnant with the whole course of the world, which contains the past, the present and the future in a supreme now." Radhakrishnan, Vol 1, p. 540. "The Silence is Full and Pregnant, and out of It flows the Stream of all formations, in endless variety: symphonies, philosophies, governments, sciences, arts, societies, and so on and on and on." Merrell-Wolff, 1994, p, 31. **Urizen**, in William Blake's visionary mythology, refers to "the figure of Jehovah but, also a symbol of man in bondage. It represents the limiting mental power of reason, an analytical and destructive force which dominates man and against which man must struggle." Benet, The Reader's Encyclopedia (2nd edition), p. 1042. "The sundering of the Absolute into the personal God and object is creation's **dawn**." Radhakrishnan, 1939, p. 125.

25. ***Brahma:*** From Brahman springs forth Brahma, "who embodies the process of evolution into name and form by which the One appears to be many." Easwaran, 1987, p. 110. ***Purusha:*** the absolute soul or conscious principle of the cosmos. ***Shiva:*** the destructive aspect of the Hindu trinity. ***Demiurge:*** deity who fashions the sensible world in the light of the eternal ideas.

indeed to the farthest reaches of sorrow and ignorance?[26] Yes, a scorched-birth policy, an experiment in higher kab-boomallistics! A self-willed division, expulsion & exile, and badda-bing, badda-

26. ***Avidya:*** Consciousness of multiplicity separated from knowledge of the One; a state of error, delusion, and ignorance. "Eternal, he assents to Fate and Time, Immortal, dallies with mortality, The All-Conscious ventured into Ignorance..." Aurobindo, 1993, p. 66. "The prime source of *samsara,* the relative universe, is beginningless ignorance (avidya)..." Nikhilananda, Vol 2, p. 25.

a wondrous thunder rends it all asunder.[27] (Ixnay on the reatio ex nihilo cay, it's a scientific blastferme and you, agape in their beloved theory.)[28] The molten infinite pours forth a blazen torrent of incandescent finitude, as light plunges an undying fire into its own shadow (oops! a dirty world) and

---

27. Divine consciousness "bursts out into manifestation, manifesting itself to itself. Only when subject is differentiated from object, when awareness is differentiated from the content of awareness, can the content of the Divine Mind, all that is potentially present within it, be unfolded across the fields of space and time." Ashish, in Ginsburg, 2001, p. 249. "[T]he fall of consciousness into matter parallels the trauma we all undergo at birth, as we are expelled from the unity of the womb. In a visceral sense, we are all **exiled** in this world." Smoley & Kinney, 1999, p. 39. **Badda-bing, badda-bang:** "[T]he universe is a laughing matter.... When you have fulfilled the Teaching of Truth, then you get the joke of human existence.... that joke is eternal and its Humor is Infinite Bliss." Da Free John, quoted in Dowman, 1980, p. 18. We might also say that the enlightenment is the Joke beyond which there is no Funnier, in the sense that it is the ultimate case of being led to believe the cosmos was one thing (the setup), only to make the delightful discovery that it is something else entirely (the punch line). A joke is a "vignette of salvation," in that "it illuminates, in a flash, the ultimate fate of man's relation to the universe. That fate is liberating laughter." Berger, 1990, p. 118.

28. **Creation *ex nihilo,*** or out of nothing, "is the highest possible expression of magic, namely divine and cosmic magic." Powell, 2002, p. 47. This explosion was not so much a bang as a blossoming seed: "It is not too difficult to imagine, because each little acorn is such a 'constructive bomb' and the oak is only the visible result of the slow 'explosion'--or blossoming out--of this 'bomb.'" op cit, p. 68. And if you understand this, you understand why the "Tree of Life" eternally exists with its roots aloft, its branches down here below. ***Agape:*** love. For a long time, scientists were very uncomfortable with the big bang, implying as it does so many scientific "blasphemies." After all, the dictionary tells us that "belief" and "beloved" are etymologically linked, so it's not that easy to part ways with a beloved belief in blind materialism.

F

A-A

L-L-L

L-L-L-L-L-L-L

S-S-S-S-S-S-S-S-S-S-S-S[29]

in love with the productions of time, hurtling higgledy-piggledy into jivass godlings & samskara monsters (Boo!) all the way down.[30] And thank-you we said, thanking the Man for this undertaking of mortality, for our daily lessons in evanescence, for this manifestivus for the rest of us.[31]

---

29. **Dirty world:** "[T]he whole order of relations among the various worlds may be conceived in images of intimate engagement, a kind of sexual contact between one world and another, between one level of being and another." Steinsaltz, 1980, p. 166. The "**fall** can be seen as an entrance into the dimension of time.... the Fall of humankind did happen, but it did not happen on any segment of history's timeline; rather, the Fall engendered time as we now experience it." Smoley, 2002, pp. 60, 65. Esoterically understood, it is a fall of "God in himself, into a dividing consciousness which brings with it all the train of dualities, life and death, good and evil, joy and pain...." Sri Aurobindo, 1970, p. 51. "The tragedy of original sin is that the world is turned upside-down." Kovalesky, in Amis, 1995, p. 205. Keep this important point in mind for later.

30 ***Jiva, Jivas*** (pl.): Brahman associated with the individual living soul, ignorant of its divine nature. **Godlings:** "only man, by virtue of his divine soul, has the potential, and some of the actual capacity, of God Himself," including the powers of will and creativity. Steinsaltz, 1980, p. 51. ***Samskara:*** habitual psychological patterns & reactions formed by one's past actions. **Hurtling higgledy piggledy:** "... consciousness scatters. It breaks up into smaller and smaller fragments, becoming increasingly heavy and obscure, forming into layers or worlds peopled with their own beings and forces, each with its particular life." Satprem, 1984, p. 303.

Wholly matterimany, how could such malkutents ever pay bhakta the One who unfurled this bhogas world?[32]

Congratulations on the equation of your cosmic birth![33] Oh my stars, He expectorated a mirrorcle, now you're the spittin' image![34] You haven't perceived the hologram to your private particle? Come in, open His presence and report for karmic duty.[35] Why, it's a Tree

---

31. The world is a **manifestation** of God's ecstatic love, which causes him "to go out from himself and create things other than himself." Ware, 1979, p. 44.

32. **Matterimany:** "Eternity is another word for unity.... Time is eternity broken in space, like a ray of light refracted in the water." Heschel, 1966, p. 112. ***Malkut*** is at the bottom of the Kabbalistic tree, the manifestation of the material world. ***Bhoga*** refers to this dualistic world of enjoyment and suffering. ***Bhakti*** is the form of yoga that emphasizes love, devotion, and worship of personal God (a ***bhakta*** practices bhakti).

33. "The essence of God is **birth**ing." Eckhart, in Fox [tr], 1982, p. 88. "How do you describe the creation of the world?... The world is created anew for each newborn person." Mouravieff, 1989, p. 143.

34. "The existence of **stars** is the key to the problem of why the cosmos is hospitable to life." Smolin, 1997, p. 29. See Book One below. "A miracle of the Absolute was born; Infinity put on a finite soul..." Sri Aurobindo, 1993, p. 101. "Understand that you have within yourself, upon a small scale, a second universe: within you there is a sun, there is a moon, and there are also stars." Origen, in Ware, 1979, p. 43.

35. **Hologram/particle,** i.e., whole/part: In our cosmos, the whole is present in each part. The experience of this fact is the key to spirituality, a point that is developed in much that follows, especially in Book Four. One way to think about your "private particle" is to conceptualize the cosmos as a Klein bottle, where the inside is the outside and *vice versa.* Alternatively, imagine a lampshade with many pinholes, each appearing as a point of light, when in reality there is only one source of light. The soul is not a "point" but more a "continuous line of spiritual being" that stretches from a general source to "the specific body of a particular person" and beyond. Steinsaltz, 1980, p. 55. **Presence:** "The world is the gift of God. We must know how to perceive the giver through the gift." Clement, 1993, p. 215. **Karmic duty:** In yogic philosophy, the cosmos is "a training ground that can advance man toward the Highest." H. Smith, 1965, p. 85.

of Life for those whose wood beleaf. What in carnation?![36] One in agni & ecstasy has given birth to Two: spirit-matter, earth-sky, knower-known, sun-moon, cats & chicks, Chaos Control, Lennon McCartney, God & Darwin, Adam & Evolution.[37] A little metaphysical diddling between a cabbala opposites, and Mamamaya! baby makes Trinity, so all the world's an allusion (that's the key to His fiat, if you know how to derive).[38] Viveka

---

36. **Incarnation:** Nature "is entirely dependent upon God, and is often described as His body or garment." Nikhilananda, Vol 2, p. 22. "In the incarnation humanity is the 'boundary' or 'frontier' between the visible and the invisible, the carnal and the spiritual, like a mediator between creation and the creator." Clement, 1993, p. 77.

37. ***Agni:*** The divine consciousness-force or will metaphorically represented as fire; the entire evolution of the cosmos "can be described as Agni's journey in four movements..." Satprem, 1984, p. 300. For our purposes, these movements are Matter, Life, Mind and Spirit. "The dancer's inside turns into the outsideness of the dance when the dancer dances. This turning inside out is **ecstasy**.... this is God's relation to the cosmos. The cosmos is a kind of dancing revelation of God. It is a kind of offspring of God. It is a kind of speech of God.... God creates the world as an act of agape-ecstasy." Bruteau, 1997, p. 39. **One gives birth to two:** "The essentially creative act is the dissociation of subjectivity and objectivity out of the primal unity. Self and not-Self then come into being, though not into independent being, for each is bound to the other by the unity of which both are polar aspects." Krishna Prem, 1969, p. 58.

38. **Mamamaya:** Matter, materia, meter, and mother all derive "from the Sanskrit root *ma- (matr-),* from which, in Sanskrit itself, come both *mata* (mother) and *maya* (the phenomenal world of nature)." Watts, 1958, p. 132. "Maya is experienced as fascination, charm; specifically, feminine charm." (de la Vallee-Poussin, cited in Campbell, 1974, p. 52). **Cabbala opposites:** Out of the unity of the eternal *ain sof* proceed "two parallel principles—appearing to be opposites, yet in reality inseparable," a masculine or active principle *(Chokmah)* and a feminine or passive one *(Binah).* Tomberg, 1992, p. 174. **Baby:** The "first born" of Brahman and maya is the empirical universe. **Trinity:** "Two is the number which separates, three the number which transcends all separation: the one and the many find themselves gathered and circumscribed in the Trinity." Lossky, 2002, p. 47. "A God

la revelation![39] Or, as one Very Old Boy put it,

> The Tao gives birth to One.
> One gives birth to Two.
> Two gives birth to Three.
> Three gives birth to all things.[40]

And His name & number shall be Immanuelent, which tranceleighted, means "Godwithinus."[41]

---

who made himself twofold, according to a pattern common in mythology, would make himself the root of an evil multiplicity to which he could only put a stop by re-absorbing it into himself," but trinity "suggests the perpetual surmounting of contradiction, and of solitude as well, in the bosom of an infinite Unity." Clement, 1993, p. 74. "Father, mother, and child constitute the natural trinity.... The seed of spirit is sown in the womb of matter, and by an immaculate (pure) conception the progeny is brought into being." Hall, 1988, p. XCIII. **Allusion:** Maya signifies the beginning of time, duality, separation, and becoming; nevertheless, every part of the cosmos is at the same time a "theophany" which "alludes" to its divine origin; or, to paraphrase Joyce, "every part so ptee does duty for the holos." Thus, for example, "the ***fiat lux*** of the first day of creation and the *fiat lux* of the awakening of faith in the soul are of the same essence. In both cases it is a question of the creative act of 'Let there be light!'" Tomberg, 1992, p. 108. More generally, "everything that is seen is related to something hidden. That is to say that each visible reality is a symbol, and refers to the invisible reality to which it is related." Origen, quoted in Clement, 1993, p. 221.

39. **Viveka:** spiritual vision, the ability to distinguish between maya and the eternally true.

40. Tao te Ching, by Lao Tzu (tr: **Old Boy**) Mitchell [Tr.], 1988. If you prefer a Christian reading, "The One enters into movement because of his fullness. The Two is transcended because the godhead is beyond all opposition. Perfection is achieved in the Three who is the first to overcome the compositeness of the Two. Thus the godhead does not remain confined, nor does it spread out indefinitely." Gregory Nazianzen, quoted in Clement, 1993, p. 65

41. "Behold, a virgin shall be with child and bring forth a son, and they shall call his name **Immanuel**, which is translated, 'God with us.'" *Matthew* 1:23. **Immanent:** that aspect of God that inheres in the world.

* * *

So begins—and ends—the most unlikely, the most thoroughly mind-boggling how-, why- and Whodunit we can possibly try to imagine. It is actually the only story that *is*, because it is the story of ALL that actually is: the improbable account of how a blank singularity evolved over 13.7 billion years to produce everything we *perceive* and everything we *are*, the marvelous all-without and the inexplicable all-within.

Until relatively recently, people looked to religion to provide an explanation for the All that Is. Today, science offers its own rendering of the totality of existence, but perhaps it is worth inquiring how much of this highly sophisticated, mostly mathematical account is based upon concepts, assumptions, and *a priori* intellectual commitments that are no more sophisticated (or critically examined) than the myths of antiquity.

Although you or I certainly do not know how a cosmos may be created out of nothing, how life may be generated from non-life, or how consciousness proceeds from matter, we are assured that science has dispelled the intellectual darkness of the ages and obviated the crude mythological fancies of our cognitive childhood. Indeed, we are told that a Theory of Everything is on the horizon, a recipe for generating a universe so concise that it may be reduced to a discrete tattoo. If, like the illiterate peasant of the Middle Ages, we don't really understand the language in which it is written, our scientific priesthood will graciously translate and interpret the texts for us.

There is *knowledge* and there is *understanding*, and it is always dangerous to conflate the two. Science *knows* a great many things, but does it actually *understand* how an exquisitely ordered yet progressive cosmos may instantaneously create itself out of nothing, how something called Life (whatever that is) can suddenly appear on a dead planet, how symphonies, paintings, cathedrals, and novels can pop out of a modified ape brain, or how a man can hit 73 home runs in a single baseball season? Religion is often accused of giving names, such as "God," to things its adherents do not understand. However, is it not equally evident that science has its own set of names for things it does not understand, names such as "big bang," "genetic program," "life," "consciousness," or even "universe"—for what scientist has ever stood athwart and observed this thing called "universe"?

The question is, does science really understand what it purports to know? According to one observer,

> modern man's attitude towards the body of scientific knowledge is almost the same as that of archaic man's towards the body of myth: He does not question or seek to understand the implications of his orthodoxy, yet it forms a vaguely defined aggregate of ideas that govern his attitude toward life.[42]

This book seeks to question and understand the implications of our scientific orthodoxy and, in so doing, provide an updated "cosmic mythunderstanding" which, like all creation stories, addresses itself to the perennial questions that have puzzled human beings ever since they became capable of puzzlement: how did we come to exist, what is the point of existing, and is there any escape from what appears to be an absurdly brief slice of existence between two dark slabs of eternity—the triune mystery of our genesis, our present being, and our ultimate end.

Of course, all creation myths emphasize the centrality of human beings in the cosmic adventure, and our mythunderstanding will be no different. This is not just for the usual reasons of cosmic narcissism or narrow self-interest, but because humans are without question the strangest and most unexpected "data" one could ever hope to encounter in a universe—we are "weird made flesh," as put in our opening genesis story, the one place where existence mysteriously becomes experience, where animal inexplicably gains access to the human, and where human is ineffably transmuted to divine. The human brain is by many orders of magnitude the most complex fact of the universe, the human subject its most arresting problem. As "facts of the universe"

---

42. Ashish, p. 57.

we must, in order to understand just what we are, "be analyzed and evaluated cosmologically."[43] And *vice versa*, for, as we shall see, virtually all esoteric spiritual traditions insist that human beings possess "inside information" about the universe, to such an extent that (according to these traditions) discovering what a human being truly *is* is the key to fathoming the implacable mystery of the cosmos itself.

On the one hand, we encounter a relative cosmos held together by cause and effect, running in the direction of past, to present to future. On the other hand, we find ourselves embedded in an absolute cosmos held together by a *wholeness* that transcends, space, time and conventional causality. As humans, we are uniquely situated between two seemingly infinite poles; looking outward, light from a distant galaxy may enter our pupil today, registering an event that took place millions of years ago, long before *Homo sapiens* were even present in the universe. Reversing our gaze and looking within, it is said that we may behold the very transtemporal Self of the cosmos, the principle of existence, the ground and source of all that is. Thus, it would appear that the boundaries of skin and lifespan that define us in space and time are completely illusory, without metaphysical foundation; or at least that is a claim this book sets out to confirm or refute.

These then are the fractally recurring themes we shall pursue and explore throughout our story: that life is not an anomalous refugee from the laws of physics, enjoying a brief triumph over the grinding, ineluctable necessity of entropy, but an intrinsic, exuberant expression of the type of universe we happen to inhabit; that the presence of self-conscious human beings explains much more about the cosmos than even the most complete understanding of the material universe can ever hope to explain about human beings; and that consciousness is not an accidental intruder that arrives late to the cosmic manifestival, but an interior, subjective landscape that may be followed forward and back, like Ariadne's thread, to reveal the transcendent mystery of our existence, an unconditioned, subjective center that, in light of its in-

43. Jonas, 1996, p. 177.

disputable existence, is as "real" and enduring as physical reality—only more so. To borrow a hackneyed phrase, "it takes a cosmos" to raise up a conscious being, and *vice versa.*

* * *

This book is intended for the general reader rather than the scholar, the cage-free intellectual or "free-range" spiritual aspirant rather than the sterile, "unfertilized egghead" of contemporary academic hyper-specialization. Having promiscuously drawn from so many different disciplines—physics, biology, philosophy, anthropology, archaeology, psychology, neurology, history, aesthetics, theology, mysticism—the book will undoubtedly offend experts in each field (with the possible exception of One).[44] Certainly it may be argued that I am presenting findings from these various fields as if they are settled facts, when each each of them—from physics on up, from mysticism on down—is beset by infighting, turf wars, academic self-promotion, unarticulated philosophical agendas, and intellectual vanity.

We have more than enough knowledge, thank you, and way too many books. The problem we face is how to relate all of this fragmented knowledge into a coherent picture of our world. Allan Schore, another "hyphenated intellectual" whose work attempts to synthesize many fields of study, has observed that the frontiers of science lie not in the further proliferation and extension of individual scientific subspecialties, but in the borderland between different existing fields.[45] In fact, this book adopts the view that human beings, by virtue of their unquestioned existence, are the meeting place of all possible scientific disciplines, the one place in the cosmos where all departments of learning harmoniously coexist in a single, multidimensional "youniversity," so to speak. In other words, as human beings, we are material, we are alive, we have minds, and we are allegedly in spirit. So the synthesis of all possible fields of study exists in us as an established

44. Although there are different esoteric systems, the Tradition is One.

45. Schore, 2003b, p. 205.

fact: we are *de facto* interdisciplinary subjectobjects, unproblematically defying any reductionistic, single-level explanation. In pondering the riddle of existence, I have merely attempted to interrogate any discipline—whether "scientific" or "spiritual"—that can reasonably claim to have discovered a piece of the cosmic puzzle. But in order to synthesize these apparently contradictory mini-truths into a coherent bangography, it is necessary to view them against the backdrop of an evolving cosmos that is in the process of progressively realizing its own higher Truth, which is ultimately One. According to Webster's dictionary, the word *evolution* is etymologically linked to the French *evolvere,* which referred to the unrolling of a scroll, or book. And as Sri Aurobindo expressed it above, "All time is one body, Space a single book." Or, putting it in a Western context, in the words of Aldous Huxley, "all science is the reduction of multiplicities to unities."[46]

For practical and aesthetic purposes, I have divided the cosmic adventure into a "four-story metanarrative" encompassing Matter, Life, Mind, and Spirit. These diverse modes of existence are so obvious, so distinct, and so different from one another, that it seems like a natural place to start our quest for a full account of reality that leaves no loose ends dangling from the cosmic quilt. If I may borrow a musical analogy, I see these modes of being as the four great "chords" constituting the song of existence. As improvisational (i.e., jazz) musicians can tell you, when they perform a solo, they are attempting to trace a coherent line, an artistically true and aesthetically beautiful pathway through the chordal structure of musical space. In so doing, and at each step along the way, there are literally an infinite number of potential pathways through the chords, some of which will be "complete" and musically satisfying, others banal, predictable, and unable to explicate the musical potential implicit in the chords. This is my best attempt at such a solo, with the full understanding that there are any number of fellow improvisational scholars who would "run the changes" differently.

46. Quoted in Easwaran, p. 15.

Of course, it is always possible to create a musically uninteresting solo by never straying from the tonic of the song, even by hitting the same note over and over. Such an academic "One Note Samba" is the musical equivalent of reductionism, which both explains everything and leaves everything unexplained. Clearly, for example, the song of existence changed chords with the appearance of Life, but our scientistic soloists largely continue to drone on in the key of matter. However, it is no longer adequate to be just a materialistic banjo-picker sitting barefoot on a little bridge of dogma; rather, one must have at least a nodding acquaintance with a few other instruments in order to play the cosmic suite. The universe is like a holographic, multidimensional musical score that must be read, understood, and performed. Like the score of a symphony, it is full of information that can be rendered in different ways. The score can support diverse interpretations, but surely one of them cannot be "music does not exist." For at the end of the day, we are each a unique and unrepeatable melody that can, if we only pay close enough attention to the polyphonic score that surrounds and abides within us, harmonize existence in our own beautiful way, and thereby hear the vespered strains of the "song supreme."

# BOOK ONE

## COSMOGENESIS: *The Gospel of Matter*

What then, I ask, is a body made of? At any given moment it is made of the world, for there is no fixed borderline between you and your surround—yet, reflecting on it at length and in the full context of time, the body progressively becomes as abstract as a melody—a melody one may with reason call the melody of life.

—Guy Murchie, *The Seven Mysteries of Life*

[I]f the presuppositions of contemporary science are made explicit, and religion is purged of superstition, the identity of the objects of their faith becomes apparent.

—Errol Harris, *Revelation Through Reason*

Blessed be you, mighty matter, irresistible march of evolution, reality ever newborn.... you who by overflowing and dissolving our narrow standards of measurement reveal to us the dimensions of God.

—Teilhard de Chardin, *The Heart of Matter*

What the... How in God's... But why... Who would have thought... I mean, really... Where in the world do we begin? Do we have any right to assume that the universe is even intelligible? If not, you can stop reading right now and do something else, something that actually has a *purpose.*[1] But if the universe *is* intelligible, how and why is this the case? At first blush, absolutely *everything* seems to be embedded in an inextinguishable mystery that no philosopher, no theologian and no scientist has ever been able to puzzle out. Yes, we are "alive," but we only pretend to know what this actually means. We are conscious, but no neurologist or psychologist has even the vaguest idea what consciousness actually *is.* As we develop through childhood, we gradually awaken to an external world that seems to obey its own rules; and yet, our life and consciousness are obviously an outgrowth of those same rules, now pondering themselves. Of course we should start our inquiry with the "facts," but what exactly is a fact? Which end is up? In other words, do we start with the objects of thought or the subject that apprehends them? And just what is the relationship between apparently "external" objects and the consciousness that is able to cognize them? Indeed, any fact we consider presupposes a subject who has selected the fact in question out of an infinite sea of possibilities, so any conceivable fact arises simultaneously with a subjective co-creator of that fact. Inevitably we are led to the conclusion that the universe is one substance. But what kind of substance? That seems to be the question.

We know from the study of physics that our universe uses the same stuff to make you and me that it uses to make everything else, from unyielding granite to gentle breezes, from rigid teeth to delicate eye tissue, from radiant stars to passing thoughts. Everything is ultimately made of the same substance and bound by the same laws—four cosmic forces, a handful of particles, a hundred or so elements; and yet, like an embryo developing within the womb of existence, the universe differentiates within itself, creating finer patterns and more complex forms as it quickens through the course of time. We can never actually stand "outside" this process, any more than the developing embryo can take a peek from outside the womb to see how things are going. Like fruit from a tree or infant from mother, we don't come into the world, but out of it,[2] a conglomeration of elements that were forged in the billion-degree heat of exploding stars, then scattered through the fathomless reaches of deep space, only to temporarily congeal into the whirling patterns known as you and me, abstract and immaterial patterns which are recreated instant by instant, like eddies given form through the flow of a rushing stream. Indeed, in a year from now, ninety-eight percent of the atoms in your body will have been replaced, meaning that you are indeed word-made-flesh, a transcendent pattern of accumulated information, not the transient material which makes a fleeting home under the organizing principle of your unrepeatable genetic logo.

In fact, as it so happens, it takes a universe—any universe—about thirteen billion years to fashion something as complex as a ewe or an eye. True, it takes only about a second for the universe to come up with quarks, protons, electrons and neutrinos, just a few minutes to knock out helium nuclei. But be patient—it takes 300,000 years for atoms to take shape, a billion years just for star-making galaxies to form, and no one knows for certain how long for solar systems and planets to stabilize.[3] After that, another couple billion years for microscopic life to appear—you get the idea. Given the initial conditions of the universe, and then assuming ideal conditions afterwards, it will take a universe a good thirteen billion years to grow complex enough at its leading edge to peer back on itself, scratch one of its newly minted heads, and wonder about its origins. Do not be impressed or daunted by the unimaginable vastness of the cosmos, for its size is simply a function of the time it has been expanding: as a matter of fact, we human observers have arrived on the scene just as quickly as this or any other universe will allow. Certainly from the standpoint of eternity, we have appeared in an instant, like mushrooms out of a lawn or offers for discreet online pharmacies in your email.

And once we did arrive, evolution (or something) picked up speed at a prodigious pace. Converting our planet's history to a twenty-four hour clock, our ancestral hominids don't arrive until 11:59 P.M., human beings till the last tenth of a second. Our physical descent—or ascent—from the apes took about 5 million years, but until about

40,000 years ago the best we could do was wonder where the next meal was coming from (and avoid *being* the next meal). As Book Three will attempt to show, humankind's continuous crisis of the past 30 or 40 thousand years is simply what occurs during the fleeting (but nevertheless catastrophic) transition period when a life form must learn to cope with the unforeseen development of self-awareness. Indeed, the mere fact that the we ex-ist (stand out), that there is existence instead of nothingness, represents a "fall," an exile from the sanctuary of the One, a departure from the timeless repose of eternal bliss.[4] But this leads to Book Four, where we hope to demonstrate that our perennial nostalgia for this Oneness also represents a "memoir of the future,"[5] where a recovery of wholeness can take place once we have passed through the gauntlet of personal and collective development, as "History moves to heal the wounds it made."[6] Thus, having fallen from being into time, we may reverse our worldward descent, reclaim the Self, and cure the dis-ease of history by crossing its last passage and fulfilling the promise of its final, never-ending chapter, as nothing returns to Nothing.

## 1.1 The Best of All Possible Bangs: Come for the Order, Stay for the Novelty

> This now tells us how precise the Creator's aim must have been, namely to an accuracy of one part in 1 in $10^{123}$. This is an extraordinary figure.... Even if we were to write a 0 on each separate proton and on each separate neutron in the entire universe—and we could throw in all the other particles for good measure—we should fall far short of writing down the figure needed.
>
> —Roger Penrose, *The Emperor's New Mind*

> It is not only that man is adapted to the universe. The universe is adapted to man.
>
> —John Wheeler

"In the beginning was, if not a word, at least a sequence of encoded information of *some* sort."[7] And indeed the creation of this universe *was* very good, for, unlike most universes, ours at least contained in its essence and origins the *potential* for the good—not to mention the true and beautiful—to appear at some point in its later development.

The exceptional event that gave birth to our universe some 13 billion years ago resulted from what physicists call a *singularity*, a tiny point of space-time so impossibly dense that it was, in effect, infinite, literally beyond our horizon of mathematical knowability, certainly beyond our ability to imagine it. But this inconceivable event—an event we mistakenly ascribe to the past (since it is happening now), and erroneously refer to as an "it" (as if we could view it from the outside)—was and is singular in another sense, in the commonly understood connotation of being a unique, one-of-a-kind, single instance of something. After all, while we may speculate that singularities also occur inside black holes, we really have no way of even conceiving what actually happens inside them, and we certainly have no reason to believe that those singularities, if they actually do exist, result in universes anything like ours.

Evidently, from the moment our universe sprang into being, and for the subsequent nine billion years or so, not a thing happened in it that wasn't completely reducible to the physical and chemical laws (or habits) it had set for itself at the very outset. But herein lies a second mystery of our universe (existence itself being the first), for just where these immutable laws came from, not a soul knows. That is to say, the laws of physics could not have theoretically existed prior to Planck time, which is $10^{-43}$ of the first second of the big bang. Thus, technically, we cannot even speak in terms of "before" or "prior" at this point in our story (indeed, there were no points, either). Whatever may or may not have been happening, physics is powerless to describe it, because physics didn't yet exist. Or did it? Einstein was convinced that the instantaneous emergence of these physical laws implied a sort of immaterial, Platonic overmind, "an intelligence of such superiority that, compared with it, all the systematic thinking... of human beings is an utterly insignificant reflection."[8] Likewise, according to Sheldrake,

> If the laws of nature were all there before the Big Bang, then they must be nonphysical, idealike entities dwelling in some kind of permanent mathematical mind, be it the mind of God or the Cosmic Mind or just the mind of a disembodied mathematician.[9]

It is indeed odd that the universe should instantaneously behave so lawfully, instead of simply degenerating into chaos. Physics tells us that our senses delude us into confusing the universe with its physical content, when in fact, a universe is simply the instantiation of the transcendent laws that govern it—it is the underlying laws that result in the relatively stable domain which our senses perceive as "matter." The laws that undergird the universe are invisible to our evolved senses; rather, they can only be "seen" with the mind's eye, the eye of reason (and even more improbably, the eye of aesthetic beauty—many mathematicians will reject a formula out of hand if it lacks "beauty"). Strangely enough, science begins with the one world we experience with our senses (where else could it begin?), but quickly saws off that familiar limb by excluding "everything that can be imagined or conceived, except in abstract mathematical terms," consequently relegating everything outside mathematical description—the very world it started with—to "an ontological limbo."[10] Only this second, abstract world is considered to disclose valid information about the universe, whereas all of our initial impressions of color, sound, texture, beauty, and meaning supposedly reveal nothing real about the universe, only about our own nervous systems. And yet, physics has no explanation for how its impressive mathematical scaffolding can relate to, much less generate, what we experience as objective reality: "The edifice of exact science, or physics as a purely conceptual structure of quantitative ideas cannot provide the very material, tangible reality, on which its equations are supposed to work."[11] In other words, while the laws make a fine blueprint, where do the building materials come from?

Nevertheless, how strange it is that we have—discovered? invented?—a human instrument, mathematical language, which so effectively mirrors the invisible, transcendent structure of the universe. We take this divinely superfluous ability for granted, but really, there is no more reason for us to have it than there is for dogs to have the ability to understand Beethoven. Our most abstract, counterintuitive ideas about the universe, such as quantum and relativity theories, are not the product of any world we can actually experience, not now and certainly not in the archaic past, during which more than ninety-nine percent of our evolution occurred. In fact, it would have been far more useful to us as a species to have a mathematical system capable of predicting the weather, something which is apparently impossible in principle due to the complexity of the atmosphere. But the agreement between our mental abstractions and the quantum world seems very simple and direct, to such an extent that it "has been confirmed by experiment to more than a trillionth percent precision."[12]

In pondering the behavior of our complex, law-abiding universe, it is as if we were watching a group of people running around randomly, and suddenly a baseball game emerges, with no one on the field conscious of the rules they are now playing under. And, just as in a baseball game, where we don't see basketball games or soccer matches break out on the fringes of the field, the universe seems somehow to "hold together" and play by the same rules across its great expanse (or so it is assumed by science). Why should everything in the universe be subject to constant change except these immaterial laws—laws of physics, laws of chemistry? "There must," says Roger Penrose, "be some underlying reason for the accord between mathematics and physics, i.e., between Plato's world and the physical world."[13] But no one—not scientists, not theologians—seems to have a clue as to why this should be so.

Given that the logic of the universe and the logic of our minds mirror each other in such a profound way, it seems almost as if "man and the world are, as it were, made for each other."[14] Although world-weary postmodern philosophers affirm that we simply impose man-made order on an otherwise chaotic universe, this view makes it difficult to explain how we are so easily able to make our way through the quantum world, and to successfully invent the many technological marvels based on our knowledge.[15]

In our universe, according to the philosopher Errol Harris, "disorder is parasitic on order," not *vice versa;* that is, the very concept of disorder presupposes some kind of prior order that is subject to the pull of randomness, chaos, and entropy. Are we therefore justified in suggesting that the deep structure of our minds mirrors the deep structure of the cosmos, and that a certain type of applied introspection may yield accurate metaphysical insights into the nature of ultimate reality? You should keep this question in the back of your mind until we address it more directly in Book Four. Suffice it to say at this juncture that to assert that humans can know *anything at all* about the universe—to affirm that the universe is in fact *intelligible*—is to make a hidden but quite revolutionary metaphysical assumption about the nature of human consciousness and its ultimate relationship to the cosmos as a whole.

* * *

And so we may trace our inception to a fantastic explosion, a "big bang" no less, but instead of randomness, we see this explosion expanding—indeed, blossoming as if from a seed—in a very complex and orderly manner. Given what we know about the tendency of things to become more disordered with time, and knowing that slight variations at the beginning of a process tend to be amplified through time, one would expect that the total chaos that prevailed at the origin of things would not diminish but accumulate through time. But this is not what happened in the case of our universe. Instead, we see such precise order that, according to no less a skeptic than Stephen Hawking, "if the rate of expansion one second after the big bang had been smaller by even one part in a hundred thousand million million, the universe would have recollapsed before it even reached its present size."[16]

We might compare the universe to a piano, which has eighty-eight finely tuned strings, each vibrating at a certain frequency. Why? So we can play something on it, a sonata, fugue, or concerto. Without those eighty-eight strings held in a constant, mathematical relationship to one another, it is impossible to produce anything higher, anything more intelligible than a cacophony of individual notes. We tune the strings so that we may produce music consisting of chords, harmony, melody, theme, all built upon one another. But just as we cannot build a piano out of the rules of music, the laws of physics that are "played" in the universe can in no way account for the physical universe itself, because a universe consisting of pure, abstract quantity could not exist:

> The laws of physics themselves emerged from a primal Big Bang, when there were no nuclear elements for the laws to operate on. So where did those laws come from? How did they come to take the supremely efficient forms they did take? And how did they come to interrelate with one another so as to make possible a coherent, intelligible universe?[17]

In short, if they weren't there from the start, how could laws that have only come into existence through time all integrate so harmoniously to produce the coherent universe we see around us?[18]

Hmm. Since we seem to have stumbled upon a perfectly tuned piano that plays beautiful music, it seems thoroughly unreasonable to avoid asking how it got that way. Scientifically speaking, there is no reason why the world should be anything other than random and unpredictable—an untuned piano, capable of no coherent or complex, much less beautiful, music. As we all know from daily experience, disorder is much easier to achieve than order: if we don't comb our hair, it becomes tangled; if we don't clean the house, it becomes dirty; if we don't close the window in winter, it gets cold inside. But one of the odd things about our universe is that it too seems "tuned" in a very precise sort of way. In fact, the standard model of particle physics has identified about twenty mathematical parameters that, if changed in any way, would make the existence of stars, planets, complex molecules—and therefore, us—ridiculously unlikely. Impossible, actually.

If a universe hospitable to life is to exist, certain very strict criteria must be met. First, we must have a stable yet flowing universe that produces copious amounts of different atoms that can form a very large number of molecules that differ greatly in their sizes, shapes, and chemical properties. Most scientists believe that carbon is the key ingredient, because only it is able to form such a variety of stable molecular structures.[19] Since all but the lightest molecular elements were produced from within stars, it is clear that in order for life to exist, stars are absolutely critical, as they literally serve as an "external organ" for cosmic biogenesis. But this is not as easy as it sounds, for a universe with stars capable of propagating complex molecules presupposes certain imponderably specific mathematical parameters that must be present at the instant of cosmogenesis.

Each of the twenty mathematical parameters that govern the character and development of the universe is hypothetically free to vary within a wide range, resulting in many possible universes—indeed, an infinite number—only a few of which would be hospitable to life. It is as if, writes physicist Lee Smolin,

> We may imagine that God has a control panel on which there is a dial for each parameter. One dial sets the mass of the proton, another the electron's charge, and so on. God closes his eyes and turns the dials randomly.... What is the probability that the world so created would contain stars? The answer is that the probability is incredibly small.... In many cases, a small turn of the dial in one direction or another results in a world not only without stars, but with much less structure than our universe.[20]

Perhaps it is just our good fortune to find ourselves living in the Best of All Possible Bangs. But what exactly are the chances of our particular universe coming into being, as against the number of possible universes? Evidently, the number is easy to calculate, coming to about one chance in $10^{123}$.[21] This number is so imposing that it actually contains more digits than there are protons in the universe.[22] And out of this virtually infinite set of possible universes, only very few are capable of sustaining the sort of functional order and evolving complexity needed for the appearance of conscious life forms.[23] Interestingly, even a cosmic intelligence conceived of in the most crude and childish manner—perhaps as a bigheaded scientist named Yacub sitting behind the cosmic console, actually twiddling knobs—is *more* likely than pure randomness resulting in that one chance in $10^{123}$. From a strictly rational standpoint, "the existence of God is not more improbable than the existence of blind laws of nature."[24] Indeed, some have made the point that it is logically incoherent to argue over whether or not a higher intelligence exists in the universe. Rather, if such a higher intelligence is even philosophically *possible*, then it is logically *necessary*, as compared with the alternative, that is, the almost impossible odds against randomness resulting in such fantastic order and complexity.[25]

There is a multitude of restrictions that must be placed on nearly every mathematical variable underlying the universe in order for the existence of a lawful and ordered, and yet open, unpredictable and evolving cosmos to exist. Let's look at some of these parameters,[26] and see why it is so important that they be what they are:

| **Setting on God's Mixing Board:** | **Result:** |
|---|---|
| energy in Big Bang too great | matter scattered too far apart |
| energy in Big Bang too weak | prompt collapse of universe |
| electric force too strong | stars extinguish before evolution reaches us |
| electric force too weak | stars can't have planets |
| change in ratio of light/heavy elements | no galaxies or star systems |
| weak force too strong | stars can't explode elements into space |
| weak force too weak | same problem |
| strong force too weak | no complex organic substances |
| strong force too strong | nothing but helium |
| change in resonance between helium and beryllium | no carbon/no life |
| change in particle/antiparticle asymmetry | no material world |

Eliminate or change the range or strength of any of these parameters, and "the universe around us will evaporate instantly and a vastly different world will come into being."[27]

This astonishing degree of order is genuinely puzzling—and a source of some consternation—to most cosmologists who, for extra-scientific reasons, reflexively wish to banish the notion of any kind of transcendent intelligence in the universe. But a more appropriately humble Einstein, in contemplating these laws, mused that scientists are not unlike children

> entering a huge library filled with books in many languages. The child knows someone must have written those books. It does not know how. It does not understand the languages in which they are written. The child dimly suspects a mysterious order in the arrangement of books, but doesn't know what it is. That, it seems to me, is the attitude of even the most intelligent human toward God. We see the universe marvelously arranged and obeying certain laws but only dimly understand these laws.[28]

More recently, physicist Freeman Dyson observed that "It almost seems as if the Universe must in some sense have known that we were coming.[29]

The incredible mathematical structure of the universe confronts us with a range of philosophical explanations, but it is impossible to choose between these based only upon mere logical or philosophical reasoning. Rather, people tend to emotionally identify with and defend an explanation that is derived more from culture or personality style than philosophical plausibility. Materialists find a materialistic explanation, theologians find a theological explanation, and narcissistic new-agers believe that they create reality themselves.

In the end, we may reduce these philosophical explanations to three. Two of these, although grounded in scientific faith, are actually 180 degrees apart. One prevalent interpretation is that the universe *had* to happen the way it did—it was strictly determined and there was no choice in the matter. This is akin to the insanity plea—the universe couldn't help it. It would mean that the creativity of the universe was indeed exhausted in its first instant, and that everything that has followed has been strictly determined based on its initial conditions. This would further mean, of course, that consciousness is fully reducible to biology, that biology is fully reducible to physics, and that physics is ultimately reducible to... to what? Here we reach a philosophical cul-de-sac that mirrors the theological problem of what caused God. In this regard, "It is a characteristic of science," writes philosopher Bryan Magee, "that it explains things in terms that are themselves left unexplained," thus exposing itself as "the philosophy of the subject who forgets to take account of himself."[30]

The converse interpretation, widespread in the postmodern world, is that the universe "just happened," that it is pointless to ask how or why (we might call this the "inanity" plea). You get enough monkeys and enough pianos, and eventually the works of Duke Ellington will appear. As pointed out above, our universe certainly could be a chance event, but the chances of a random universe being so tuned that it may, after 13 billion years, produce conscious life forms capable of dismissing themselves as a chance event, are dauntingly remote. No, this is a very unusual and puzzling universe, and we will not make the problem go away by simply dismissing it either as a completely determined or purely chance event.

A third approach, which generally reaches us through religious thought or philosophical idealism, essentially holds that the universe cannot be explained within itself. Just like everything else, it can only be explained with reference to something transcending or undergirding it, something outside or beyond its purely physical laws. This "ultimate something," whether conceived of as immanent ground or transcendent other, has gone by the name of Brahman, Tao, YHVH, The Absolute, The One, Bob Dobbs, among countless others. And in fact, if we are so inclined, we are on scientifically firm ground to conclude, as does Stephen Hawking (for the record, an atheist), that it is "perfectly consistent with all we know to say that there was a Being who was responsible for the laws of physics."[31] I believe we may go further than Hawking, and advance the metaphysical conclusion that this Being or principle "cannot be rejected, because in its absence, there could be no thinker in the world to seek philosophical comprehension of the nature of things, and so no metaphysician."[32] Or, as trumpeter Dizzy Gillespie once said about the first great jazz improviser, Louis Armstrong, "No him, no me."

* * *

And yet, our wonderment at the mere order of the universe—marvelous though it may be—is misplaced. Both the scientific priesthood and the creationist countermovement make much of this order, but to opposite ends (one to prove the necessity of a creator, the other to prove a creator unnecessary). Either way, a metaphysics of order is a metaphysics of the dead-on-arrival past, an eternally frozen or repetitive universe seen through the rearview mirror of mathematical invariance. Order alone cannot form a metaphysical basis for what is in fact the case, that is, an unfolding, evolving, creative universe capable of sudden, punctuational change, even ontological discontinuities, most notably, the sudden appearances of Life and Mind. In fact, in order for evolution to occur on a cosmic scale, both randomness and order must be held in check, because both are fatal conditions to any open system. If there is an intelligence behind or beyond the order of the universe, it seems that it must have more to do with placing constraints on probability than in producing predetermined, mechanistic outcomes, because a purely mechanical universe would be as incapable of evolution as an entirely random one. Our evolving universe *must* be more than its laws, because a merely ordered world could never become separate or distinct from its source: an element of contingency is necessary for anything truly novel to come into being.

In short, while order is a necessary condition for a functional, evolving cosmos, it is not sufficient. If two plus two equals four every time, then we never leave the evolutionary starting gate; rather, there must be some way for two plus two to occasionally equal five, some means of "escaping" rigid order for there to be the possibility of novel emergence of higher levels of complexity. As we shall see, only the "arrival" of an open future saves us from the mindless repetition of settled forms and unvarying processes. Novelty and possibility, renewal and emergence—perhaps even liberation and salvation—are only made possible because the future meets the past in the now, the only "place" where the universe is, paradoxically, both what it *is* and what it is *not yet*.

## 1.2 Temporal Wholeness: Turning the Cosmos Upside Down

> [M]an *is* the measure of all things—not, of course, by virtue of laws promulgated by his reason but by the paradigm of his psychophysical wholeness, which reveals the maximum degree of concrete ontological completeness known to us. *From this pinnacle downwards*, the classes of being would then be described in terms of privation, by progressive subtraction down to the minimum of mere elementary matter. In other words, instead of the higher forms of life being reduced to the lowest, beings would be characterized in terms of "a less and less," an ever more distant "not yet." Ultimately, the deterministic nature of lifeless matter would be interpreted as sleeping, not yet awakened to freedom.
>
> —Hans Jonas, *Evolution and Freedom*

> We gain a truer perspective of the whole evolutionary process if we study it from its most recent results rather than only from its beginnings.
>
> —Charles Birch, *Neo-Darwinism, Self-Organization, and Divine Action*

There is no reason to spend a great deal of time picking through the erroneous assumptions of the Newtonian, mechanistic approach to reality, or explaining how the "new paradigm" of quantum physics has overturned the mechanical, deterministic world as envisioned by reductionistic philosophers of the seventeenth and eighteenth centuries. This has been ably (if polemically) addressed in any number of recent works, and this book assumes some familiarity with those arguments. That is to say, based upon the scientific evidence, it is no longer possible to avoid the conclusion that our perceived world of separateness and fragmentation is only superimposed on a more fundamental, seamless web of subatomic activity, a vast realm of unbroken wholeness. The universe as revealed by quantum physics is so intrinsically interconnected—such an undivided "whole"—that each individual "part" of the universe can be understood to simultaneously exist, to some degree, "within" every other part. Because "any local agitation shakes the whole universe," wrote Whitehead, "there is no possibility of a detached, self-contained local existence."[33]

The point here is that the universe as we understand it today is an astonishingly different place than what we thought it to be just one hundred years ago: it is not your great-grandfather's universe. But because of the counterintuitive nature of modern physics, the necessary revisions in ontology and epistemology have not trickled down to the commonly understood, consensus reality. Indeed, it is a banality to point out that the mechanistic-materialistic stance elucidated by Newton in the seventeenth century remains the axis of our tacit metaphysic even today, simply because it mirrors the way the solid bodies of reality interact with our locally evolved senses. "Our mistake," according to Nobel prize-winning physicist Steven Weinberg, "is not that we take our theories too seriously, but that we do not take them seriously enough."[34] So long as scientific theories "work" in a narrower, technical sense, most physicists are content to live in a pre-Einsteinian, "common sense" universe, ignoring the unavoidable metaphysical implications of quantum and relativity theories. But, because science has failed to draw out these implications, it "increasingly finds itself enmeshed in a cosmic tapestry of the impossible":

> The subatomic physicist must incessantly account for what he cannot intellectually believe: an electron changes from one orbit to another without ever having traveled through space; an electron fired at a screen with two holes in it goes through both apertures at once; a positron... can only be explained as moving backward in time; a neutrino, which has no mass, no charge, and no magnetic field—and which hence cannot be truly said to exist—passes through our bodies and through the crust of the earth as if those "objects" did not exist for it—in fact, quite like a ghost.[35]

Without going into a great deal of detail, I would like to spend a little time exploring just what has happened to the foundations of that pre-Einsteinian universe to make it now seem so quaint. This is important, because the very framework of science continues to stand upon a number of outmoded concepts that are not the outcome of its methods, but are rather, *a priori* assumptions projected onto reality—not outcomes of the search, but scientifically unwarranted preconceptions that simply helped get the search under way. Three of these pivotal concepts are determinism, materialism, and reductionism, and none of them any longer have any compelling force in providing an accurate description of reality. Let us briefly look at each of these in order to show why their continued application needs to be reexamined.

*Determinism* draws its central metaphor from the mechanical clock. Its thesis, stated bluntly, is that all processes in the universe are entirely determined, and that if we could know the exact location and velocity of all the particles in the universe at a given moment, then it would be theoretically possible to have complete knowledge of the universe for all times antecedent or subsequent to this.

*Materialism* means that the universe is ultimately composed of stable, individual parts that interact with other parts, all of which are fully *external* to one another. Importantly, it is assumed that a material body remains fully itself regardless of the passage of time. In other words, an entity is the same no matter how long or short the span of time involved.

*Reductionism* is really a hybrid category containing elements of each of the above. This is an approach that attempts to account for all of the phenomena of any level of reality in terms of a more simple or basic one. The most immediate examples are the belief that consciousness may be reduced to the level of biological activity, or that the workings of biology may be reduced to the level of chemistry, chemistry to physics, and so on.

Now, one of the startling discoveries of quantum physics is that an electron does not travel continuously through space, but rather appears at discrete positions (quanta) in space for successive durations of time. It is as if, while observing an automobile moving at sixty miles per hour, the car appeared successively at each street corner, remained for a few seconds, and then disappeared again—all the while "averaging" sixty miles per hour.[36] Matter, in the quantum view, appears to have this same "on-off" vibratory character as sound or light.[37]

Recall that in a Newtonian, materialistic universe, a "thing" is always itself, no matter how infinitely the time is subdivided. But in the quantum view we see time taking on an entirely different, primary importance. For, just as "a note of music is nothing in an instant, but requires its whole period in which to manifest itself," so too a vibratory entity of primordial matter "requires its whole period in which to manifest itself."[38] Even the most solid, unchanging matter is actually a reiteration, only with little or no novelty entering into it: the same note, so to speak, played rapidly, over and over. Really, the experience we call "matter" has nothing at all to do with whatever it is that matter actually *is*. So-called "solid" matter is mostly a property of fingers and eyes, only the end result of a perceiving subject projecting its experience onto a world of vibratory energy, a "floating condensation on a swarm of the indefinable," as Teilhard de Chardin put it. If even physicists agree that their most "fundamental" aspect of the universe—matter—is a process in time, this naturally leads us to regard the entire universe as a process which, like all processes, requires time in order to manifest the fullness of its being. Time, therefore, is not mere featureless duration but the essence of creative evolution: "since there are no instants," wrote Whitehead, "there is no nature at an instant."[39] Rather, the essence of everything is *transition* and *participation* in the creative advance of the cosmos.

Whitehead referred to what he called "the fallacy of simple location," the assumption that a bit of matter "is where it is, in a definite finite region of space, and throughout a definite finite duration of time, apart from any essential reference of the relations of that bit of matter to other regions of space and to other durations of time."[40] As it so happens, the idea that we can say exactly when and where anything *is* is an error, a confusion of mistaking our abstraction for the concrete reality of the situation. In fact, there is no element of material reality that is simply and unambiguously *over there*, or happening *right now*, because "each volume of space, or each lapse of time, includes in its essence aspects of all volumes of space, or all lapses of time."[41] For Whitehead, the unavoidable conclusion is that, "in a certain sense, everything is everywhere at all times. For every location involves an aspect of itself in every other location. Thus, every spatio-temporal standpoint mirrors the world."[42]

Whitehead's views, although conceived shortly after the dawn of modern physics, have not been surpassed. The most recent theories of physics agree that the properties of elementary particles "are in the end influenced by the history and state of the whole universe."[43] If an event endures and has a future, then it follows that the past participates in the present, that the present anticipates the future, and that the future may affect that part of the present which is "open" and not fully determined; there is both upward, deterministic causation (part-to-whole, past-to-future) and downward, teleonomic causation (whole-to-part, future-to-past) in the form of mathematical attractors, hierarchical control of lower levels, and boundary conditions exerting their influence on levels below them. And the ultimate implication of this view would be that, just as the universe had an origin, it has a destiny; but in the end, the origin and destiny must be One, since the universe is only separable in our imagination. (This possibility will be further explored down in Book Four.)

In any event, it is clear that the notion of a static, mechanical universe must give way to that of a dynamic, "processional" one, because even material reality is involved in a continuously evolving becoming:

> Material entities assume the character of an event; apart from process, there is no being. A thing is what it is by virtue of the serial unfolding of pattern through time; if one attempts to isolate an object at a single, non-temporal instant, apart from the instants preceding and following it, the object loses its essential identity. Thus nature becomes a structure of evolving processes....[44]

The logical outcome of all this is that the entire foundation of the materialistic, deterministic, and reductionistic world view has dissolved. Those bedrock, "primary" qualities described by the old physics—mass, locomotion, simple location—are no more real, and just as much a synthesis in the mind of the observer, as the so-called "secondary" qualities of color, taste, smell, an so on. Every quality we can possibly imagine is a projection that takes place between an observer and a phenomenon, like a rainbow that results from eyes in relation to light waves striking rain drops in a certain way. Our cognized world is no more—or less—real than a rainbow.

In searching for a more appropriate metaphor to better understand this new metaphysic, we might again look to music. Normally when we consider models of the universe, we rely upon our sense of sight, picturing in our mind a three-dimensional panorama, with everything co-present at one time in the picture—like a photo of the Milky Way, or a shot of the earth from space. But relying on our sense of vision is particularly problematic in attempting to think metaphysically about the world, because it suggests that it is possible to isolate a particular moment in time, cut off from everything preceding and following it. Nothing whatsoever in our vision can tell us anything about the intense interconnectedness of the world, both spatially and especially temporally. As Whitehead puts it,

> The information provided by mere sight is peculiarly barren—namely external regions disclosed as coloured.... [T]here is nothing intrinsic to the mere coloured regions which provides any hint of internal activity whereby change can be understood.... Nature is thus described as made up of vacuous bits of matter with no internal values, and merely hurrying through space.[45]

But what if reality is better understood through analogies drawn from the world of hearing than the world of sight? Zuckerkandl notes that,

> The knowledge of space that hand and eye possess is exactly matched by their ignorance of time.... A true image of time must be an image for the ear, an audible image, an image made of tones.... Thanks to music, we are able to *behold* time.[46]

If we listen, say, to a symphony, the whole point is that it cannot be understood merely as an aggregate of individual notes played together in an instant. No, the symphony obviously requires a certain amount of time, not only to reveal its essence, but to demonstrate how all of the individual parts relate to the whole, both harmonically (vertically) and melodically (horizontally). If we don't wait until the end of the symphony, we shall never come to understand how all of the parts have served the ends of the symphony taken as a whole. A process, as opposed to a thing or mechanism, only reveals its nature with a backward, top-down, or holistic view, not by looking at a particular, static slice of time.

As is true of subatomic particles, which are not absolutely distinct, but "smeared out" over a probability wave, a single note of music also doesn't really exist as a discrete entity. Rather, it consists of innumerable overtones and vibrations that are latent within musical "space" but which "collapse" into what is heard as a single, dominant tone. Like the quanta that comprise physical reality, music creates continuity out of discontinuity, a flowing musical surface that is suspended over time.[47] Furthermore, just like subatomic particles, individual notes are "non-local," in the sense that each note in the "line" of a melody "is also a participant in other relations, intersecting and interacting with them."[48]

> Musical compositions are organizations of time, which, unlike space, is given its shape by the events occurring within it.... A single point in musical time can be host to a contrapuntal assemblage of events. This temporal space is so laden with crossroads that we can choose, in our listening, any number of paths through it.[49]

Here again, like subatomic particles, the musical notes are *internally* related to one another, with no essential being except as reflected in all the others. The same note will obviously be experienced in a completely different way, depending on its musical context (just as an atom behaves differently in your body than a rock).

Likewise, if the universe is indeed a whole system, then its parts can only be understood in the context of the whole:

> If the whole did not participate in and serve as the ground for the existence of the parts, the parts would not exist. If one, therefore, seeks to disclose this whole by summing the parts, one is seeking to explain their existence in the absence of the ground for their existence.[50]

Persisting in this metaphysical delusion is akin to abstracting an ocean current from the totality of the ocean, or seeing clouds as separate from the weather system that produced them. Ultimately, every "thing" in the universe is somehow "inside" everything else, much more like an organism than a machine:

> ...[H]ere organic phenomena are not being simply *likened* to musical phenomena; instead, musical phenomena give us the decisive indication that leads us to an understanding of organic phenomena. Because there is music, we can comprehend the genesis of an organism.[51]

The point here is that there is no possibility of analyzing the universe into parts and then additively coming to understand the whole. Wholeness is the primordial condition of the universe, not anything we can inductively construct from multiple observations; the solid matter we construct out of our locally evolved senses cannot in reality be dissected from the sea of energy underlying it:

> Simply put, the classical assumption that the collection of parts constitutes the whole has proven invalid. We now know that the properties of parts can only be understood in terms of the dynamics of the whole, and that what we call a "part" is a pattern in the inseparable web of relations.[52]

In a holistic, temporal universe, points become lines, lines become planes, planes become volumes, and space-time itself becomes a hyperdimensional plenitude, with past and future somehow co-present in the now. According to Huxley, since all phenomena in our universe (including human beings) are *processes,*

> they can never be evaluated or even adequately described solely or mainly in terms of their origins: they must be defined by their direction, their inherent possibilities..., and their deducible future trends.[53]

As such, looking at the universe *from the bottom up*, that is, from matter to life to mind, the appearance of life and mind seems inexplicable, even impossible. But many of the most puzzling aspects of the universe disappear if we *begin* at the top, and ask ourselves the question, "What *must* the universe be like if such thoroughly bizarre modalities as life or consciousness can exist?" Science, by its very nature, is engaged in the project of "pulling" all subjective and qualitative elements in the universe back into the realm of the purely quantitative and objective, ultimately located in the distant past.[54] But there is no philosophical obstacle whatsoever preventing us from reversing this view, and considering the possibility that the movement of evolution involves a "pulling" of the objective back into the subjective, located in the future. Only by changing our perspective to a "top down" one, from spirit to mind to life to matter, does the cosmos become intelligible in its totality, a totality that unquestionably includes biological and psychological dimensions.[55]

Let's put it another way: when we talk about a "relationship" between life and the cosmos, we are dealing quite literally with a tautology, a statement of equivalence; that is to say, as we have seen, our universe is so narrowly suited to life, that in order not to mislead, we cannot refer only to "the universe" but to something along the lines of "the living universe" or "the universe in the process of coming to life." Ours is exactly what a universe hospitable to life looks like: everything in it points to or implies life, just as life implies it. From our privileged vantage point of being alive, there is actually nothing surprising about the nature of this universe, because it had to be almost exactly the way it is in order for life to exist in it—if any of those twenty parameters were even slightly different, we wouldn't be here. So really, when we talk about Life as such, we are necessarily presupposing everything that made it possible for Life to exist at all. In other words, it turns out that our universe is not contingent at all, but a necessary consequence of the fact that we are alive. To put it even stronger terms, for some very odd reason—a reason science is simply not equipped to understand, but which should become clear by Book Four—Life is actually *indispensable* to the cosmos. Or as poetically expressed by the mystic Rumi, "Though it seems the branch is the origin of the fruit, in truth the branch only exists for the fruit."

Reductionistic scientists will naturally object that this is placing the living cart before the material horse, but in fact, they are making the unwarranted assumption that physics is more general than biology, and that biology can be completely subsumed by physics.[56] However, if we wish to get past some of the longstanding philosophical stalemates that have prevented us from truly understanding the whole of reality, then I believe we must free our minds of unnecessary and unwarranted preconceptions, and agree with the eminent physicist John Wheeler that,

> Like a strange botanic specimen newly arrived from a far corner of the earth, [the universe] appears at first sight so carefully cleaned of clues that we do not know which are the branches and which are the roots. Which end is up and which is down?[57]

Indeed, which end is up, Life or Matter? While we are certainly free simply to assume that life is contingent on a certain very specific kind of universe, we may argue with equally sound logic that the universe is a necessary consequence of a metaphysical principle called Life. Make no mistake: in order to forever rid ourselves of the pernicious mind/matter dualism, one side will have to go. (But ultimately, this is a dispute that we will not be able to resolve before discussing in Book Two exactly what Life *is*, and whether or not it is even synonymous with biology, or something else entirely.)

This notion of top-down wholeness is a profoundly important one, with implications that will (as we shall see in Books Two, Three and Four) resonate on every level and mode of existence, both subjective and objective. A "whole" represents a unity, a single thing, with all parts subordinate to and harmoniously integrated with it. In order for something to be called whole, there must be some hierarchical, organizing principle that is present in all of the parts that constitute the whole. A genuine whole is like a living organism, wherein the parts have an internal relationship to one another, all subordinate to a transcendent principle of organization that is present in the material of which the whole is made. The organism grows, differentiates and develops from *within*, in contrast, say, to a machine, whose externally related parts are assembled from the outside. And, unlike a machine, which may be composed of various materials, the universe ultimately represents a unity of substance—it is all the same "stuff," whatever we wish to call that stuff. And finally, an organism is internally related not just in space, but in *time*: it is internally related to its own past and future, something we experience as *memory, anticipation,* and *fulfillment.*[58]

Without the principle of wholeness woven into the very fabric of the universe, it would be impossible for true wholeness to later emerge at the levels of life and mind. The integrated wholeness we see in a living organism discloses a fundamental principle that is absolutely intrinsic to the universe. Likewise, Kant's "synthetic, transcendental unity of pure apperception"—the ordered whole we all effortlessly refer to as "I"—is another accurate intuition of the wholeness of nature. That is to say, without the principle of wholeness, there is simply no explanation as to how the billions of individual cellular processes taking place in your brain and body so neatly resolve themselves into the simple, transcendent and unitive experience called "I." In fact, in order for the universe to exist as an integrated, ordered, and undivided wholeness, it must, on some level undisclosed (and undisclosable) by science, be aware of itself. Wholeness, as we shall presently see, implies at least a rudimentary degree of consciousness and interiority. Without it, there is no way to account for how "the physicist's desire to study atoms emerges from them,"[59] or even how the billions of independently living cellular creatures that constitute "me" (but cannot know of my existence) have somehow become sufficiently unified to type this sentence upon my command.

## 1.3 Spatial Wholeness: Turning the Cosmos Inside Out

> If consciousness is an emergent property of the universe in the case of human beings, would not this also imply, given the underlying wholeness of the cosmos, that the universe is itself conscious?
>
> —Menos Kafatos & Robert Nadeau, *The Conscious Universe*

> Inconceivable as it seems to ordinary reason, you—and all other conscious beings as such—are all in all. Hence this life of yours which you are living is not merely a piece of the entire existence, but is, in a certain sense, the *whole*....
>
> —Erwin Schrodinger

Among living things, human beings are unique for the fact that we are aware of simultaneously existing in two seemingly distinct realms, an external, objective world of material substance, and an internal, subjective world of private thought, emotion, meaning, and creativity. Even though this latter world is the only one we can ever really "know" first hand—all knowledge of the external world supposedly being based on mere inferences filtered through an evolved and species-bound nervous system—our mysterious inwardness is dismissed by most scientists as a side effect—perhaps even an illusion—produced by a brain which happens to be particularly complex. Although most religious traditions regard our inwardness as a primary fact of existence, they are just as thoroughly dualistic as science, positing a soul that has somehow been implanted into us by God. Either way, this phenomenon of inwardness as such—without question the most interesting, even shocking fact of the universe—is really not explained, but explained away.

But our subjective dimension is an ontological fact, perhaps, as Descartes believed, the only fact of which we can be entirely certain. And it is indeed a mysterious fact, because there is simply no amount of knowledge of physics, biology, or neurology that explains or has any purchase in the inner world of subjectivity:

> Nor would the fullest objective description of the brain, down to its minutest structures and most delicate ways of functioning, provide any clue of the existence of consciousness, if we did not know about it through our own inner experience—precisely through consciousness itself.[60]

Analogously, we could spend a lifetime studying the exact properties of the electricity passing through a telephone line, but it would not give us even the slightest bit of information as to the content and meaning of the conversation taking place. In short, the Subject for whom the world is Object is absolutely and irrevocably invisible to the methods and models of science: only consciousness itself can know consciousness, or even know of its existence in others.

It is more than mere tautology to state that we inhabit a universe that gave rise to subjectivity; true, we are here, so this is an obvious statement. But if we wish to construct a complete account of existence, we must, at the very least, grant to matter an original potentiality with astonishing capacities far beyond what physics can deduce from its models. Physics can no more capture subjectivity in its current paradigm than a two-dimensional plane can capture a three-dimensional cone. One might well ask if it is possible that subjectivity was latently present from the very outset of the cosmos; but from our surpassing vantage point, 13 billion years from the origin, one might more appropriately ask if it is possible to conceive of our universe *without* this latent inwardness entangled throughout creation.

You may, as most scientists are apt to do, argue that matter came first, so that subjectivity, mind, must be subordinate to it. But we now know that this is rather misleading. In the beginning, the universe was completely unstable, with temperatures in the billions and billions of degrees, nothing (outwardly, at least) but a cauldron of energy, an indistinct miasma of elementary particles. In fact, matter didn't emerge for hundreds of thousands of years into the big bang, so that both mind and matter may be looked upon as relative latecomers in cosmic evolution. Scientists continue to view matter as primary, simply because this is what our senses tell us. But physics long ago ruled out this kind of coarse, common-sense picture as a reliable indicator of what is really real or primary in our universe. Perhaps we may even stipulate that both matter and mind reduce to something called *energy*, so long as we stop pretending to know what this energy *is*.

According to biologist Charles Birch, we have run into a metaphysical dead-end because "we think of mentality and subjectivity as elements that do not enter the evolutionary sequence until quite high up." But "there is an alternative, and that is that from its beginnings *evolution is the evolution of subjects*."[61] So to suggest that our inwardness was implicit in the origins of the universe should be no more controversial than pointing out that matter too was an implicit possibility contained in the seeds of the big bang. Matter, no less than the mind, is an historical *achievement* of something much more general that preceded it.

Among the various interpretations of quantum physics, there is only one that makes the inwardness of the cosmos—and by extension, ourselves—philosophically non-problematic. The interpretation I am referring to rests on the controversial concept of non-locality, which many physicists seem to have difficulty accepting despite the fact that it is fully permitted (some say demanded) by the research:

> A very interesting question, for those of us who feel uncomfortable with the quantum theory, is whether it could be replaced by any other theory that is local. The answer is no.... This means that we can only give a complete description of any part of the universe to the extent that we describe the whole universe.[62]

Despite the misgivings of many physicists, recent experiments in physics imply that all subatomic particles once in close proximity, even from the origin of the cosmos, remain a single quantum system, forever linked and interacting together. In what has been dubbed "experimental metaphysics," a number of researchers, including Alain Aspect at the University of Paris and Nicolus Gisun at the University of Geneva, have demonstrated that a pair of photons will remain instantaneously correlated with each other, regardless of their distance in time and space. As such, we may assert with some confidence that "non-separability is now one of the most certain general concepts in physics."[63]

It is difficult to overstate the importance of these experimental findings as to their extraordinary metaphysical implications. The non-separability or quantum entanglement of subatomic particles is also referred to as non-locality, because it implies that the entire universe must be, at some level, instantaneously in contact with itself despite its vast dimensions in time and space. It is probably easier to imagine spatial non-locality; the idea of temporal non-locality is perhaps more mind-boggling. Nevertheless, if the universe is spatially non-local, then it is necessarily temporally non-local (because time and space are complementary aspects of one another). Therefore, if consciousness emerges at *any* point in cosmic evolution, it is as if it were there at *all* times. Moreover, because non-locality appears to be a fundamental, unavoidable property of the cosmos as a whole, this means that the universe must somehow, to employ Whitehead's term, "prehend" itself, because all particles within it remain in some sense part of a single system. Thus, the discovery of quantum non-locality makes it possible—actually, necessary—to view the universe as a whole system that maintains contact with itself across space and time. As such, then, the principle of non-locality requires us to posit some dimension of "awareness," regardless of how inchoate or infinitesimal it might be. But the fact that this primordial, non-cognitive awareness has presumably been present from the very start—and is now demonstrably present in us—provides an elegant solution to the insoluble mind-matter dualism that has always plagued Western philosophy. What matter is "trying to say" through quantum mechanics, seems to be "that all matter has a rudimentary degree of mind..."[64] The universe, as Eddington put it, is made of "mind stuff," of matter with mind-like qualities, of mindmatter. Indeed, the brilliant philosopher Schopenhaur, using pure reason unaided by modern physics, argued the same point: that the "noumenon"—that is, whatever reality is in itself, uncolored by our perceptions—must, if nothing else, be an undifferentiated One, directly and non-cognitively known unto itself, without "knowing" in the usual subject-object way (for that would imply twoness, not wholeness). Similarly, mystics from time immemorial have attested that the universe is actually composed of a single "divine substance" that may be known through identification with it to reveal the Oneness of All. (But this is something we won't be in a position to confirm or refute until Book Four.)

It is quite possible that non-locality provides the missing key that explains how consciousness is able to work in a "top-down" fashion on the brain. For example, the eminent biophysicist Werner Loewenstein has speculated that the "all-excluding oneness" of our consciousness—a phenomenon that takes place over what is an immense space in molecular terms—might be explained by the *quantum coherence* that arises from non-locality. In pondering what it is that could possibly account for the rapid spread of information over so vast a molecular space as the brain, he notes how the principle of non-locality might make this unproblematic. Again, because of non-locality, "one part of a system is able to affect other parts instantaneously," just as if the entire assembly were the quantum state of a single particle: "To start with, the particles are milling around randomly (their usual behavior); but all of a sudden many of them begin to move, like well-drilled soldiers, in unison."[65] As such, he wonders whether a similar "quantum state over a space transcending the cell boundaries—a single state with a large number of quantum activities occurring simultaneously in many neurons," might be "the stuff of our conscious thoughts."[66] If thought is the only phenomenon we know of that is faster than light,[67] it makes sense that it would operate non-locally.

My point is this: While there is widespread agreement among physicists as to the "facts" of physics, there is little agreement as to how these facts are to be interpreted. As it stands, there are probably at least a dozen mutually incompatible major theories that account for the phenomena of physics equally well. If we take only physical reality into consideration, there is no rational way to choose between these interpretations. Instead, various scientists choose one interpretation over another based upon non-scientific, unarticulated (and usually faulty) metaphysical assumptions. But there is no ironclad rule that says we must limit ourselves to the physical domain in attempting to sort out this problem. Rather, if we begin our inquiry with the obvious fact that we are alive and conscious, then perhaps we have to look to the interpretation of physics that permits these exceedingly strange conditions to exist. Or, as genially expressed by philosopher Holmes Rolston, "if physics presents a theory of quarks that implies that I cannot wave to my friend, so much the worse for that theory."[68] I believe there is only one such interpretation, and that the other interpretations, if true, would mean that we couldn't be here contemplating them (or be able to wave to our friends, for that matter). According to Birch, it is nigh impossible to metaphysically

> understand how something with an inside, something that is for itself, could emerge out of things that have no inside, that are nothing for themselves. Because this seems *prima facie* impossible, the burden of proof is on those who think that it is possible."[69]

That is to say, the placement of an arbitrary boundary between mind and matter, and the assumption of an objective world completely independent of consciousness, leaves everything on "our" side of the line unexplained and unexplainable, in theory, in fact, and even in principle.

* * *

But in the meantime, what really existed ten billion years ago? Five billion years ago? To ask it in another way, what was the universe like with no separate individual there to experience it? In just what sense are we entitled to say that the universe even existed at all? This is not as easy a question as it sounds. In order to answer it, you must first of all remove the concept of perspective, both temporally and spatially with no living beings, there is no "point of view" from which to survey the universe, there is only all places at once. There is no finite time from which to look backward or forward, no before or after, no relative position from within time's flow. What about scale? Do we look from the scale of a billion light years, where the universe appears rather boring and homogeneous? From the point of view of an atom? A quark? But don't think in visual terms, for vision is a property of eyes, and eyes do not exist. Do not think in terms of hot or cold, hard or soft, solid or gas, loud or quiet, bright or dim, violent or gentle, because these are all properties of senses and perspectives which do not exist. As Hegel knew, "there is no unmediated knowledge of the particular."[70] "Apart from the experiences of subjects," wrote Whitehead, "there is nothing, bare nothingness." Likewise, according to Schopenhaur,

> If I take away the thinking subject, the whole material world must vanish, as this world is nothing but the phenomenal appearance in the sensibility of our own subject, and is a species of this subject's representations."[71]

And yet, there are certain universal truths that must be the case for any conceivable observer, overall features that we may deduce about the noumenal universe as a whole, even before the appearance of Life or Mind, and regardless of the limitations of our perspective, our sensory faculties, or our mode of cognition. Certainly we may agree that the cosmos we eventually awakened to possessed an unexpected degree of mathematical order and a puzzling tendency toward greater differentiation, complexity, and novel self-organization through time; it also manifested an undivided wholeness suggestive of some type of interiority, or self-prehension. But, as far as we could have known, it possessed no freedom, no destiny, no meaning beyond itself—just an unevolving cosmic stalemate with no ontological options. God was apparently a fabulous mathematician, but nothing more—certainly not a biologist, neurologist, or historian. Clearly no amount of knowledge of physics or chemistry could have discerned the fantastic potential that only time could reveal; or have foretold the luminous fissure that was about to break open in this heretofore dark, impenetrable circle. Here, the dawning of an internal horizon in a universe now divided against itself, the unimaginable opening of a window on the world, a wondrous strange mutation as unique, mysterious, and altogether surprising as our first bang into material space-time; that is,

*A luminous fissure appeared in this herefore dark, impenetrable circle, the unimaginable opening of a window on the world.*

# BOOK TWO

## BIOGENESIS: *The Testimony of Life*

[L]ife poses the most serious kinds of challenges to physics itself.... More specifically, the expectation that phenomena of life or mind could be assimilated directly into physics as merely a minor technical bubble, of no conceptual significance, was mistaken.

—Robert Rosen, *Essays on Life Itself*

The basic objection [to Darwinism is] that it confers miraculous powers on inappropriate agents. In essence, it is an attempt to supernaturalize nature, to endow unthinking processes with more-than-human powers—including the power of creating thinkers.... I find it impossible to share this faith that supra-human achievements can be encompassed by sub-human means and sub-rational mechanisms.

—Richard Spilsbury, *Providence Lost*

Yes, the miraculous does exist, for *life* is only a series of miracles, if we understand by "miracle" not the absence of cause..., but rather the visible effect of an invisible cause, or the effect on a lower plane due to a cause on a higher plane.

—Anonymous, *Meditations on the Tarot*

...portions of the universe—*what, on Earth?!*—somehow declared their independence from the strict, physiochemical laws that had held matter in their death grip up to that time, and began exchanging energy and information with the "outside," so as to maintain and reproduce themselves through time. In setting up this dynamic exchange with the outside, the universe now had undeniable evidence of an "inside," with new, unprecedented categories of being, such as intention, perception, sensation, emotion, and, eventually, freedom, thought, and moral and aesthetic judgment:

> The nondogmatic thinker will not suppress the testimony of life.... It is in the dark stirrings of primeval organic substance that a principle of freedom shines forth for the first time within the vast necessity of the physical universe—a principle foreign to suns, planets, and atoms.[1]

With Life, *existence somehow became experience*, and a new world literally came into being, outwardly dependent upon the previous one, but at the same time inwardly transcending it: a universe beyond itself, a restless declaration of subjectivity from the mute algorithms of opaque material repetition. Only with the appearance of life can we retrospectively understand that matter was endowed from "before the beginning" with vibrant possibilities that no physicist could have then predicted or can now explain, any more than we could have looked at sodium and chloride and predicted that salt (sodium chloride) would taste good on tomatoes. Since Life, with its inwardness, will, and purpose, has emerged from the material substance of the cosmos, it is difficult to avoid the conclusion that

> these qualities cannot be entirely foreign to this substance in its essence; if something cannot be foreign to its essence, then it also cannot be foreign to its beginning; thus in the matter under formation in the "Big Bang" there must have already been present the possibility of subjectivity—the inner dimension in latency, which awaited its external opportunity in the cosmos for manifestation.[2]

Indeed, it is illogical and metaphysically incoherent to argue that life has somehow been superimposed on a "dead" material universe. That is to say, the concept of death can only be understood in the context of life: the two define each other and arise simultaneously, like "inside and outside" or "husband and wife." Thus, while life arose through the universe, by no means are we justified in saying that it was a dead universe; rather, it was a universe prior to the outward manifestation of the life/death duality:

> At first sight it may appear that birth and death are attributes of Life, but it is not really so: birth and death are processes of Matter, of the body. The Life-principle is not formed and dissolved in the formulation and dissolution of the body.... Life forms body, it is not formed by it.[3]

In other words, *all death is local.* Unlike Life, which must be a nonlocal, immanent spiritual principle of the cosmos, there can be no metaphysical principle called "death." Rather, there are only cadavers and corpses, strictly local areas where Life is no longer concentrated and outwardly visible at the moment. As we shall come to see in Book Four, we will not be able understand either Life *or* death by studying the universe prior to their outward manifestation in the world. Rather, to comprehend our cosmic ecosystem we must "read the fine print" represented by Life itself, not just the large-print, condensed version of reality produced by physics. Again, the universe has an entirely different character depending upon our spatial or temporal vantage point, just as our body does not look alive at subatomic or galactic dimensions.

Just as scientists cannot say what actually preceded the big bang and caused the material world to come into existence, they do not know what life *is* or what caused it to emerge—how the cosmos managed to pull a live rabbit out of its material hat. While there are models of how life might have started, these models simply reframe the phenomenon in such a way that it is no longer problematic, like saying that the mind consists of "neural networks," "information processing," or "id, ego and superego," so that the enigma of consciousness is spuriously solved through mere sleights of language. In fact, when it comes to problems of genesis—the origins of the cosmos, life and mind—science simply substitutes questions it can answer for ones it cannot. According to the eminent biologist Richard Lewontin, scientists are too clever and perceptive (let alone, tenure-seeking) to spend their careers working on particularly thorny problems

> where they have little hope of success. When faced with questions that they really don't know how to answer—like "How does a single cell turn into a mouse?" or "How did the structure and activity of Beethoven's brain result in Opus 131?"—the only thing that natural scientists know how to do is turn them into other questions that they do know how to answer. That is, scientists do what they already know how to do.[4]

So submitting to a biologist the question, "What is life?," is a bit like asking a watchmaker to explain the nature of time. The watchmaker may be able to tell you all about springs, gears, and pendulums, but he is obviously unqualified (based only upon his knowledge of watches) to say anything meaningful about time itself. Or, to put it another way, biology can tell us everything about life except for what it *is.*

Instead of dealing with life on its own mysterious terms, conventional biology provides answers that are on the same logical plane as those provided by the benighted watchmaker: ask about the origins of life, and you are likely to hear about cellular automata, catalyzing chemical reactions, protein synthesis, dissipative structures, clay ions, or flowing information circles—but not about Life as such. Science is simply a method for asking questions of reality, so we should not confuse the answers we get with an actual description of reality, any more than we should confuse intelligence with an IQ score, a musical performance with the digital encoding of a CD, or a baseball game with a box score.

But despite what biologists may tell us, a universe that contains even the potential for life is utterly different from one that does not, and different in ways that simply cannot be articulated by science as presently understood. For one thing, only such a universe may be *experienced* and *known.* As the philosopher Hans Jonas put it,

> The science of biology—being limited by its methods to external facts—must ignore the dimension of inwardness that is a part of life. In so doing, it leaves material life, which it claims to have totally explained, more mysterious than when it was unexplained.[5]

Surely, it doesn't advance our understanding for biologists to affirm that life may be reduced to matter, when physicists can't tell us what matter actually *is.* In other words, it is insufficient for scientists to tell us

> that the nature of matter is such that what we call life and consciousness develop out of and as qualities of physical forms wherever the environment permits the formation of their characteristic compounds. We want to know how the capacity to develop these qualities got there in the first place.[6]

True enough, before the appearance of life, the universe could be thought of as objectively One, a single-level totality of integration and therefore of potential *understanding.* But the first living being shattered that unity, for it represented a new and distinct identity over and apart from the prior unity of self-sufficient material existence. Any possibility of understanding the totality of the cosmos using physics alone ended abruptly with the appearance of life. The physicist's search for a mathematical "theory of everything" is about 3.8 billion years late. After that, the material numbers will never add up to the living sum, any more than the physicist can articulate a metaphysic that accounts for himself.[7]

With life comes the possibility—actually, the necessity—of transcendence, a category of being that is not accounted for by physics. In order to stay alive, an organism must constantly transcend itself by maintaining an open exchange of matter, energy, or information with the environment. Science cannot appreciate the qualitative leap to a self-transcendent universe, because the practice of science *presupposes* the existence of transcendent selves (that is, scientists) standing in opposition to the world: "science must transcend itself to remain science. It stands as evidence that something beyond its own limits is inherent in the very consciousness which makes it possible."[8] Scientists are able to practice science because they regard the universe as an objective, public *outside* capable of being embraced (and therefore transcended) in its totality by a private, subjective *inside.* The living beings called scientists are themselves *a priori* benefactors of a transcendent wholeness that is not conferred from the outside, but through an internal, non-cognitive "prehension," a self-integrating, self-unifying, and self-renewing process that cannot be located in or reduced to its constituent, external parts. The "identity" of a living thing is not located in its material—reduced to its material substance, it is no longer living. Rather, it is located across time and space, in its dynamic and transcendent functional wholeness. Once again, we see that the very possibility of life presupposes the non-local wholeness described in Book One. As philosopher Errol Harris succinctly puts it,

> The type of property that must be presumed to make possible the emergence of life is that which has already been adumbrated in quantum physics. It is that type of property which is holistically determined by the structural principle of the system to which the properties belong.[9]

In other words, *already existing wholes* are a prerequisite for the operation of Darwinian evolution, so that "Ordered totality is thus logically prior to natural selection."[10] Or, to take it one step further, "From the very start, nothing less than Life itself (to speak strictly) has ever lived."[11] Life necessarily pervades space and extends infinitely forward and back in time. The simplistic notion that we may reduce subjective to objective, inside to outside, life to matter, is "tantamount to postulating a simple world,"[12] a world too simple for life, mind, or even natural selection to exist in it.

* * *

How then did living beings—local benefactors of the non-local Life principle—appear? How did matter ever escape from the dark, dense, utterly predictable prison house of physical law that supposedly rules the cosmos? Think of it: for nine, ten billion years, nothing but the blind rearrangement of matter, just one blunt, senseless fact after another—or so we are asked to believe. In actuality, as explained by Teilhard de Chardin,

> [W]e can no more fix an absolute zero in time (as was once supposed) for the advent of life than for that of any other experimental reality.... Everything in some extremely attenuated extension of itself, has existed from the very first.... But... that each new being has and must have a *cosmic embryogenesis* in no way invalidates the reality of its *historic birth*.[13]

In other words, although a latent or embryonic principle of Life surely must have existed during the first nine billion years of cosmic evolution, the second singularity nevertheless occurred in an historical instant, when the universe did something that no one could have anticipated, a flagrant violation of everything that had happened up to that point: matter wrapped around itself, turned outside in, and awakened to an obscure but utterly determined intention to go on being, to develop a new universe, or "microcosmos," within the existing one. One day, no life. The next day, Life!, "a fateful eddy..., a wheensy whirl in the cosmic stream where information, instead of flowing straight as everywhere else, flows in circles."[14] If physicists had been there on that day—or any of those preceding four thousand billion outwardly lifeless days—they surely would have told us that it was impossible—what, for unprecedented novelty to occur, for a categorically new domain to emerge, dependent on matter, but somehow existing independently of it, with an inexhaustible capacity not only to creatively modify and complexify itself, but to continuously extend and deepen its newfound inwardness as well? Sorry, can't happen. Not in this universe.

## 2.1 Is Life Necessary?

> ...[O]ut of all possible universes the only one which can exist, in the sense that it can be known, is simply the one which satisfies the narrow conditions necessary for the development of intelligent life.... The essence of our presence in the Universe today is that *we* require the Universe to have certain properties.
>
> —Bernard Lowell, *A Contemporary View of Man's Relation to the Universe*

Here we are, then, at the dawn of life, 3.85 billion years ago, with a lot of debris from the primal explosion strewn everywhere. Nine billion years or so have passed since the big bang, and we have no reason to believe that the next nine billion years will be any different from those first nine. In their attempt to account for the origins of life (and discourage creationists), biochemists like to blur the distinction between life and matter, so they now talk about a period of "pre-life" preparing the way for the emergence of life. Really, this kind of "junk metaphysics" is an attempt to sneak the principle of natural selection into the universe before there is a biology for it to operate on. In any event, it makes no philosophical sense, for the term "pre-life" assumes something—life—which supposedly did not exist and could not have been predicted by merely looking at its molecular constituents. If a period of pre-life did in fact prefigure life, then it is unnecessary to qualify it as "pre-," because it was part of the process of life and therefore indistinguishable from it. In other words, if we wish to be intellectually honest, we must place "pre-life" on the life side of the matter/life divide, not on the matter side, unless we fatuously rename life "post-matter."

The above problem just serves to illustrate how biology represents such an annoying quagmire of conceptual puzzles for physics, puzzles that in principle it can never eliminate. If the materialistic explanation of life is true, it can't be true: matter is dead, life is matter, therefore life is dead. Nevertheless, most scientists take it for granted that life does not exist as anything separate and distinct from matter. In the fashionable reductionist view, this is simply the way it must be: biology is in the end nothing more than an unlikely but mildly interesting property of physics. (Why interesting? Why should matter be interested in anything?) But this is hardly a suitable explanation for such a profound mystery. Rather, it is a "question-begging fallacy" that "demands an initial acceptance of the doctrine of naturalism before any explanation is offered."[15] In other words, only matter is ultimately real, so that life may be reduced to, and fully explained by, the electrical and chemical properties of atoms and molecules. It is a presupposition of science that we learn nothing new about the properties of matter through the study of matter that happens to have the shocking property of being alive. Knowledge must always be a one-way, bottom-up affair:

> One must never pass to a larger system in trying to understand a given one, but must invoke simpler sub-systems.... From simple to complex is only a matter of accretion of simple, context-independent parts.[16]

But unfortunately, this means that biology can never be reached by physics—you can't get here from there. Instead of looking "forward" at what all the parts of an organism are always converging upon—that is, the living organism—biology looks backward at that which the organism uses to express its functional wholeness, thus destroying the very thing—life—it is attempting to explain. This is odd, because it is not possible to even begin a discussion of life without an unstated intuition of the dynamic wholeness that is always manifested through it. After all, no biologist ever starts out by looking at a bunch of parts—a mouth here, a leg there—and inductively leaping to the conclusion that these parts must constitute a living whole.

The existence of life cannot be proven by science, any more than the existence of the cosmos can be proven by astrophysics; rather, both are metaphysical assumptions that are immediately ignored, and therefore never explained.[17] At the same time, scientists seem to be under the mistaken impression that, since science cannot define life quantitatively, it doesn't exist as a scientific problem whereas, in reality, life simply exceeds the limits of what quantitative science can explain. For those of us among the living, life is more than just a case of very improbable mathematics.

But as we saw in the case of physics in Book One, it is an unquestioned dogma in science that all qualities in the universe are ultimately explainable in terms of quantities; that everything not only may be assigned a number, but *is* a number.[18] Thus, in a very real sense, everything that has happened subsequent to the dawn of life may, according to the materialistic paradigm, be legitimately "pulled back" into the purely material domain prior to life, without loss of anything vital or fundamental: all qualities are reduced to quantity, freedom to necessity, life to matter. Of course, this arbitrarily ignores the critical issue of *time* discussed in Book One, that is, the question of how long it takes for something to become itself. Who's to say how much time a living universe requires to express itself locally and to eventually reveal its maximum degree of diversity-in-unity, or whether a living organism is simply a ripe old galaxy seen up close?

But this is exactly how reductionistic biologists are able to make the problem of life disappear: first, they create abstract mathematical models with the unstated assumption that everything outside the models has an exact image inside them; once everything is inside the model, they may claim objectivity, because everything is now a number, no longer tainted by any subjective quality; and finally, in order to complete the illusion, biologists forget that they are only using a simulated, abstract model of their own invention, with no actual external referent: in short, "one begins by abstracting from concrete existence, and ends by attributing concreteness to the abstraction."[19] But once life is identified with an impoverished, simplified mathematical model, *voila*, not only is the problem of life solved, the problem cannot even arise! However, there is a slight difficulty here; that is, the universe described by these models is so impoverished that life could not exist in it, any more than one may obtain nourishment by eating a recipe. The "life" in these biological models is actually more similar to a motion picture, which consists of innumerable photographs

> of something which is always moving, and by means of these successive static representations—none of which are real, because Life, the object photographed, never was at rest—recreates a picture of life, of motion.[20]

In other words, the gap between the orthodox scientific model of life and Life itself is conceptually as great as the gap between a Saturday cartoon show and the San Diego Zoo. And when we confuse the model with the thing itself,

> the properties we ascribe to our object of interest and the questions we ask about it reinforce the original metaphorical image and we miss aspects of the system that do not fit the metaphorical approximation.[21]

This actually reflects a kind of intellectual idolatry, for "when the nature and limitations of artificial images are forgotten, they become idols."[22] Science bows before the idolatrous "high abstractions" it confounds "with the primary reality,"[23] thus attributing an independent reality to its own fragmented viewpoint (all the while accusing metaphysically-minded "heretics" of doing the same thing by positing "unnecessary" worlds of life, mind, and spirit, when there is only the one presumtive material world). And why do these prickly, hypersensitive materialists defend their abstract idols with the same fervor of the religious fundamentalist? Because if humans are "cut off from the spiritual plane," they "will find a 'god' to worship on some lower level, thus endowing something relative with what belongs only to the absolute."[24]

Of course, prior to the emergence of modern science, human beings made the habitual mistake of subjectivizing, or "mentalizing" the environment in order to comprehend it; now they commit the opposite fallacy of objectifying the subjective in order to understand life and mind. Ironically, biologists today are studying the universe of four billion years ago, when biological entities were not there; they are seeking a kind of Platonic truth that is unsullied by Life, independent of the scientist. In order to recapture the lost material "unity" of the cosmos, they bring in the reductionist wrecking ball to level all of its upper stories, so that "the aristocracy of form is replaced by the democracy of matter."[25] Thus, regardless of how close scientists come to a complete understanding of the cosmos, if they are employing the standard ways of materialistic science, it will be an understanding from before the instant life became manifest. In order to place a bright line between observer and observed, subject and object, science must retreat to a time when no subjects apparently existed. In short, science tries "to pull the subjective into the objective by pulling the present into the sufficiently remote past.[26]

But in so doing, science can never leave the ground floor of the cosmic eschalator (sic). As we already know from Book One, it is impossible to draw such a line between the subjective and objective worlds without some annoying mind-stuff ending up on the wrong side of the artificial dualism. "Trouble arises," according to Rosen, when we attempt to divide a universe into two parts so as to satisfy some property (such as objectivity), and end up with "some consequent of the property back into one or the other class as defined *by* the property."[27] In this case, we end up with way too much biology on the material side of the divide. Biologists—and scientists in general—proceed as if living things are "clues only to what the universe is *not* like,"[28] but the more they prove this point, the more they disprove it. To borrow an arboreal analogy from Harding, these scientists are like the branches of a tree trying to show that the trunk is dead by growing more leaves, only proving Gilson's point that the question of what makes science possible is not a scientific question susceptible to a scientific answer.

## Life: The Accidentally-On-Purpose Phenomenon

A huge conceptual problem for biology, according to Rosen, is that it is completely organized around the paradigm of natural selection, which turns out to be metaphysically incoherent. Natural selection does not in fact bear on the problem of Life itself, but on the origins of *species* of life. As such, orthodox biologists are committed to the view that any and all changes in life forms occur absolutely blindly, governed by chance mutations presided over by an environment which selects the winners whose genes will pass on to the next generation. At no point, according to the standard model of biology, is there a violation of any known physical principle.

But whereas the ongoing evolution of life is completely random, the origin of life itself is supposedly not; rather, the origin of life is to be explained completely mechanistically, as an inevitable consequence of "simple downhill reactions," of underlying chemical processes. Here we are being asked to accept a stark contradiction; that is, despite no unambiguous evidence, it is assumed that life as such must be a necessary outcome of chemical properties, potentially present at the outset of the universe. But once life appears, it is then regarded as completely contingent, guided only by random, unpredictable and accidental mutations, with no purpose or necessity whatsoever. Here we are confronted with an incoherent, ad hoc metaphysical dualism of the first order. Even on purely logical grounds, according to Michael Denton,

> [It] is far more likely that, if the chemical evolution of the first cell was built in, then the far less complex process—the biological evolution of life—will also turn out to be built in.[29]

In fact, it is logically impossible for a true novelty (such as life) to arise from chemical necessity. Take, for example, the twenty-six letters of the alphabet. The reason why these letters may be combined to form words is precisely due to the fact that the letters, with a few exceptions (such as Q and U), do not have to go together in any particular way. Imagine playing a game of Scrabble, but instead of picking seven letters which may be combined in an infinite variety of ways, each letter dictated that the next letter could be combined with it in only one particular way. Obviously, not only would any kind of game be impossible, but it would be impossible to make any meaningful statement with such an alphabet. As Polanyi expressed it,

> Whatever may be the origin of a DNA configuration, it can function as a code only if its order is not due to the forces of potential energy. It must be as physically indeterminate as the sequence of words is on a printed page.[30]

In fact, it is only the physical *indeterminacy* of a DNA sequence "that produces the improbability of occurrence of any particular sequence and thereby enables it to have a meaning…."[31] Again, physics can only deal with this improbability by pointing backward, toward a single-level, chemical framework, so that these unlikely patterns of genetic information are regarded only as rare instead of meaningful. To apprehend any meaning—such as the meaning of this sentence—one must look forward, to where the words are pointing, not back to that which is doing the pointing (i.e., the words or letters themselves).

What is true of words and the meanings they converge upon is equally true of the molecular constituents through which Life expresses itself. Over one hundred years before the development of modern biology, Kierkegaard, on purely philosophical grounds, recognized that the *necessary* cannot come into existence, because coming into existence is a transition from not existing to existing. The purely necessary in fact cannot essentially change, because it is always itself. In other words, novelty is truly creative and therefore contingent and unnecessary. If something is strictly determined, it cannot be novel or creative, for the same reason that you cannot compose a symphony by merely applying a predetermined rule for the combination of notes. According to Maritain, reality is composed of *nature* and *adventure,* which

> is why it has a direction in time and by its duration constitutes an (irreversible) *history*—these two elements are demanded for history, for a world of pure natures would not stir in time; there is no history for Platonic archetypes; nor would a world of pure adventure have any direction; there is no history for a thermodynamic equilibrium.[32]

Again, if we say that necessity governs the emergence of life, we run into insurmountable conceptual problems because it is not possible to encode *information* in molecules that can only combine in one way. In other words, our problem is not really the emergence of life from non-life, but the encoding of information by non-information. And not just any information, but the inconceivably complex information entailed in the simplest biological system. Even a single cell "must utilize close to a million unique and adaptive structures and processes—more than the number in a jumbo jet."[33]

But there is an equivalent problem if, in order to be philosophically consistent, we decide that chance, or pure "adventure," should govern things on both sides of the matter/life divide, not just the life side. Until quite recently, science believed it had the answer to this problem: the mighty god of Chance, opiate of the scientisic multitudes. That is, given the vast amount of time available in the universe, it was assumed that random processes alone could account for the development of life. But scientific faith in this view has come under strain for a number of reasons. First, we now know that there was not nearly as much time as previously thought for life to be set in motion. No one believes any longer that infinite time was available for earth to randomly experiment with every possible combination of elements, like the hundred monkeys who, given enough time, will eventually produce the works of P. G. Wodehouse. Rather, the earth only began to form about 4.6 billion years ago, just as soon as it was possible to do so. Then, for the subsequent 1.62 billion years, earth was, among other inconveniences, simply too hot and radioactive for complex, stable biological compounds to form.

Now the current fossil record indicates that life emerged on earth 3.85 billion years ago. From 3.98 billion years ago, when the earth was too hot to sustain life, to 3.85 billion years ago, when life appeared, is a paltry (in geologic terms) 130 million years. As such, a window of just 130 million years was available for random chemical processes to result in living beings. Remember, science permits no intention here, no teleology, no purpose, just chemicals floating around, doing what they are constrained to do.

Could it happen? Well, yes and no. Any number of mathematicians have calculated the exact odds of random processes producing even a simple (but critical for life) enzyme, and it comes out to about one chance in ten to the twentieth power, or 1 in 100,000,000,000,000, 000,000. As for the odds of random processes resulting in a single cell, that would be more like one in ten to the eightieth power. Mathematicians have a word for this: impossible (for some reason, a probability of less than one in ten to the fiftieth power is considered a mathematical impossibility),[34] something like walking blindfolded into the Sahara and picking out a single grain of sand three times in a row:

> [T]he formation within geological time of a human body, by the laws of physics (or any other laws of a similar nature), starting from a random distribution of elementary particles and the field, is as unlikely as the separation by chance of the atmosphere into its components.[35]

Not only that, but the very purpose of scientific hypothesis is to rescue us from chance and randomness, to explain how and why something happened, not to explain it away as a miraculous coincidence. Jaki summarizes the situation by noting that "chance remains a glorious cover-up for ignorance," while strict determinism, for that matter, "is refuted by the very freedom whereby it is posited."[36] Or, as bluntly expressed by Barfield, "Chance, in fact, = no hypothesis."[37]

Scientists who wonder about these things are fully aware of the daunting odds, and are beginning to understand that they had better come up with a better explanation than randomness or determinacy to explain the sudden emergence of life. They are caught in a sort of "catch 22 to the nth power" because both scenarios imply guidance from some type of creative intelligence. (It has been remarked that "Teleology is a lady without whom the biologist cannot live but with whom he would not appear in public.")[38] It seems almost impossible that random processes could result in a living entity. But it really doesn't advance their materialistic cause to embrace determinism either; according to Morowitz,

> It is widely assumed that to hold the idea that life began by deterministic processes on the surface of the earth is, of necessity, an antireligious point of view. This is certainly not the case.... Indeed, the idea of life as necessary would seem, at the very minimum, to presuppose that the universe is infused with something like a creative intelligence.[39]

Morowitz goes on to say that "the short time required for life to emerge argues that either life was a unique event, or spontaneous life is highly probable. I favor the second of these possibilities."[40]

Unfortunately, rather than viewing the problem with this kind of detached objectivity, most scientists seem to be more preoccupied with not ceding an inch to creationists, as if the only viable alternatives to the problem of life's origins are chance, determinacy, or a literal reading of the Book of Genesis. For example, Francis Crick, the co-discoverer of DNA, has conceded that

> An honest man, armed with all the knowledge available to us now, could only state that in some sense, the origin of life appears at the moment to be almost a miracle, so many are the conditions which would have to be satisfied to get it going.[41]

As such, because there simply was not enough time for life to arise randomly, Crick has put forth the theory that it must have been "seeded" by intelligences from other galaxies. But even if true, those galaxies would be dealing with the identical time constraints, including a 13 billion-year-old universe and probably several billion years for hospitable planets to form. In short, Crick's theory, known as "directed panspermia," can only result in at best a slight improvement of the odds, and quite possibly even worse odds.[42]

Nevertheless, the vast majority of biologists continue to maintain that every last bit of the mind-boggling diversity and undeniable progress of life, right through the emergence of human beings, may be attributed to an inconceivable number of completely random, contingent, and unnecessary, but very lucky, accidents. In fact, if we could somehow "rewind" evolution and start over from the beginning, it is assumed that the entire process was so governed by chance, that it is unlikely that anything resembling humans would ever happen again.[43] In one sense, this is true: there was nothing inevitable *from the past,* or from the world of physics, that was sufficient to cause the evolution of molecules to amino acids to single cells to human beings. But what if the ultimate cause of human beings is located not in the past, but in the future, operating not from part-to-whole, but whole-to-part? And what if Life is more general than physics, the more encompassing principle to which the laws of physics must conform?

## 2.2 Is Life General?

> It is clear, therefore, that whatever the original source of life may have been, it can neither have been by the natural selection of nonliving chemical processes, nor by purely accidental and random synthesis of proteins, that it arose. It seems that there must be some principle of unity, creating and maintaining coherent wholes, already inherent in the process of the world from which life originally emerged.
>
> —Errol Harris, *The Reality of Time*

Alfred North Whitehead once wrote that "It is a well-founded historical generalization, that the last thing to be discovered in any science is what the science is really about."[44] If this is true, then perhaps it shouldn't surprise us to learn that the rank-and-file biologist hasn't a clue as to what Life is or how it came to be, any more than the physicist understands what energy actually is or the psychologist can say what consciousness is. Few people ever stop to consider the fact that biology cannot explain biology. How could it? Biology is a closed system of knowledge referring to already existent biological entities, so only something outside this system of knowledge can explain the presence of those biological entities. Only a view from outside the closed system of biology can tell us whether the emergence of life reveals anything new about the properties of matter. Thus, the biologist defers to the physicist on this point, who confidently informs us that the presence of life in our universe is of no significance whatsoever. Therefore, in assembling our ultimate metaphysical principles, we are free to ignore and exclude life, because the the laws of physics are general, while the realm of biology is just a special case of those more general, transcending principles. "In effect," says Rosen, "contemporary physics is based on the belief that *no complex systems exist in nature.*"[45]

Certainly it is a puzzling philosophy that holds that the person espousing it does not really exist. But what is a living, thinking universe supposed to look like, anyway, if not like ours? Is there any *scientific* reason for believing that the laws of physics are the most general, and that everything in the universe is ultimately reducible to them? In fact, no.[46] The belief that physics is more general than biology is just that, a belief. And this belief is not the result of any scientific methodology, but the basis *for* a scientific methodology; it is by no means *what* we are looking at, but merely *a way* to look. Again, these extra-scientific, metaphysical beliefs ordain that we always look downward, toward the particulars, for an ultimate explanation, never upward, toward wholeness or finality. So Life itself, which exhibits both wholeness and finality, is in fact incomprehensible to our paradigmatic science, physics. Indeed, there is actually no way for physics even to tell us whether or not something is alive or inert. Only something alive can detect the presence of life, just as only a mind can detect the presence of mental life.

As Ken Wilber reminds us, it is axiomatic that "if one philosophical system can embrace another, but not vice versa, then the more encompassing is the more valid."[47] And, just as Newtonian physics cannot embrace Einsteinian physics, physics itself can in no way embrace biology. This is because the laws of physics actually apply only to a rare type of system: one that is closed and not at all complex, unlike biological systems, which are both open and extraordinarily complex. And this is the real reason why there is such a conceptual abyss between the laws of physics and the most simple biological system, why physics can tell us nothing of interest about Life, much less Mind or Spirit. No wonder Einstein conceded that "One can best feel in dealing with living things how primitive physics still is," or that Schrodinger spoke of the utter failure of physics "to say anything significant about the biosphere and what is in it." So why do we go on pretending we know how a leaf transforms sunlight into thought, music, and poetry?

Let's look at it this way: Is it really plausible that the universe could be governed by the same laws whether or not life is present in it? In other words, does it matter to the physicist whether he is dealing with a living or dead universe? Now an open-minded physicist might allow for the emergence of novel biological laws, as long as they do not contradict the underlying physical laws. But what, aside from modern superstition, prevents us from looking at the situation in reverse, and suggesting that: the laws of physics are a special case of those governing biology, permitted to exist so long as they do not contradict the ability for biological entities to exist at some point in the development of the universe? In short, what if we hold to the view that biology explains much more about physics than physics can ever explain about biology?

The obstacle here results not so much from actual physics as from the fact that normative science continues to cleave to the same pre-Einsteinian view of reality discussed in Book One. With that obsolete viewpoint, there are certain features of the universe, including Life, that will forever remain mysterious and paradoxical. But there are some key findings in the new physics which are very much relevant to a discussion of life. In an organism, just as we have seen with respect to the universe, everything is inside everything else, that is, internally related. In fact, one of the things that defines an organism is that everything about it is a necessary consequence of everything else in it, in a way that defies any conceivable linear or mechanistic explanation involving only external relations. Indeed, even in a single amino acid chain, the position retained by

> each one of the thousands of atoms is influenced by all the other atoms in the molecule and... each atom contributes, via immensely complex cooperative interactions with all the other atoms in the protein, something to the overall shape and function of the whole molecule.[48]

The science of genetics can no longer be understood using metaphysic of logical atomism—the commonsense but ultimately naive idea that genes are like separate "particles" that have some sort of one-to-one effect on a phenotypic trait: "Genes are not like particles at all. What a gene does depends upon neighboring genes, on the same and on different chromosomes, and on other aspects of its environment in the cell."[49] In short, "The genome has been shown to act as a whole and not as a collection of separable effects."[50] What this means, in Rosen's phraseology, is that "semantics cannot be reduced to syntax," or meaning to order. Rather, in some ultimate sense, semantics must be prior to syntax, meaning to order. In its functional wholeness, everything in the organism implies and is implied by everything else. As an organism develops, it is

> governed and directed by the organized structure of the mature individual, which is immanent in every phase and differentiates itself in the process.... Each phase presents the whole, but in a different and contraposed degree of integration and articulation"[51]

And this serial articulation of wholeness is only possible because we live in a universe of internally related parts which reveal an underlying wholeness, a dynamic wholeness that keeps mysteriously recurring at each level, whether chemically, organically, psychologically or, ultimately, spiritually. If the wholeness were not there from the start, it could not manifest later. While we could have agglomerations and aggregates, gobs and blobs, we could not have the property of true wholeness, of parts participating in a higher entity which unifies them and reveals their meaning. And this is the reason why, in the final analysis, "Contrary to the claim that DNA is the secret of life, life remains the secret of DNA."[52]

We know that we live in an organismic universe by virtue of the undeniable fact that organisms exist in it. And this biological fact, it turns out, tells us a great deal about our physical universe. Specifically, it is my contention that not only biological, but mental (and later, spiritual) wholeness could not exist if wholeness were not woven into the very fabric of the universe. And furthermore, because of the principles of non-locality and non-separability discussed in Book One, we may logically deduce a very critical point—that the transcendent power of Life is temporally symmetrical: "if it had no beginning, it can have no end. And if it occupies any point in space, it must fill the universe."[53]

## 2.3 Is Life Meaningful?

> How can the machinery of the universe ever be imagined to get set up at the very beginning so as to produce man now? Impossible! Or impossible unless somehow—preposterous idea—meaning itself powers creation. But how?
>
> —John Wheeler

Among other things, what differentiates life from non-life is that in an animate system, something can go wrong, which introduces the possibility of *pathology* into the cosmos. Prior to the appearance of life, we cannot speak of pathology, of things going wrong; there are no diseased stars, no dysfunctional galaxies, no disordered and victimized rocks. Inanimate nature accomplishes nothing, and is therefore infallible, incapable of making a mistake. But as Polanyi points out, "a living function has a result which it may achieve or fail to achieve."[54] And "achievement," "success," "attainment," whatever you wish to call it, these are *values* that do not exist prior to the appearance of life, and are unexplainable in terms of any principle known to physics. From the standpoint of physics, a living system is nothing more than a statistically rare lump of matter; there is actually no principle in physics that can tell us whether or not something is "living," much less "meaningful."

Current evolutionary theory also does not speak of such values, in fact, banishes them from its purview. There is no higher or lower, no better or worse, no direction or aim in nature. True, biologists do speak of the value of *survival*, and survival is not a concept that we generally apply to the inanimate. But all survival is nevertheless value-neutral, even tautologous, in the sense that survival is equivalent to survival and does not surpass itself: the survival of bacteria is no better than the survival of human beings (and in fact, ranking biological entities in terms of the value of survivability, human beings would undoubtedly fall below insects, bacteria, and Fidel Castro).

It seems pointless to hold an ideology so counter to the way we actually live in and experience the world. Indeed, no one but the autistic, the sociopath, and the dogmatic materialist actually thinks of life in this bloodless, value-free way. However, even the most uncompromising materialist cannot really think of himself "as a simple aggregate of the calcium, iron, phosphorus, and other elements to which he is reducible chemically," but as "a creation consisting of more than the sum of all these..."[55] In fact, it is more interesting to contemplate the source of the materialist's passion for truth—which, let's face it, is a fervent metaphysical quest, however misguided—than it is to evaluate the fruitfulness or intellectual viability of a belief in blind materialism.

But deep down, no one really believes any of this—the barren idea that one may logically devote "one's life to the purpose of proving that there [is] no purpose."[56] Beneath the veneer of academic correctness, beneath the counter-reaction to some naive or distorted version of religion inculcated in childhood,[57] we all intuitively understand that human beings are by far the most interesting and unexpected fact of evolution, the most philosophically arresting and conceptually paradoxical problem in the cosmos, if solely for the fact that only humans can look at themselves and conclude that, after all, it's not so odd that a dead universe should come to life and start wondering about itself.

According to Polanyi, even if we agree with standard evolutionary theory that living systems are really nothing more than "Darwinian machines," we must acknowledge that the operation of any machine relies upon the presence of two distinct principles. Specifically, a machine involves the imposition of boundary conditions on the underlying laws of physics and chemistry in order to harness their workings. Analogously, the notes in a musical scale do not by themselves compose a symphony, or the letters of the alphabet compose words, sentences, and paragraphs. Rather, at each level of development, a higher principle exploits what is left open on the lower level, imposing boundary conditions on it in order to produce something higher. We cannot understand a great poem or work of music by focusing our attention on the individual notes or words that constitute it. Rather, in order to understand a work of art, we must blind ourselves to its particulars and see past them, toward the wholeness that reveals the meaning of the particulars.

The same is true in our attempt to comprehend the phenomenon of Life. All of the parts of a healthy, living entity point toward and converge upon the whole organism. If we study only the parts themselves, we specifically lose sight of what they are pointing toward, their meaning: the living organism. Not only does conventional biology fail to follow the arrow that the particulars are pointing toward and converging upon, but it introduces its own reverse arrow, which points toward the even smaller, less meaningful particulars of physical and chemical reality. But there is actually nothing at all barring us from viewing life as a transcendent, cosmic power, an irreducible, dynamic *whole* that reveals the meaning of the parts that constitute it, parts that we mistakenly thought were just floating around meaninglessly in the universe until life revealed otherwise.

A good analogy, if you are familiar with them, is provided by those three-dimensional stereoscopic images which appear to jump out of the page when you change the way you look at the parts that comprise them. These images are constituted of thousands of seemingly random markings on paper. If you specifically focus on the markings, they make no sense at all. But if you relax your eyes and see through and beyond the markings, quite suddenly a three-dimensional image leaps out from the page. It turns out that what we thought were meaningless, unrelated two-dimensional markings are actually parts of a higher dimensional object that has revealed their meaning. With this analogy in mind, is there any doubt that the countless atoms joyriding through your body have no idea of the greater meaning of which they are participants? Or that the billions of individual cells constituting your body simply go about their daily business, with no idea whether they are participating in writing a novel, or launching a three-point shot from way downtown, or even situated in some other life form, such as a tree?

Clearly, any detached observer can see that the universe has a long and distinguished record of creating more comprehensive, integrated, and complex "wholes" as it has evolved through the course of time, including in the biological realm addressed by natural selection. Most biologists deal with this progress either by attributing it to chance, or by denying that it is even progress at all—in other words, affirming that the apparent progress is just a random, meaningless drift in the direction of complexity. However, as it so happens, there is a much more adequate and intellectually credible explanation for how and why the universe inevitably keeps advancing and surpassing itself, and it has to do with the the sort of logic that governs any holistic structure, such as our cosmos. In short, strict Darwinians—and scientists in general—tackle the problem of progress by looking at it as if it were occurring in a universe of disconnected fragments, with no underlying wholeness. The "formal logic" reflexively and unconsciously employed by most scientists presupposes what is known as "logical atomism," a metaphysical assumption that

> conceives the world as made up of, or as a collection of, facts, each independent of all the rest, so that any one of them may be the case or may not be the case without making any difference to any of the others. The facts are therefore atomic and their mutual relations are external.[58]

However, if we abandon the mistaken assumption that the world is merely an assemblage of unconnected facts, and assume rather that it is a *whole* that displays internal relations, then an entirely different type of logical theory is required to make the universe intelligible. This is "dialectical logic," the logic of system. With dialectical logic the progress of the universe may be seen as an inevitable (but not determined) result of its very structure, whereas with formal logic that same progress is simply unintelligible, so that ad hoc, incredible theories must be put forth to explain it, such as the pure luck of natural selection.

Clearly, based upon the findings presented in Book One, we must conclude that the universe is a diverse but ordered unity that displays underlying wholeness. Obviously the universe contains innumerable parts, but those parts are only parts by virtue of their participation in the whole. As such, the universe is an infinitely diverse unity, with the diversity extending into both space and time. But because of its temporal nature, "this diversity is not given all at once, but proliferates in a continuously changing process."[59] Now, if these diverse parts of the universe were not connected by an underlying wholeness, then there could be no development in the universe at all, because each part would truly be just one event in an unending process going nowhere, with all changes necessarily averaging out to "zero" progress.

But our universe does not operate that way. Rather, each part of the universe is suffused with the non-local holistic principle of which it is a local expression, and the non-local whole is by definition outside finite space and chronological time. Again, as explained by Harris, a developmental process can only occur "if the totality is already in some sense actual, and the whole can be actualized only in and through the process."[60] In other words, the whole must by definition deploy its wholeness in time if it is truly a whole; if it has no parts it is not truly a whole, but simply a blank and featureless unity devoid of any characteristics at all (including change of any kind). Only in time and space is it even possible to deduce the presence of a whole; otherwise, we are dealing with an unintelligible, self-identical entity that cannot even be entertained in thought, because there is nothing differentiated within it, no possible ground or basis for thought. Just as the existence of chronological time necessitates the positing of an atemporal whole, the whole, as a unified diversity, must be differentiated in time. Thus, an eternally complete whole that is logically prior to the process that manifests it "is the very condition of there being any real progress in time."[61] Differentiation which is more than mere fragmentation "is possible only if there is a center toward which the parts look for their meaning and validation."[62]

But why must the temporal deployment of the whole necessarily be progressive? Again, assuming the underlying wholeness of the cosmos, that wholeness applies to both time and space, and implies the prior existence of the already complete whole in each part. Because the whole is deployed in time, each phase of the developmental sequence will necessarily be a more adequate expression of the whole, if not in the short term, certainly in the long term, as our universe forcefully demonstrates to us in a self-evident manner, at every stage and level of development, from matter to life, life to mind, and mind to spirit. At each successive phase of cosmic evolution we see "a fuller realization of the totality to which they all belong. Consequently the later phases will include and integrate the earlier ones into more complex structures." Thus,

> the totality, as a developed outcome of the process, reveals itself equally as the beginning and source of everything that was involved in the process of its own development. That process can occur only if the totality is already in some sense actual, and the

> whole can be actualized only in and through the process.... [The whole] is at once eternally realized and continually realizing itself by means of a process throughout which it is immanent.[63]

Evolution is progressive because our holistic universe can be no other way, so that later forms are the meaning, truth, source, and destiny of earlier ones. Which is why we may affirm with Richard Weaver that ,"If a series of things is hierarchically ordered, it is conditioned from top to bottom and so cannot be infinite. If it is infinite, it cannot be conditioned from top to bottom, and there is no higher and lower."[64] Or with Wolfgang Smith, who concludes that "the evolutionist picture is but an inverted image" of truth, and that it is paradoxically more accurate to say that "the more primitive forms of life have actually descended from man."[65]

Once again, by turning the cosmos upside down, we see that Life is a higher-dimensional, transcendent principle that reveals the *meaning* of matter; although all biological organisms are alive, Life is not synonymous with biology, any more than the One Living Being, if such a One exists, is a mere biological entity (although It is surely alive). Rather, Life must be a middle term, linking matter with something quite beyond itself, a principle descending from above, a bridge between the merely endless and the truly eternal.

* * *

But exactly what does life point toward? What is the greater whole of which it is a part? This is a critical question, because absent what life was patiently converging upon, its mere appearance in the universe did not seem to be any cause for celebration (or cerebration), perhaps not even worth the bother. "Marvelous gift, useless gift," cried Pushkin, "for what purpose were you given us?" Why this living, struggling little sub-universe consisting of mindless circles of lateral mutation, so much variety yet so little meaningful novelty: the "mere sport of nature" in a "vain, unnecessary world,"[66] with all the pointless pageantry and nonexistent morality of a Mike Tyson fight. For billions of years, countless little portions of the universe vainly declared their independence, lived for a few days, a few weeks, and returned to the purportedly dead matter from whence they came. These rebellious little beings, each a novel, whirling focus of inwardness, grew more complex, learned a few more tricks, lived a little longer, but still, the only point seemed to be to hold out against the universe for as long as possible before falling back into blind nothingness, ashes to ashes, dust to dust. Even in more complex life forms, to the extent that consciousness existed, it was indistinguishable from the sensations of the nervous system. These life forms did not feel hungry, they *were* hunger. They did not become frightened, they *were* fear, merely a certain repertoire of hard-wired responses. There was alarm, but nothing to be anxious about; tranquility, but nothing to be calm about.

Now, the adventure of life is already two thirds over. In another two billion years, the expansion of the sun will incinerate the earth, putting a final end to the anxious struggle. Especially for such a fundamentally dead and meaningless universe, life seems to have been an extraordinarily elegant and complex, but nevertheless bizarre and pointless solution to a nonexistent problem, a "a cancerous growth on the body of nothingness."[67] In fact, it only created a new, more pressing problem, the problem of avoiding or delaying the return to non-being. Before life, there were no problems in the universe—nothing could go wrong because nothing had to go right. But life's reckless emancipation from matter brought forth a nagging tension, an unresolvable conflict, an inherent incompleteness in the cosmos. In a sense, life was and is a dis-ease of matter in a literal sense, just as mind is a dis-ease of biology, an alien condition with no *backward-looking* cure (short of death or unconsciousness) that can return it to a state of ease or wholeness. The only way out of this deadly predicament seemed to be forward and inward, in a never-ending balancing act between helpless dependence upon, and open defiance of, matter. Life groped blindly on, because that was the only alternative.[68]

But then something altogether surprising happened. From our vantage point outside time, we now see that the boundary of life did not end with its own precarious little dance along the precipice of non-being. Rather, we see that life was bound by two infinite frontiers, one side down and back into dark death and obscure material dissolution, the other up and beyond, into more subtle regions of Mind and Spirit. Crossing that radiant upper threshold we are witness to…

*Wandering along the precipice of non-being, one side down and back into dark death and material dissolution, the other up and beyond, into more subtle regions of Mind and Spirit.*

# BOOK THREE

## PSYCHOGENESIS: *The Presence of Mind*

A belief in the gradual emergence of man from an inanimate universe reveals to us that the dead matter of our origins was fraught with meaning far beyond all that we are presently able to see in it. To set aside an achievement as full of meaning as this—as if an emergence of this sort could happen any day as if by mere accident—is to block the normal sources of inquisitive thought.

—Michael Polanyi, *Meaning*

There is nothing in the paleontological record of the evolving human body that rivals the rapidity with which *Homo sapiens* began to evince advanced "out-of-body" culture—cave art, music, burial of the dead, clothing, personal ornamentation, diverse tools, and so on.... If one is drawn to dramatic "hiccups" in the history of life on this planet, this certainly ranks near the top.

—Noel Boaz, *Eco Homo*

[T]he individual, in his short history, passes once more through some of the processes that his society has traversed in its long history.... If one wished to express recurrent processes of this kind in the form of laws, one could speak, as a parallel to the laws of biogenesis, of a fundamental law of sociogenesis and psychogenesis.

—Norbert Elias, *An Outline of the Civilizing Process*

...*BOO!!!* another startling explosion—or perhaps, implosion—this one into a *subjective* space that was somehow awaiting the primate brains that had to learn to navigate, colonize, and eventually master it. Just as the first singularity was an explosion into (and simultaneous creation of) material space-time, and the second singularity a discontinuous "big bang" into the morphic space of biological possibility, this third singularity was an implosion into a trans-dimensional subjective space refracted through the unlikely lens of a primate brain. Up to the threshold of the third singularity, biology was firmly in control of the hominids, and for most of evolution, mind (such as it was) only existed to serve the needs of the primate body. Natural selection did not, and could not have, "programmed" us to know reality, only to survive in a narrow "reality tunnel"[1] constructed within the dialectical space between the world of phenomena and our evolved senses. But suddenly, about 40,000 years ago, mind crossed a boundary into a realm wholly its own, a multidimensional landscape unmappable by science and unexplainable by natural selection. History is the chronicle of the ongoing break with nature caused by the unexpected dawning of self-consciousness that vaulted *Homo sapiens* into this subjective world space.

Just as the second singularity represented an escape up from blind mechanical necessity into a new biological dimension with a greater degree of freedom, the third singularity represented a way out from biological necessity, and into a realm with a vastly greater degree of freedom, well beyond the confining prison walls of the senses. However, most humans failed to exploit this new freedom, and instead found themselves in a virtual straitjacket mirroring the dimensions of their misused imaginations. Just as it required aeons for matter to become harmoniously subordinate to biology, millions of years passed before biology harmoniously reconciled itself to mind, even in a few individuals, much less the human group (which obviously still struggles with this mastery). The poet Blake was among the few who have realized that the imagination is nothing less than "the Eternal Body of Man," the "real and eternal World" of which our local universe "is but a faint shadow."[2] It took many thousands of years for any human beings to understand that the imagination was *the new environment where they actually lived*, and that this realm was capable of infinite elaboration and expansion (as well as metastasis into hellish dimensions of cruelty and evil).[3]

And even then, the most fortunate humans quickly discovered that the relative freedom of the mental dimension was easily overshadowed by an increased, sometimes acute awareness of a truly dire existential dilemma: the grim inevitability of death, loss, and meaninglessness in a world of apparently local and contingent being. In his classic *Denial of Death,* Ernest Becker asked,

> What does it mean to be a *self-conscious animal?* The idea is ludicrous, if it is not monstrous.... This is the terror: to have emerged from nothing, to have a name, consciousness of self, deep inner feelings, an excruciating inner yearning for life and self-expression—and with all this yet to die. It seems like a hoax....[4]

As such, soon after acquiring the dubious gift of self-consciousness, humans almost immediately began fumbling around for an escape hatch beyond the boundaries of the mental, a side door into other unexplored dimensions, other possible singularities with even greater degrees of freedom. After all, given that the most astonishing developments in this universe were totally unpredictable, who could say what other uncanny surprises remained enfolded in the ground of being? Certainly not the scientist armed only with yesterday's mechanical paradigm, already so inadequate to account for the unlikely appearances of Mind and Life. But in the meantime, humans had first to pass through the gauntlet of personal and collective development before discovering whether or not another singularity lay at the end of history's troubled riverrun.

## 3.1 The Big Bang of the Mental Universe

> The mind, even more so than the physical world and bodily organisms, possesses its own dimensions, its structure and internal hierarchy of causalities and values—immaterial though they may be.
>
> —Jacques Maritain, *The Degrees of Knowledge*

> I was like a monkey in a net.... only with great pain, effort, and struggle did I break through these "walls around art." Thus did I finally enter the realm of art, which like that of nature, science, political forms, etc., is a realm unto itself, is governed by its own laws proper to it alone, and which together with the other realms ultimately forms the great realm which we can only dimly divine.
>
> —Wassily Kandinsky, *Reminiscences*

At this writing, it has now been 3.85 billion years since the appearance of the second singularity, Life. The third singularity, Mind, occurred after more than 3.84 billion of those years had passed, perhaps as recently as 40,000 years ago, when a certain undistinguished line of primates (our upright furbears, as Joyce called them) became conscious of consciousness and ventured into an intangible dimension of inward space: that is, our initial *exterior* diaspora out of Africa was soon followed by an *interior* one, with various cultures carving out their local, more or less misguided encampments within the greater light of consciousness as such. This chapter will review what is known about the beginning of truly mental life, both individually and collectively, and attempt to trace its temporal evolution to the threshold of something beyond time, self, and history.

* * *

Until fairly recently, it was assumed by most experts that evolution is a slow, gradual, and continuous process caused only by minute, random genetic mutations creating the variety which is then disinterestedly pruned by the environment on the strict basis of reproductive fitness. However, this account of our descent has never really jibed with the fossil record, which instead shows long periods of genetic stagnation followed by the sudden appearance of new species. As it turns out, those old textbook renderings of apes gradually standing more upright, losing their hair, growing big brains and appearing more human are no more accurate than the obsolete drawings of atoms that look like miniature solar systems. For example, one of our immediate ancestors, *Australopithecus*, roamed Africa for 1.5 million years, stuck in an evolutionary dead end with only a slightly larger brain than the apes. And then, after 100,000 generations of stasis, they suddenly disappeared, only to be replaced by *Homo ergaster* and *Homo erectus*, who bumbled around for another million and a half years before taking their bows and leaving the evolutionary stage, clearing the way for us, *Homo sapiens*.

A mere 40,000 years ago, something dramatic happened to the human *mind*—not brain—an unprecedented outpouring of innovation, creativity, and inspiration. Oddly, the last spurt in brain growth had occurred between about 500,000 and 200,000 years ago, with no corresponding change in the archaeological record. Instead, what we see during those thousands of years is unimaginable monotony, endless variations of the same unimpressive tool, the infamous handaxe. After millions of years of human evolution, idle hands, and a brain the size of ours, what had it all come to? "As a whole, the archaeological record between 1.4 million and 100,000 years ago seems to revolve around an almost limitless number of minor variations on a small set of technical and economic themes."[5] Archaeologist Steven Mithen, after sifting through the rubble of "handaxe, after handaxe, after handaxe," pulls no punches and calls it what it really is: "tedious stuff" with no evidence of art, science, or religion, produced by what must have been a "rolling, fleeting, ephemeral consciousness" with swift memory loss and no capacity for introspection. Paleoanthropologist Alan Walker goes further, describing these early humans as "tall, strong, and stupid," a statement that Richard Klein says is probably applicable "to everyone who lived between 1.8 million and 600,000 to 500,000 years ago."[6] Ouch.

* * *

Although the fossil record of our descent from the apes becomes increasingly detailed (or at least decreasingly sketchy), this provides us primarily with knowledge of *exteriors*, no definitive understanding of *interiors*, of what it was like to be one of these proto- or early humans, prior to the great awakening of the cultural explosion.[7] We know, for example, that the human descent from the apes began somewhere between 7 and 5 million years ago, with the first partially upright hominids, the *Australopithecus* species. *Homo ergaster* enters the picture around 1.7 million years ago, archaic *Homo sapiens* about half a million years ago. Only between about 130,000 and 200,000 years ago do we see the full emergence of genetically modern *Homo sapiens sapiens*, that is, *us*. During this time we know that the brain triples in size, but this actually tells us very little about what might have been going on "inside" one of those brains. In fact, as will be discussed later, when it comes to brains and their psychological activity, size clearly isn't everything. (In fact, average brain size has actually declined sharply in the past 15,000 years, from an average of around 1500cc to more like 1200cc.)[8]

I believe some psychological inferences may be made based upon the fossil record, which tells us that primitive tools are present about 2.5 million years ago, use of fire about 1.5 million years ago,[9] and probably some archaic language by a million years ago, most likely consisting of some directive pointing and grunting, by no means similar to our state of living in an almost infinitely rich, expanding linguistic world space. There is the occasional Venus carving from as far back as 100,000 years, the odd cave painting from 75,000 back, and some isolated instances of burial of the dead 60,000 years ago. However, these occasional finds do "nothing to alter the impression of a creative explosion afterwards."[10] No offense to *Homo erectus* (or to romantically inclined anthropologists), but based on commonsense inferences we can draw, there is no reason to believe that there was anything of much interest taking place in their primitive minds (as compared to any other animal). For example, the fossil record tells us that *Homo erectus* did indeed have tools, or more accurately, one simple tool, the above-noted handaxe. And that tool shows no significant change at all for a *million* years, from about 1.4 to .4 million years ago, for perhaps 40,000 generations! If handaxes didn't change for a million years, it is quite possible that they weren't even products of "culture" as we know it at all, that they were much more akin to a beaver's dam or a bird's nest. Archaeologist like to talk about how difficult it is to produce a handaxe, but this proves nothing—I can't build a spider web or an anthill either.[11] The point is, this slightly modified rock was apparently the technological "solution" to every problem encountered by primitive human beings. And as we all know, if your only tool is a handaxe, you will treat every problem as a… as a thing to be smashed with a handaxe.

* * *

Let us make it clear then that it is no mere exaggeration to call our sudden ingression into psychological and cultural space an explosion, an explosion as vast, monumental, and singular as the big bang itself. Pierre Teilhard de Chardin called it the "psychozoic era," a truly catastrophic revolution undergone by the biosphere, a time when consciousness somehow managed to "double back" upon itself, the result being that the human being was

> in a flash able to raise himself into a new sphere. In reality, another world is born. Abstraction, logic, reasoned choice and inventions, mathematics, art, calculation of space and time, anxieties and dreams of love—all these activities of inner life are nothing else than the effervescence of the newly-formed centre as it explodes into itself.[12]

John Pfeiffer, who coined the term "creative explosion" to describe this sudden, punctuational change some 40,000 years ago, wrote that art, for example, "came as a bang as far as the archaeological record is concerned. There is nothing to foreshadow its emergence, no sign of crude beginnings…"[13] Similarly, Jaynes emphasized that "It is as if all life evolved to a certain point, and then in ourselves turned at a right angle and simply exploded in a different direction."[14]

And although natural selection was necessary to set the stage for the ontological mutation of human self-consciousness, it was in principle not sufficient, as we shall see, to account for it. For example,

McCrone, in *The Ape That Spoke,* writes,

> One of the biggest evolutionary puzzles is not that humans are self-conscious, but that we could have become self-conscious with such phenomenal speed.... [I]t is as if the human race had spent all day walking just to travel as far as the ape brain, then reached the rational, self-aware human mind in just three minutes' extra journey.... There has simply not been enough time for evolution to make major changes in the way our brains work.[15]

What we are analogously dealing with is the difference between the hardware of the brain and the software of the mind, and the two are by no means identical. Indeed, we know full well that brain hardware has changed only negligibly in the past 130,000 years, so that even if we had in our possession a fully preserved brain from that time, it would be anatomically no different from, say, Wayne Gretzky's brain, and reveal absolutely nothing as to whether that brain supported a consciousness resembling ours. In all likelihood, it did not.

Given the fantastic, almost infinite potential of the human mind, the question naturally arises: Why should a brain that was selected by evolution so that it might be able to mate, hunt, and forage a little more successfully than apes, also be capable of art, music, literature, science, moral ideals, religious truth, slapshots from the blue line? Everything needed for survival out on the open savanna could probably have been done just as effectively in an unconscious, robotic fashion, without the annoying burden of our self-awareness. Most everything humans have done with their minds for the past 40,000 years—at least all of the really interesting things that define us as human—has been completely and utterly superfluous from the standpoint of natural selection:

> [T]he evolution of the human brain not only overshot the needs of prehistoric man, it is also the only example of evolution *providing a species with an organ which it does not know how to use*; a luxury organ, which will take its owner thousands of years to learn to put to proper use—if he ever does.[16]

And why was there such a long interim between the evolution of our large brain and our eventual putting it to such good (and bad) use? For example, while our brain was tripling in size during the course of evolution, there was no discernible payoff in terms of technological innovation. In fact,

> one could not ask for a worse correlation between growth in a biological organ and evidence of its supposed survival benefits.... How could evolution favor the expansion of a costly organ like the brain, without any major survival benefits becoming apparent until long after the organ stopped expanding?[17]

Similarly, Ridley concludes that culture appeared so late in evolution as to have no effect on the size of the brain:

> The truth is that however you look at it, the mute monotony of the Aucheulean hand ax stands in silent reproach to all theories of gene-culture evolution: brains got steadily bigger with no help from changing technology, because technology was static.[18]

It is axiomatic that natural selection does not plan ahead, so there is simply no conventional way to "understand how a costly investment in big brains today may be justified by cultural riches tomorrow."[19]

So for at least 100,000 years, *Homo sapiens*, despite our big new brains—fully loaded with all the optional equipment—behaved identically to early humans who were, frankly, not all that different from apes. "As far as the archaeological record is concerned, the outstanding feature of the vast stretch of time from the first hominids to early *Homo sapiens* is that nothing much seems to have happened.[20] Prior to the emergence of mind, the subjective side of human beings—like all organisms—consisted mostly of information about the external world: a no-frills, relatively closed system with a one-to-one correspondence between information and environment. But while drifting along with the tide of mere Darwinian change, a "miracle in human history" occurred, in that "Man arose and raised himself above the plane of natural evolution," and a "non-empirical idealism lit up within him.[21] That is, with the creative explosion, humans began to inhabit a third area, a virtual space that, surprisingly, did not contain "no information." Instead, the opening of this space meant that humans were now susceptible to influences from other domains—nonempirical spiritual, scientific, aesthetic, and moral dimensions that clearly seemed to operate through a "top-down" causation on the psyche, not in a conventional, deterministic, "bottom-up" way. Natural selection simply cannot account for most of the traits and capabilities that suddenly arose in this virtual space, such as our profligate creativity, our love of music and art, our ethical capacity, our sense of humor, and a linguistic ability that far surpasses mere survival needs. From a Darwinian standpoint, all of these things must be explained as adaptations to some problem we faced while attempting to survive on the plains of Pleistocene Africa. But in fact, there are no plausible evolutionary theories that can make sense of these seemingly superfluous extravagances. In short, Darwinian anthropogenesis cannot, by itself, account for emergent psychogenesis. Ironically, what E. O. Wilson once remarked about Marxism is equally applicable to his own field of sociobiology: "Wonderful theory. Wrong species."[22]

* * *

There are actually two major hurdles faced by a strictly Darwinian explanation of our humanness. First, as we have seen, is the suddenness with which it occurred. Second is the issue of what was awaiting us when we arrived there. That is, leaving aside the matter of how and when the creative explosion occurred, the question remains, exactly what did humans discover when they discovered art, religion, love, truth, beauty, language? In other words, what is the ontological status of this new mental dimension? Is this realm really nothing more than the banal and meaningless side effect of a complex neurological system? Or is it an ontologically real (but more subtle) world that we have the unique privilege of entering, an independent, virtual space with its own laws, attributes, categories, and characteristics?

For mainstream anthropologists, archaeologists, and evolutionary psychologists, this question does not even arise, for they assume at the outset that the mind is nothing more than a brain-based local adaptation to transient environmental circumstances. It is not ontologically real, but is strictly a reaction to something that is real: the external, material world. But here they run into a bit of a snag. In short, how can the discovery of something—for example, the spiritual dimension—represent an adaptation, when the thing discovered doesn't really exist? In order to get around this problem of giving humans credit for "discovering" a made-up world, these theorists must invoke some ulterior factor, such as the fostering of social solidarity, in order to place religion in a biologically adaptive context. In other words, religion is not really "about" spirit, but about group cohesion achieved through collective self-delusion.[23]

Modern scholars run into the same problem in considering the discovery of beauty in the creative explosion. Why, all of a sudden, do humans all over the globe begin expressing an urge to create, to bring into being beautiful artifacts that have no utilitarian purpose? Today we live in an age in which works of art are no longer felt to convey any intrinsic meaning, much less an ontologically real spiritual presence. Sociobiologists inform us that art is really about our drive for status (the flaunting of "conspicuous leisure," thereby making males more desirable objects of female sexual interest),[24] or perhaps about the innate pleasure we feel in knowing our neurological system is functioning properly when we recognize auditory and visual patterns in artistic productions. Likewise, from the blinkered standpoint of modern literary theory, we would have to conclude that overnight, as it were, privileged human primates developed the adaptively useless drive to create texts of political domination for other tenured primates to deconstruct. Something about that doesn't sound right.

It is beyond the scope of this book to carry out a complete analysis of all of the new capacities that emerged with our sudden discovery of mental space. At any rate, of the three traditional transcendentals, the good (our moral nature), the true (our rational mind), and the beautiful (our aesthetic sense), it is this final category that poses the greatest obstacle to any Darwinian explanation, and which opens a door to something clearly beyond the merely biological or material, where "rational understanding is overpassed and a higher faculty opens, suprarational in its origin and nature."[25] In fact, genuine art "must rank with science and philosophy as a way of communicating knowledge about reality,"[26] specifically, spiritual reality; it is, said Malraux, the "currency of the absolute," or as Hegel put it, "the Spiritual making itself known sensuously."[27] Great works of art, according to Balthasar "appear like inexplicable miracles and spontaneous eruptions on the stage of history."[28] In the words of Plotinus, they "reascend to those principles from which Nature herself is derived."[29] Art and beauty, as expressed by Cutsinger, are "intrinsically linked to the very structure of the universe," in that they represent "on a small scale what the world itself is on a large scale," an "objective point of conjunction between visible creatures and their invisible Source."[30]

What I would like to focus upon here is the demonstrable capacity of a genuine work of art to transport us out of the phenomenal world through its mysterious resonance with a trans-empirical beyond. The "radiance" and "transparency" of art allow us to experience in it a tangible exteriorization of spiritual presence, but also to see through and beyond its material form, to the living spiritual source that is instantiated in it. Sacred art (which all art once was), according to Schuon, facilitates "the mysterious introduction into one realm of existence of a presence which in reality contains and transcends that realm...."[31] It points "not to the world as such, but to what the world itself points toward, to that invisible Reality which the world reflects."[32] To the "connoisseur" of spirit, the ability to intuit the noetic light in a painting or poem is really no more problematic than, say, a psychoanalyst who is able to "see" (not with the eyes of course) the workings of the primitive unconscious in the outward behavior and verbalizations of a patient.

* * *

The most spectacular examples of prehistoric art are found in the Lascaux cave located in southern France, one of more than two hundred such caves in western Europe dating back approximately 30,000 years. We might begin with the obvious question, "Why are these cave paintings so literally breathtaking, so much more beautiful than they have to be?" As described by Pfeiffer, "No matter how many caves one has explored," their majesty "always comes with a catch of the breath."[33] Aesthetic beauty is never necessary and always truly creative, bringing into being something uniquely beautiful that never existed before; part of what defines it is that it is entirely superfluous—it did not have to be, and yet it is. Why should eyes that were evolved for the sole purpose of avoiding danger and finding food and sexual partners suddenly be able to create and discern such beauty, "rendered with a fluency and grace of line, as alive as life itself"?[34]Those who are open to the effect of these magnificent cave visions speak of a tangible "presence" inhabiting them, and the impossibility of imagining "by what miracle of inspiration" such works were conceived and realized: "No crude anthropological theory of 'primitive magic' suffices to explain [their] extraordinary beauty, the aesthetics of [their] organization, or the magnificence of [their] forms."[35]

Of course, it makes no difference what these first explorers of the imagination were consciously thinking about when producing these aesthetically fully realized images. In any event, art cannot be something so mundane as the local manifestation of a complex nervous system in the form of a skillful drawing of a bison, stag, or horse. Rather these paintings document the first halting, transitory revelations of a nonlocal reality enfolding and penetrating our local one. The fact that the paintings retain a capacity to "astoneage"[36]us and reveal their splendor can mean only one thing: these genetic *Homo sapien sapiens*, so recently submerged in the body and engulfed in the senses, had stumbled across the gate of access into the realm of the fully human. Here the analogy with biology is exact: for just as life in all its explosive variety may be traced to the first metabolizing substance that escaped material necessity, so too, all of the aesthetic creations freely produced by human beings in the last 40,000 years may be traced to this sudden escape from the "idiot hierarchies of speechless apes,"[37] into a realm as radically different from biology as biology was from matter.

Perhaps no major western philosopher more than Schopenhaur appreciated what happens when human beings are in contact with the aesthetic dimension, whether today or 40,000 years ago. With art,

> we are in touch with something outside the empirical realm, a different order of being; we literally have the experience of being taken out of time and space altogether, and also out of ourselves, even out of the material object that is our body.[38]

Further, Schopenhaur recognized that art "penetrates to the level at which the phenomenal (the part of the universe available to our senses) makes contact with something that is not phenomenal. It brings us closer than anything… to a perception of the inner significance of life."[39] To use one of Schopenhaur's metaphors, the merely talented man is like a marksman who hits a target others can't hit, while the great artist is like a marksman who is able to hit a target that the ordinary man—not to say mere animals—cannot even see. And it goes without saying that aesthetic beauty is a target natural selection cannot strike, know, or even conceive of. Either there was no beauty in the world until human beings crossed over the monkey bridge to the transcendental realm from which beauty radiates, or life just happened to evolve in a universe of stunning beauty that was already there waiting for someone to appreciate it. I don't know which explanation is weirder.

Everything we know about art makes no sense if it was something only "invented" by the manipulations of a clever primate species. However, the problem disappears if we adopt the same view we have been taking throughout this book, that by "turning the world upside down," many of its most intractable enigmas disappear. Thus, with a top-down view, we see that the newly revealed dimension represented by primitive art was not invented but "discovered" in the course of our outwardly random evolutionary walk out of biology and into a specifically non-biological, human realm. This and other mental realms "do not depend on us or on what we think of them any more than the sea depends on the anemone; they exist *independently* of man."[40] Just as we may deduce the existence of hands from the archaeological discovery of axes, so too does the discovery of primitive art necessitate the positing of an inward realm, the soul, which corresponds to the outward object of its contemplation. Although *Homo sapiens* were still a mixture of human and mostly animal at this early stage in our evolution, we had clearly begun to make a break from the realm of the purely biological and, with the first halting steps into our local imagination, to bring down a glimmer of the nonlocal Divine Imagination:

> The imagination argues for a divine spark in human beings. It is absolutely confounding if you try to see imagination as a necessary quantity in biology. It is an emanation from above—literally a descent of the world soul....[41]

A true work of art points beyond itself in two directions, toward an "unseen reality" that can only be grasped by an intuitive response in the soul: "The soul of beauty in us identifies itself with the soul of beauty in the thing created...."[42] The palpable depth we perceive in a work of art is literally the measure of our soul, in that "soul" *is* the dimension of depth in human existence. And depth, profundity, wonderment, rapture, the revelation of cosmic meaning or deep inspiration—these are all "luxury capacities" without any Darwinian utility, iridescent signals coming at us from the future, the mysterious penumbra around something radically beyond both the biological and the human. In channeling artistic beauty, humans were no longer confined to "an external existence," but had instead gained "a momentary penumbral glimpse of Himself,"[43] the non-local Being "casting its luster" upon an otherwise aesthetically barren mindscape.

To say that human beings are "made in the image of God" is another way of saying that the creativity of the universe operates on us in a top-down fashion, and that by submitting to its influence, we may participate in the ongoing, creative revelation of Divine Being. In other words, humans are the self-aware locus of divine Self-revelation, and works of art memorialize the flow of intelligibility that proceeds from this ultimate ground. Thus, art represents a kind of knowledge of the absolute which, unlike profane scientific knowledge, can never transcend, dominate, or become "superior" to the object known. And this is why genuine art is so endlessly and inexhaustibly creative, even (or especially) upon repeated exposure to the very same work—the work is perpetually "enlivened" and renewed by its link to immortal Being.

Prior to the nineteenth century, it was understood that all art had religious connotations, that "the human artist—every authentic artist—must participate to some degree in the eternal wisdom"[44] The artist was "but an agent; to achieve perfection in his art he must make himself an instrument in the hands of God," acting "as the gods did in the beginning."[45] And, just as a timeless ground must underlie the temporal cosmos, the artistic act does not take place in time, but through an atemporal *now* into which the plenitude of divine creativity flows: the authentic artist captures somehow that effulgent moment at the frontier between time and eternity, which accounts for the inexplicable and enduring vitality, charisma, harmony and radiance which flow back to us through real art. And the living wellspring from which art originates is truly infinite, for just as no plant or animal could ever fully disclose or exhaust "the hidden vitality of the earth, so has no work of art ever brought to expression the depth of the unutterable, in the sight of which the souls of saints, poets and philosophers live."[46]

* * *

We have been focusing on the visual arts, but obviously all of the same things can be said of music or language. To paraphrase Luther, theology begins where music leads to. Consider the fact that the "rules" for writing bad music are identical to those for writing profound music. So, what is it that gives us chills upon hearing certain performances of a great masterwork, and how are we, within a few notes of hearing it, able to differentiate it from a merely technically proficient performance? What is it in us that allows contact with an undefinable mystery behind the sound phenomena, and what is it we are contacting? Or even more implausibly, what is it in us that allows us to make such a fine discrimination, to discern spirit in what is, for example, in Beethoven's late quartets, nothing but vibrating air molecules produced by rhythmically scratching catgut tautly suspended over pieces of wood? Or even more preposterously, how is it that an individual growing up in the most grinding poverty, oppression, and cultural deprivation, such as a Louis Armstrong or Muddy Waters, can take a limited musical form such as blues, and use it to express a sort of luminous musical genius that completely transcends its time and place? Saint-Saens writes that "music takes up where speech leaves off, it utters the ineffable, makes us discover in ourselves depths we had not suspected, conveys impressions and states of being that no words can render."[47]

Among the neuronal modules built by natural selection into human brains, it is easy to understand why we would have ones for, for example, intuitively understanding the properties of physical objects or differentiating human faces. But how on earth, by "monkeying around" with paint and noise, did early humans stumble upon a way to liberate spirit from air and matter, to achieve a radiance and harmony well beyond the physical properties of light and sound?

Consider language as well. Why, for example, do we have a 60,000 word vocabulary, when the most frequent one hundred words account for 60 percent of conversation? Indeed, for basic English you can get by with only 850 words,[48] and say everything you really need to say from a survival standpoint, such as "food," "beer" and "channel changer." The mystery of language, like the mystery of Life, is one of the keys to understanding the nature of our cosmos. According to the great philosopher of science, Stanley Jaki, the theory of natural selection must ironically "be proposed in the medium called language which remains even today as unexplained on a Darwinian basis as it was when Darwin tried to cope with it."[49] In other words, language easily accounts for (and therefore transcends) Darwin's theory, which is precisely why Darwin's theory cannot account for language: language is always one step ahead of the game, and to think otherwise is to attempt to give birth to one's mother. Language "is not just a set of signs which have meaning in virtue of referring to something, it is the necessary vehicle of a certain form of consciousness which is characteristically human.... [Words] not only describe a world, they also express a mode of consciousness...."[50]

If language was not a gift from the gods, handed down to human primates fully formed, then it might as well have been. If God's emanation of the logos creates the cosmos, our utterance of the word creates a "cosmion," or "little world of order" reflecting the larger divine reality.[51] Animals do not possess a flexible, symbolic language, only concrete signs at best. In a profound sense, language is what a human being *is,* the very thing that drives a wedge between man and chimp, perception and thing, now and then, here and not here. As such, it is language that gives us access to time, space, meaning, and a rapid-response creativity that can take place in the absence of the object or immediate problem. Of course, most people do not actually *speak* language but are passively *spoken by it,* so that their thought becomes subservient to the coarse and the concrete. However, it is possible to loosen the grip the material world exerts on words, and to allow language to become more fluid, mercurial, and receptive to higher things. (More on which below, in Book Four.)

To employ a reverse-tautology, words are much more than mere words. With language we are no longer an animal living in a nervous system, but semi-divine creatures living in an ever-expanding world of meaning that takes us far beyond the mere moment given to us by naked perception. Our primate ancestors once looked upon a relatively impoverished world with eyes designed to negotiate only three of its dimensions, not the higher worlds from which it is a declension. But when language piggybacked onto our nervous system, the world suddenly revealed itself to be a hyper-dimensional hologram with literally inexhaustible layer upon layer of gratuitous meaning. And of course, only through language were human beings vouchsafed the authentic scriptures of the world, through which they could articulate their higher selves and exit the closed circle of material existence. No wonder Sri Aurobindo wrote to a disciple that "It has always seemed to me that words came originally from somewhere else other than the thinking mind, although the thinking mind secured hold of them, turned them to its use and coined them freely for its purposes."[52]

So let's make one thing clear: in no way does language refer to mere things, as assumed by babies and nominalists; nor is language merely a self-referential, closed circle of signifiers, with no inherent meaning or objective referent; rather, it is specifically an open system in dynamic rapport with a transcendent source that imbues it with the noetic light we all use to get through the day. Indeed, the world itself is a book full of ideas, an antecedent reality that comes into view through the fusion of imagination and symbol. The senses alone provide no such knowledge, and to think otherwise is to shrink the world down to a mirror image of our most primitive way of knowing it. Without imagination, the world is nothing more than the "brute fact" presented to our untutored senses.

* * *

Obviously, the brain was already fully evolved long before the creative explosion. What was suddenly discovered were mind, imagination, spirit, and creativity. But how? One wonders what barrier had to be overcome in order for *Homo sapien* brains to break out of the closed circle of animality and begin hosting human minds. In the following two sections, we will discuss how it happens today, on an individual basis (3.2), and how it might have happened collectively, in the archaic past (3.3). In 3.4, we will take up the matter of what seems to have gone wrong with the human species, some sort of "aboriginal calamity" that occurred after such a seemingly auspicious start—our much rumored *fall.*

## 3.2 The Acquisition of Humanness in a Contemporary Stone Age Baby

> The truth is that the least-studied phase of human development remains the phase during which a child is acquiring all that makes him most human. Here is still a continent to conquer.
>
> —John Bowlby, *Attachment and Loss*

> From the child of five to myself is but a step. But from the newborn baby to the child of five is an appalling distance.
>
> —Leo Tolstoi

In December of 1952, a young biochemist at the University of Chicago, Stanley Miller, attempted in the laboratory to create the building blocks of life by sending a bolt of high-voltage electricity through a chemical soup made up of the simpler elements thought to have been available on earth some four billion years ago. Although some of the theories underlying Miller's efforts turned out to be fatally flawed, one must nevertheless applaud his Promethean (not to say Frankensteinian) effort to pry the secret of life from a test tube.

Nearly three years later, in October of 1955, my parents conducted an equally important if quixotic experiment. That is, they attempted to recreate in a suburban ranch-style laboratory the identical conditions that permitted "humanness" to emerge from an upright, bipedal primate in the archaic past. This they did by giving birth to a helpless, utterly dependent, pre-reflective and neurologically incomplete packet of genetic material, and by providing the proper conditions, transforming it into the thinking, self-reflective, perhaps a bit eccentric social animal that I am today. Here we should make it perfectly clear: the DNA bestowed on me at conception, while necessary, was entirely insufficient to create what any of us would call (and some still don't) a proper human being. Rather, the genetic material provided only a flexible mainframe for the storage and retrieval of a human being. Absent the very specific environmental conditions (i.e., my parents) that coaxed my humanness out of an otherwise Stone Age baby, "I" would be something else entirely, perhaps similar to Uday Hussein, or to the Wild Boy of Aveyron, found living by himself in the woods of southern France in 1800:

> [O]ne can perceive in him only animal behavior. If he has sensations, they give birth to no idea. He cannot even compare them with one another. One would think that there is no connection between his soul or mind and his body, and that he cannot reflect

> on anything. As a result, he has no discernment, no real mind, no memory. This condition of imbecility shows itself in his eyes, which he never keeps on any one object, and in the sounds of his voice, which are inarticulate, and discordant.[53]

My parents' little experiment just highlights one of the truly odd things about human beings: unlike every other animal, we are not just genetically *determined*, but genetically *permitted*. In other words, we are the only species that comes into the world with an almost infinite *potential* that may or may not be fulfilled, depending upon the familial and cultural environment we happen to encounter. Indeed, even under the most ideal circumstances, it is safe to say that none of us will, in the span of a single lifetime, actualize even a fraction of the potential enfolded in our minds (which is one of the inherent tragedies of worldly existence).

For much of the history of psychology, human beings were looked upon as isolated, closed systems that dissipated instinctual tension only in order to return to a state of blissful equilibrium. For example, Freud viewed the infant as primarily motivated to discharge id energy so as to maintain a sense of "primary narcissism," with no interest at all in the *object* of the instinct, the human being at the other end. Indeed, it was thought that the only reason infants were interested in mothers was because mothers fed them. Until fairly recently, no one considered bonding and attachment to have any great significance for how the human mind actually develops.

But modern attachment theory—by far the most fruitful and profound approach to human development—has turned this theoretical situation on its head. We now know that the antiquated view of the mind developing as a closed system is utterly false, and that the infant is exquisitely attuned to the human environment right from the start, even in the womb. It is now well understood that the only way to "become human" is to be immersed in an interpersonally rich environment in which we are treated as subjectively human right from the start. We all come into the world with a primary interest in maintaining a secure, meaningful relationship with a nurturing other, so that the dissipation of instinctual energy is now regarded primarily as a pleasurable "link" between two subjects, not an end in itself. In short, human beings are now regarded as uniquely open systems on our "ground floor" neurological/emotional level, onto which all later psychological development will piggyback.

Allan Schore, whose work brilliantly integrates cognitive neuroscience, developmental affective neuroscience, psychoneurobiology, developmental neuropsychoanalysis, and other emerging "hyphenated" disciplines, observes that,

> More than anyone could have predicted, observational and experimental research of infants interacting with their mothers has turned out to be the most fertile source for the generation of heuristic hypotheses about not only early development but also psychic dynamics.[54]

This is because our earliest social interactions "are imprinted into the biological structures that are maturing during the brain growth spurt that occurs in the first two years of human life, and therefore have far-reaching and long-enduring effects."[55] Strange as it may sound, immature babies interact with mothers in such a way as to use them as an "auxiliary cortex" for the purpose of "downloading programs from her brain into the infant's brain."[56] The infant's brain, "when coupled with the mother's, allows for a brain organization that can be expanded into more coherent and complex states of consciousness."[57] Of note, this "downloading" mostly occurs in the nonverbal right brain, which develops earlier than the syntactically organized left brain, and is dominant during the first two or three years of life. Furthermore, recent research indicates that early experience lays down many deep connections between the right brain and the emotional limbic system, so that it is fairly clear that the "unconscious" is located in the right brain. The right brain is where early traumas take root, where disowned parts of the self reside undetected by language and logic, where the parents' unconscious conflicts are imported, where the deepest psychosomatic representation of oneself endures, where dysregulated systems are locked in, and where "mind parasites"[58] and other ghostly psychotoxins hide out.

Bear in mind that it has only been in the past fifty years or so that we have begun to appreciate just how subtle the relationship is between caretaker and infant, what with the continuous functioning of various projective (outgoing) and introjective (incoming) mental processes. For example, as recently as the 1920's, John Watson, the well-known behavioral psychologist, could warn parents that "Mother love is a dangerous instrument," which "may inflict a never healing wound," so that parents should never hug or kiss their children, or even allow them to sit in their lap.[59] Of course, this sounds "crazy" to most of us now, but that is only a measure of how far we have advanced in our ability to understand and empathize with the experience of infancy (very similar to our modern ability to empathize with the suffering of animals, which did not trouble the vast majority of people in the past). Especially during early growth and development, the psychological feedback between the baby and its caretaker is so intimate that the two (infant and caretaker) can only be artificially separated. In fact, the brilliant pediatrician and psychoanalyst D.W. Winnicott made the farsighted observation that there is actually "no such thing an infant." Rather, because the baby comes into the world without any firm psychological boundaries, there is only a fluid, shifting, unitary space between (usually) mother and infant, as if they were a single organism. And it is within this "virtual space" that we all initially locate our minds, but only with the assistance of an emotionally sensitive and responsive parent.

The dynamic, back-and-forth interplay between mother and infant actually creates reverberatory autocatalytic loop which is internalized by the infant, forming the most primitive basis of what we call "thinking," that is, the ability to operate on and modify the content of one's own mind—thoughts, impulses, emotions, and mental states. Furthermore, it is now well established that many disturbances in mentation can be readily traced to the earliest relationships, and that most forms of mental illness, in one degree or another, involve difficulty in "thinking one's thoughts" or "feeling one's emotions." Indeed, one way of putting it is that disturbed minds do not generally think their thoughts, but are thought *by* them; thoughts, emotions and mental states abruptly "intrude" in an unpredictable, uncontrollable, unassimilable, and bewildering way, preventing any real continuity in being and identity. The real self fails to "come into existence," because "the personality becomes built on the basis of reactions to environmental impingement."[60] Further psychological evolution for these individuals is "checked," as they seem to be

> attached to an insurmountable object. Unable to integrate traumatic memories, they seem to have lost their capacity to assimilate new experiences as well. It is... as if their personality development has stopped at a certain point, and cannot enlarge any more....[61]

Thus, what we call our "mind" is not something only located inside our brain. Rather, the mind is actually discovered and developed in the virtual area (what Winnicott called the "transitional space") generated between various neurophysiological processes and early interpersonal relationships. One of the most revolutionary findings in all of modern science has been the discovery and elaboration of the "attachment system" bequeathed to human infants by evolution. It is no exaggeration to say that this system is the very means by which we create virtual connections to the mental world, so that individual brains may be functionally linked to one another. We take our thoroughly entangled mental connectedness to others for granted, but it is actually a quite unusual condition only brought about by the specific circumstances of human infancy. Through the medium of attachment, the immature brain of the infant is able to enlist the services of a mature adult brain in order to help regulate, organize, and understand its own mental states (which will otherwise remain a disordered and irritating jumble of chaotic, discontinuous and uncognizable intrusions on the surface of being, like the Wild Boy described above).

Our capacity to form social bonds with others has to do with our ability to "mindread," that is, to perceive and share mental states with others. Children are evidently born with a template for this ability, known as a "theory of mind." However, if this template for reading the mental states of others is not engaged by a sensitive caregiver, the result may be a condition of "mindblindness," in which we are not only unable to access the subjective states of others, but more or less unable to understand, explore, and deepen our own. According to Pinker, "A mind unequipped to discern other people's beliefs and intentions, even if it can learn in other ways, is incapable of the kind of learning that perpetuates culture."[62] Thus, we may put forth the psychological/evolutionary law that "if your mind wasn't read (as an infant), then you are mentally dead (as an adult)." In other words, our capacity to navigate around and enlarge our own mental space will very much depend upon whether or not we were cared for by parents who themselves had the ability to read and respond to our mental states, to empathically enter our mental world by being able to understand their own. Our ineffable experience of "I" is actually not an independent discovery, located through some kind of applied introspection or intuition (as in "I think, therefore I am."). If anything, we probably first discover the "I" of the (m)other, by trying to read the minds and intentions of our early caretakers (who simultaneously treat us as a subjective center with an "I" of our own, before we even know we have one). Often—*very* often—the true self is never discovered at all and an authentic person does not come into being, only the hardwired reactions to a psychologically toxic childhood environment—emotional deadness (or uncontrolled emotionality), lack of empathy, unregulated shame, absence of curiosity, unreflective acting out of conflicts, and an abundance of envy, guilt, rage, distrust and ingratitude. Remarkably, we are discovering that early experience can be *literally* neurotoxic, inducing increased destruction of synapses in the brain.[63] This occurs at the worst possible time, because this is when the brain is growing most rapidly, going from 400g to over 1000g in the first year of life. During this stage of development, synaptic connections will either be reinforced and "etched" by experience or ruthlessly weeded out and "pruned,"[64] to such an extent that the latter process actually resembles neurodegenerative disease:

> the early social environment, mediated by the primary caregiver, directly influences the final wiring of the circuits in the infant brain that are responsible for the future social and emotional coping capacities of the individual.[65]

This, as we shall see, has extraordinary implications for our human evolution in the archaic past. Specifically, because of modern research in attachment theory, we now understand that "humanness" did not, and could not have, emerged from individual brains, but only in an irreducible system that was able to link brains together in an evolving, virtual space known as "mind." Individual brains "link up" to one another in the virtual space of parent/child attunement, which is precisely where the self-reflective mind emerges.

Other social animals, such as dogs, have relatively hardwired means of sending and receiving messages from brain to brain, e.g., baring the teeth, pointing the ears forward, or stretching their front legs out and arching the back in the "play position." If this were the extent of our mindreading capabilities, I do not believe we ever would have become human. Rather, our becoming human required a much more flexible mindreading capability geared to the *individual* infant. The evolution of mindreading set in motion the primordial process whereby early human beings were able to break through the animal wall and eventually colonize the realm of mental space. The gradual extension and deepening of maternal empathy promoted a virtuous cycle of mental evolution, as more effective mindreading created more effective mindreaders. In this regard, the development of the mindreading cycle is analogous to the emergence of metabolizing molecules upon which all further biological evolution rested.[66]

* * *

One of the reasons we know so much about the attachment system and its implications for mental evolution, is that we may readily perceive what happens when something goes awry with it. This is not the place for a full explication all the psychopathologies that are now known to result from insecure, ambivalent, neglectful, chaotic or traumatic attachments. Suffice it to say at this juncture that the attachment system, while it provided our gateway into humanness, also included a subsystem to deal with the the great variability in the quality of (mostly inadequate) parenting that has been available throughout the course of history. This subsystem, known as the "unconscious," is responsible for the intergenerational transmission of psychopathology, and helps to explain the violence, madness, and irrational mayhem that comprises so much of human history.

* * *

Just as babyhood has traditionally been oversimplified and misunderstood by science, so too has parenthood. As Bowlby accurately described it, "when a baby is born, it evokes feelings in the parents that are as profound as those of a young child for its mother or as the passions of new lovers." However, most critically, the feelings evoked in the parents are by no means uniformly positive. Rather, an array of primitive feelings is usually aroused, including envy, resentments, hatred, and anxiety, all stemming from a reawakening of unconscious feelings first experienced in their own distant infantile past. The problem is that to allow oneself to be fully receptive to the emotional needs of the baby

> is to become reacquainted with oneself as a baby, to reexperience the pain of being totally dependent and desperately in love and yet being shut out and feeling unwanted. People construct their defenses in order to prevent being reengulfed by such feelings. But when one becomes a parent, the buried, unresolved pain is shaken loose, the defensive wall is breached, and new defensive efforts are required, which, in the case of the dismissing parent, means keeping the baby and its needs at some distance.[67]

And this is where the dark underside of the attachment system comes into play. That is, negative aspects of our own attachment experience that cannot be remembered tend to be *lived out* in adulthood, generally through cultural institutions and intimate relationships, but especially toward our children and other loved ones. As such, it is simply axiomatic that, despite what we may say to the contrary, we are often driven to recreate relationships that repeat early negative experiences, no matter how unsatisfying. For example,

> The fact that many people find romantic excitement in a lover who displays the qualities of a rejecting parent, an excitement that they do not find in others, suggests the degree to which they remain not just committed to but enthralled by early attachment figures. They can't let go of the mother or father who who didn't love them the way they needed to be loved. And they continue to be bewitched by the hurtfulness that compromised their care.[68]

In short—and I have seen this in literally hundreds of cases—the poorly attached child generally grows up to become "magnetized" by the rejecting quality, so that to relinquish it

> feels like giving up love itself. And so one seeks love in repetition.... An obvious corollary is that the prospect of being [cared for] in a truly loving way is undermined at every turn; indeed, it feels perversely unacceptable.[69]

Consider some of the adjectives used in the above paragraphs to describe the enduring, internalized bond with the inadequate or frustrating parent: *profound, passionate, overpowering, engulfed, excitement, enthralled, magnetized.* Not only are these not hyperbole, but one could add to the list *entranced, addicted, hypnotized, compelled* and *obsessed.* As the preeminent psychoanalyst James Grotstein put it, these internalized patterns (or "objects").[70]

> can acquire sovereignty over our psyche at any given moment as we find ourselves (unconsciously) identifying with that internal object and behaving as if we are in hypnotic subjugated thralldom, spell or trance—*becoming* it at that moment or enacting the scenario or agenda that it subjugatingly compels us to follow.[71]

These "internal objects" are subjectively experienced as a

> strange yet familiar distortion—a demon or monster, alien, misbegotten chimera, or homunculus. These entities may be internal or external, although the externally feared one may not be consciously *perceived,* only *experienced* as such. A person fears not only the fearsomeness inherent to other persons but also the negative attributes that we projectively—subjectively—attribute to them or that their provocations selectively release into our awareness from our inherent repertoire of preconceptual possibilities.[72]

The point I am emphasizing is that our earliest relationships, in the degree to which they are unsatisfactory, lead to a paradoxical situation in which the poor parental bond is internalized and turned into a psychic entity that compulsively seeks to reenact the situation later in life. If this sounds strange, just think about it from an evolutionary standpoint for a moment, and you will see its perverse beauty. As LaBarre fully recognized, *Parents are a serious adaptive problem for the infant.* The most fundamental dilemma faced by all humans is the fact that we come into the world utterly dependent upon parents who may be ambivalent, neglectful, preoccupied, not too bright, or even frankly hostile, and who may or may not be adequate to the task of raising us. In any case, because of the absolute dependency of the infant, combined with the complete uncertainty as to the quality of parenting that would be available, human infants had to evolve a way to maintain attachment to parents while denying the frustrating, coercive, or outright abusive aspects of the relationship. What we now call the "unconscious" is not, as in Freud's highly romanticized view, a seething cauldron of uncivilized drives, but a latent structure designed to hold childhood trauma in escrow for later processing, so as to not threaten the bond with the parents. As such, the content of the unconscious is actually quite variable in different people, cultures, and historical eras, while the structure itself is a constant, something that I believe was subject to normal evolutionary selective pressures—no different than the thickened skin we evolved on the bottom of our feet to deal with upright walking. The unconscious is merely a "container" for a "contained" that may vary considerably, in the same way that culture may be thought of as a particularized container of different civilizational content.

This is an important point, because there has been a persistent misunderstanding of the unconscious in academic circles. Again, there is the mistaken belief that we are born with certain universal drives inherited from our animal past, and that these become the troublesome content of the unconscious due to the effects of civilization—that is, because of repression. This mistaken view implies that the content of our unconscious is universal, somehow more "real" than our false, local, civilized selves. In fact the reverse is true: like all other biological entities, we come into the world a "whole" organism, not something riven and tortured by drives, impulses, and instincts. This is not to say that most people are not distressed by a subjective feeling that they are pushed around by drives and emotions: they are. It is just that this fractured condition of feeling like an ego driven by impulses or punished by a tyrannical conscience is a result of something that happened during childhood: it may be "average" but it is not "normal."

The common condition of multiple "subselves" in conflict with one another is actually a result of what I call the "parental purification system," the original unconscious structure that was evolved in order for us to maintain the illusion (if necessary) of parental love. We certainly don't have to reconstruct the distant past to see this mechanism in operation, as it is present to a greater or lesser degree in everyone. We all come into the world with the problem of managing the two most basic but difficult human impulses, *desire* and *aggression.* To the extent that our desires are overly frustrated, they are driven underground to constitute an unconscious, semiautonomous, split-off domain of insatiably greedy or destructively envious desire which was called the "id" by Freud. Likewise, to the extent that our aggression is unmanageably triggered as small children, it simply cannot be expressed directly toward those upon whom we absolutely depend. It too is driven underground, forming the nucleus of the superego, which either retroflects the aggression toward the self (experienced as guilt), or reverses it and expresses it toward others (which is known as identification with the aggressor). In this regard, the hypertrophic superego can literally be thought of as a psychological autoimmune disorder, as it functions to attack and prevent the expression of our normal desires and impulses.

According to Grotstein, "From one point of view one can consider all psychopathology as due to the failure, to one degree or another, of proper attachment and bonding."[73] Interaction between caregiver and infant "directly influences the evolution of structures in the brain," and "is imprinted into the child's developing nervous system."[74] This process is now fairly well understood and may be easily observed in oneself, for example, in psychoanalytic psychotherapy (or even through honest, disciplined introspection of the Gurdjieffian variety). In psychoanalytic parlance, the psychic structures that form in early childhood are known as internalized "object relations," in that they are "unconscious representations of the self interacting with the social environment."[75] Specifically, internalized objects create an emotional template, or psychic cartography, "constituted by a self-representation, an object-representation, and an affect [emotional] state linking them…"[76] These enduring, preverbal templates are reactivated throughout life, shaping "the individual's interpretation of interpersonal experiences and thereby his outwardly observable behavior." In this way, internalized object relations—or what I am calling "mind parasites"—are more than just inaccurate and ineffective working models of the world, but lifelike "beings" with their own autonomous agenda that "psychobiologically mediate psychiatric *and* cultural psychopathology."[77]

While the idea of a parental purification system may sound abstract, speculative, or overly theoretical, it is actually as commonplace as can be. As a psychologist, I know I am not alone in my observation that the more people were mistreated by their parents, the more they tend to defend them with statements such as "I deserved it," or "I was really a handful." Furthermore, these same individuals are generally *driven* to recreate the poor relationship as adults, and they are uncannily adept at finding parental stand-ins with whom they may act out their unconscious resentment, hostility, envy, "pay back," or perverse idealization later in life. Because both poles of the parent-child relationship are internalized during childhood, the adult individual, in acting out the relationship, may adopt the role of either member, that is, the child in relationship to the projected parent, or the parent in relationship to the projected child. For example, it would not be uncommon to see an abusive or controlling man in relationship to a needy, dependent woman (who contains his projected infantile part), or a weak, victimized man in relationship to a magically powerful, alluring, sexually "omnipotent" woman (who now contains the parental part). Either way, the critical point to bear in mind is that most people are quite literally "not themselves." Rather, they are inhabited by other "selves" internalized during childhood which, like viruses, commandeer the machinery of the host (in this case, the mind) in order to "reproduce" themselves in the form of toxic, unsatisfactory relationships later in life. Indeed, we might go so far as to say that many people are driven to have children, not only to get their genes into the next generation, but to get their parasitic "memes" into the next generation; natural selection applies to the mind parasites no less than to our DNA.

For example, a typical case of mine involved a self-defeating woman who had been abused by her mother throughout her childhood. She recalled asking her mother why she beat her so often, and her mother responded with unusual candor, "When I was little I got hit.... Now it's my turn.... When you grow up, it will be your turn." More recently, another depressed patient described alcoholic parents who neglected her to such an extent that she was repeatedly hospitalized for malnutrition, even during infancy. When I asked if she had ever been physically abused, she responded that "my dad loved us dearly.... He would never think of anything like that." Again, the lie is erected so as to maintain the illusion of love, while the reality is shunted into the nonverbal right brain, where, in this woman's case, it caused a lifetime of loveless relationships with much older men for the purposes of protection and dependency.

It is safe to say that nearly all human beings are inhabited by at least a few personal and cultural mind parasites, while most people have considerably more than a few. Remember, evolution doesn't care if you are happy, only if you survive and reproduce, both materially and psychically. Evolution always makes do with whatever is at hand, and the parental purification system was the best solution it could come up with to solve the immediate problem of how to secure the life-preserving bond between parent and child regardless of its quality. Nevertheless, one of the reasons why these mind parasites are so difficult to eradicate is that they are internalized during the same time our brains are neurologically incomplete and being shaped by the environment. Again, our earliest experiences become "hard wired" in the right neocortex, extending down into the more primitive emotional centers of the brain. Only the neural connections reinforced by experience will survive, so that the brain we end up with is not a deterministic result of genes, and the person we end up becoming may or may not be "us" at all, but a lot of hard-wired responses to a stressful environment, fated to act themselves out until death do us and our parasites part. Interestingly, Steven Pinker, in his book *The Blank Slate* makes the point that humans seem to be born with a true, individual personality that is not merely a result or outcome of good parenting; however, at the same time, our true self can be crippled or obscured by bad parenting. In other words, there appears to be scientific confirmation (not that it is necessary) for the view that the true self is not a temporal, environmentally created entity, only the false self that we internalize through experience.[78]

But whatever you wish to call them—complexes, fixations, repetition compulsions—there is no question that human beings serve as the unwitting hosts of "parasitic organisms" that operate independently of our conscious will and tend to subjugate it: "these perverse tendencies can deprive us of our freedom and enslave us. Worse still, they can avail themselves of our imagination and inventive faculties and lead us to creations which can become the scourge of mankind."[79] That is, because these self-replicating "psychoviruses" keep reproducing themselves on both a personal and historical basis, they are, as we shall see, "a source of social infection as real and serious as are carriers of diphtheria and typhoid."[80]

## 3.3 Humans and How They Got That Way: Putting the *Sapiens* Into *Homo*

> It seems as if grown-up people, in thinking about their origins, involuntarily lose sight of the fact that they themselves and all adults came into the world as little children. Over and over again, in the scientific myths of origin no less than in the religious ones, they feel impelled to imagine: In the beginning was a single human being, who was an adult.
>
> —Norbert Elias, *The Civilizing Process*

> [W]e may reasonably view an infant's dawning of awareness on two levels: as a consciousness arising in the individual and, simultaneously, in the universe as a whole.... we can watch an incredibly condensed version of the growth of awareness on this planet, and in the cosmos, in each developing child.
>
> —David Darling, *Equations of Eternity*

At this point, I would like to shine the light of attachment theory onto human prehistory and see if it can help illuminate just how, in *Homo sapiens,* cosmic evolution transcended biology and finally became conscious of itself. The specific question I would like to explore is what our present understanding of developmental psychology can tell us about our sudden ingression into mental space in the archaic past. As we have now seen, most anyone (or anytwo) can make a baby, but that does not mean that the baby will grow up to be fully "human" as we understand the term—that is, fulfill its human potential. Rather, a baby requires certain non-genetic experiences and conditions if it is to develop a coherent, flexible, creative, and self-reflective mind, relatively free from the reproductive, antievolutionary cycle of mind parasites. So the same theory that explains how a contemporary baby becomes a mature adult should provide some insight into how our Pleistocene ancestors acquired their humanness, since no human baby will grow into adulthood without certain distinct behaviors on the part of its caretakers. Since our genotype has not changed in at least 130,000 years, all babies today start out life just as they did then. What I will be arguing is that the human baby—both now and in the archaic past—is the "missing link," the narrow neck we must all pass through on the way to humanness, a bridge over the "awesome chasm" separating the instinct-bound ape, or merely genetic *Homo sapiens*, from the truly human, which is characterized by a capacity for, among other things, freedom, love, and creativity.

## Nature's Greatest Invention: The Helpless Baby

At this point we might review just what is known about how early humans came into being in the pre-mental soup of Africa.[81] Without question, we are descended from tree-dwelling primates that eventually became upright and earth-bound. Probably the best explanation we have for this at present has to do with a major geological event that occurred in Africa some 5 to 10 million years ago, the collapse of the Great Rift Valley. This enormous fault line effectively split the primate population and left them isolated from one another in completely different environments, the western side continuing with rain and trees, the eastern portion increasingly dry and treeless.

The contented primates on the western side were able to carry on as before, eventually resulting in the monkeys, gorillas, and chimpanzees we see today. But on the eastern side, nature (literally) forced our hand, leading to the emergence of a new primate species, the hominids. The field here is open to speculation, but most of the experts assume that much of our transition to humanness took place in this new, more challenging environment of the open savanna.

According to Steven Stanley, the evolution of our large brain depended on our being forced down from the trees, something he calls the "terrestrial imperative." In short, before we could evolve large brains, it was necessary for our hands to be free in order to hold, transport, and take care of helpless infants. And in order for our hands to be free, we had to come down from the trees and evolve the ability to walk upright. Obviously, babies are very demanding creatures, drastically restricting the activity (and survival prospects) of the mother, so there must have been a great side-benefit that accompanied the evolutionary development of these quadriplegic eating and crying machines. In general, evolution cannot normally afford the luxury of a species so utterly helpless at birth. For example, a baby zebra, giraffe or deer must be able to run away from predators almost immediately after birth. If evolution ever tinkered with the idea of creating a deer that could not immediately run with the pack, obviously those genes were long ago eliminated. Likewise, a chimpanzee infant can grip the mother's fur with its hands and feet, so the chimpanzee mother, whose arms are otherwise occupied by constant climbing, is able to pay much less attention to the baby.[82]

Why the relationship between helpless infants and large brains? As our brains became larger and larger (and pelvises became narrower due to bipedalism), the Biblical curse of bringing forth children in pain became very real for our primordial Eve, so recently banished from the Edenic paradise enjoyed by her peaheaded primate cousins to the west. Many hominid females undoubtedly perished as evolution sought a balance between our useful big heads and the ability to give birth to them without dying in the process. Nature's "solution" was to shorten the span of pregnancy and allow much of the brain's development to take place *outside* the womb, a pattern completely unique among the primates.

More than anything else, it was this delayed development, or "neotany," that created the possibility of our acquisition of humanness. In an ingenious evolutionary trade-off, human beings possess the largest brain possible given the limitations of the female pelvis (who knew?). But because of this trade-off, this meant that all humans had to literally be born premature—to be exact, about twelve months premature—so that we are completely helpless and uncoordinated at birth:

> babies must continue their still unfinished brain growth postnatally during a period of helpless dependency. Only much later can the body afford to catch up, because brains are needed *from the*

> *beginning* for the business of becoming a new human being.... It is to this strikingly unfinished bodily dependency that the human female's specialty in maternity is the response....[83]

It has been estimated that, to achieve maturity, the term of human gestation "should" last about twenty-one months, which means that our first years are spent as extrauterine fetuses with the world as our psychological womb, for better or worse. As it so happens, that virtual womb turned out to be the psychic laboratory where an awkward evolutionary solution to the problem of how to make a bigger brain created an unanticipated byproduct: the self-awareness needed to bridge the gap between the animal and the human.

* * *

There is indeed evidence from the field of cognitive archaeology that something unusual happened to the human mind some 50,000 to 100,000 years ago, leading up to the creative explosion. In his book *The Prehistory of Mind,* Steven Mithen agrees that the rather sudden development of our human mental capacity did not involve a new brain *per se*, but a newly developed ability to integrate and link up various specialized "intelligences" that had previously been separate. As he explains it, "A cognitive fluidity arose within the mind, reflecting new connections rather than new processing power."[84] Somehow the brain went from a lot of personal computers working on individual tasks to a hyper-connected internet with much greater flow of knowledge and ideas between domains. But how did this happen, and what does it have to do with babyhood? Klein and Edgar note that "humans virtually everywhere had achieved modern or near-modern brain size by 200,000 years ago. Any neural change that occurred 50,000 years ago would thus have been strictly organizational..."[85] But what kind of organizational change? According to Mithen again, if we look at Neanderthals and other extinct humans, there is evidence that their brains became fully developed at a much earlier age than ours do, before neural networks integrating the various modules of intelligence could be linked together. In other words, because these earlier humans were not, as we are, born as premature, the window of brain development slammed shut more quickly, before cognitive fluidity could be wired in. Mithen agrees that it was not our large brain alone, but the gradual lengthening of the period of extra-uterine brain development—and therefore, infantile dependency—that must have been central to our creative explosion.

As touched upon above, where all other animals possess hard-wired, species-specific traits, human beings emerged from a species-specific *situation*, that is, the tripartite family of mother-father-infant. According to the great psychoanalytic anthropologist, Weston LaBarre,

> We should not take human babyhood so much for granted! Babyhood is manifestly a *human specialization*. We make much of the sexual dimorphism of the human male and female. We should take note, more properly, of the human *trimorphism*—male, female, *and* infant—and the reciprocal influence of these three upon one another.... *[A]s a new animal environment*, the family shapes all three of its members, morphologically as well as psychologically.[86]

In short, what we need to investigate is how this trinitarian family situation came about, and how it led to the unique possibility of a template for human potential in the form of a developmentally delayed, neurologically incomplete ape: the baby.

This situation of giving birth to helpless, big-brained infants out on the open savanna had a number of extremely important consequences. With it, human beings were now fully *trimorphic*, with each member of the family able to focus to the hilt on its own area of specialty. For men, this meant hunting; for women, nurturing the young; and for babies, being dependent and *learning*.

> [I]t is specifically the new biological situation of a long childhood that gives rise to this new kind of culture-bearing animal. Male and female sexual dimorphism and physical specializations are plainly the *enabling factors* behind the baby's specialization in babyhood....[87]

It is this ability of the baby to specialize in dependency, attachment, and slow maturation that holds the key to the emergence of humanness. It is the baby[88] who is the wild card in human evolution, the flexible template through which culture has the opportunity to continuously update itself:

> [I]mmaturity—an *absence* of maturely functioning instincts—allowed, indeed required, the replacement of wild-animal instinct with the new adaptation: culture. Culture, however, must be learned. And learning in turn demands malleable, labile, instinct-poor, dependent, immature animals, so that there is a circular and cumulative feedback in this cultural-physical process....[89]

We are accustomed to looking at human evolution only from the point of view of mature, adult members of the species. But in keeping with the spirit of our trimorphism, it seems obvious that, in order for helpless babies to survive, they had to become adept at "evoking" the environment they needed to survive—specifically, an intelligent, caring mother. Perhaps it sounds odd, but it seems an inescapable conclusion that, in order for babies to be able to specialize in babyhood, they had to "select" mothers who were intelligent, capable, and empathic enough to be up to the task of caring for them. Think about it: caring for a helpless infant is at least as complex and challenging on a moment-to-moment basis as hunting for game. Modern research by attachment theorists has shown that babies will literally waste away and die if not given the proper amount and type of attention. Let's face it: those mothers who did not develop these complex mothering skills may have gotten their genes into the next generation, but not long enough for that generation to do the same. Thus, the selective pressure of helpless infants might well have contributed to a runaway positive feedback loop for greater intelligence in the species, as babies became more helpless (because premature) and mothers became more intelligent and attuned to them (so that babies could survive their prematurity). In fact, there is scientific evidence that the "mutual entrainment" between mother and infant

> triggers an amplified energy flow, which allows for a coherence of organization that sustains more complex states within both the infant's and the mother's right brains.... [E]vidence indicates that *the organization of the mother's brain is also being influenced by these relational transactions.*[90]

Did the baby also select for monogamy and fidelity? According to Morgan, when a nuclear family (which involves monogamy and parental assistance in raising the young) occurs, "it is driven by the needs of the offspring and the female's inability to cope on her own."[91] Geoffrey Miller, author of *The Mating Mind,* writes that "the minimum investment human female ancestors could have made in their offspring would have been a nine-month pregnancy followed by at least a couple years of breast-feeding."[92] Moreover, if females became pregnant and gave birth after weaning, they would be further incapacitated by pregnancy and having to care for multiple children. Sociobiologists often suggest that males and females developed radically different sexual strategies, with females focusing on the quality of a mate (because of the great burden of raising a child), males on quantity, that is, trying to impregnate as many females as possible in order to maximize their chances of getting their genes into the next generation. While there is surely some truth to this, I believe it ignores just how difficult it would have been for a Stone Age mother to raise a brood of infants and children on her own without some assistance and commitment from the male. This problem was solved, to a certain extent, by our ability to bond with another for an extended period of time beyond mere sexual mating. Helpless babies that survived into adulthood did so because of the care (which they experienced as love) they received as infants. And when they grew to adulthood, they unconsciously searched for relationships in which this blissful bonding could be recreated. That is, our unique desire and ability to fall in love have to do with attachment experiences we all had very early in life, before we even knew what was happening to us. Attachment leaves such a lasting impression that much of our later life is spent trying to recreate its specific character, for better or worse. We are intensely attracted to those particular individuals who resonate with our earliest emotional map.

Here again we see the helpless baby as the hinge of psychogenesis, as the infant "selects" for caring mothers in committed relationships in order to ensure its survival. The fact is, we are not an innately or even habitually promiscuous species; rather, "almost all human pregnancies arise in sexual relationships that have lasted at least several months, if not years."[93] Furthermore, "when it comes to choosing sexual partners for long-term relationships, men and women increase their choosiness to almost identical levels."[94] Why? Not necessarily because of genetic strategy, but because of psychological needs. In the case of humans—because of the issue of infantile helplessness—natural selection could never have worked just through copulation or even babies being born; that would not have been enough. Rather, copulation must result first in birth, and birth must then result in a baby who in turn survives to grow up, bond, and reproduce. And as we have seen, this requires a certain behaviors from caretakers, not just the fact of its physical birth. Babies can only serve the genetic interests of their parents if parents ignore their own short-term interests in order to serve the immediate needs of the baby.

In addition to the psychological needs shaped by one's own infantile experience, there is new evidence that babies produce measurable changes in a man's testosterone levels (it has long been known that they have this effect on females, triggering the production of the powerful "bonding" hormone, oxytocin). So profound is the impact of a baby, that recent research by a team of anthropologists at Harvard University[95] has demonstrated that a man's testosterone levels drop significantly from the mere act of holding an infant—even from holding a baby doll. Testosterone is the sometimes troublesome hormone that mediates fighting, competing, and mating, which means that babies are able to control adult male behavior in a direct, endocrinological way, attempting to rein in testosterone-fueled behavior so as to increase the likelihood that their fathers will settle down and take care of the family. In a very real sense then, an adult who falls in love, bonds with a mate, and takes care of his family, is just a baby's way of making another baby, and the invention of the helpless baby would appear to be a critical step in the further evolution of the cosmos. Therefore, perhaps religious myths that refer to a "divine child" are on to something. For that matter, if I recall correctly, it is a sword-wielding baby who, for reasons you may wish to ponder, has guarded the tree of life ever since the fall of man. We close this section with a quote from the brilliant author of Meditations on the Tarot, who wished to remain anonymous:

> There is nothing which is more necessary and more precious in the experience of human childhood than parental love;.... nothing more precious, because the parental love experienced in childhood is moral capital for the whole of life.... It is so precious, this experience, that it renders us capable of elevating ourselves to more sublime things—even divine things. It is thanks to the experience of parental love that our soul is capable of raising itself to the love of God.[96]

*What is Man!*

*Answer: a baby's way of making another baby. The helpless neonate is the missing link, the hinge of evolution, the narrow neck we must all pass through on the way to humanness.*

## 3.4 Adapting to Mindedness: Why the Past Is So Tense

> In light of the fact that many… mothers have suffered from unresolved trauma themselves, this spatiotemporal imprinting of the chaotic alterations of the mother's dysregulated state facilitates the down-loading of programs of psychopathogenesis, a context for the intergenerational transmission of trauma.
>
> —Allan Schore, *Affect Dysregulation and Disorders of the Self*

> It is time to accept the *irrational* as a component of human affairs, to recognize that men adapt both to an outer, rational, secular world and to an inner, irrational, sacred world whose locus they have misplaced as being outside.… The pattern of this projection lies deep in human biology and real childhood experience.…
>
> —Weston LaBarre, *The Ghost Dance*

I am about to put forth a rather sweeping generalization about the meaning and direction of history, and I will undoubtedly be accused of oversimplification due to the fact that I am seeing things from the narrow perspective of a psychologist, no different than, say, a dentist who sees the long march of history revealing a tendency toward better dental hygiene. However, I have a very specific view of history in mind, and it is quite different from that of the typical historian. First of all, historians—contemporary ones, anyway—no longer presume to know the "purpose" of history. Without question they tell us about causes and motivations *within* history, but they steer quite clear of asking what is the actual *point* of history. And understanding the point of history is admittedly quite difficult—if not impossible—if you do not know what a human being *is.* That is, history is simply an account of human actions and reactions, so if you don't know what a human *is,* how could you possibly know what history is *for?* The problem is only compounded if you are only a human working with merely human sources, for how then can you stand outside the flow of historical events and gain any perspective on history, or have any stable frame of reference? In other words, if the historian is just a historically conditioned product of history, why should we pay any attention to him at all?

But no historian really believes they are nothing more than another anonymous historical "fact" embedded in the march of time. Historians always stand outside time and take a transcendental view of history, but conceal the transcendental agenda or ideology that has guided their selection and shaping of facts, which gives their work a false air of objectivity. I will make no such effort to conceal my agenda. Rather, I believe that history must be understood in the total context of cosmic evolution, and agree with the great hermeticist Valentin Tomberg that the leading edge of this cosmic evolution involves a path of "ongoing interiorization," starting "from the latent stage of mere existence" toward

> further interiorization in reflection, leading to consciousness of self, and lastly from that to a conscious cooperation with the whole evolutionary process. Eventually the path leads to the attainment of the ultimate summit of this process of interiorization, the omega-point, or God.[97]

Another way of saying it is that history is "the way in which humanity and the individual work out the great Cosmic Process, of Fall and Return."[98] This short description suggests a great deal. First, it means that history is a *cosmic* process, part of the general evolution of existence. Secondly, it suggests that *individual* humans are participants in this cosmic process as well. And thirdly, it suggests that cosmic history has a destination (more precisely, a "deustination") but that there is some sort of problem we must first "work out" in order to arrive there.

Occult lore speaks of an "akashic record" which, like a sort of cosmic memory bank, purportedly contains a complete record of everything that has occurred in the past. However, even if we were in possession of every raw historical fact, we would no more understand the "point" of history than a complete mapping of our genetic blueprint would reveal the purpose of our life. Historians unavoidably make what amounts to a partial selection from the totality of the akashic record, and then attempt to link these facts through logic, common sense, ideology, and conventional cause and effect (among other methods). But this is why such narratives are vulnerable to the corrosive effect of "deconstruction," in that the next scholar is always able to come along and assemble the same facts into a very different, even completely contradictory, narrative. (In other words, the same facts may be used, say, to describe Columbus' discovery of America as a great advance for western civilization or a great colonialist oppression of indigenous peoples.)

Therefore, the only way to construct an objective history is with reference to its final cause, not material, efficient, or necessary causes from within. Any historical narrative that falls short of taking into account the end of history will necessarily be a subjectively biased narrative superimposed on the jumble of disconnected historical facts drifting along in the wake of temporal progression. (I should emphasize that I am specifically *not* talking about a naive Marxist or Hegelian historicism, in which general laws guide history in a deterministic fashion. Rather, I am treating history as an *open* system that is non-deterministically lured by a trans-historical eschatological "subject/object" located outside space and time.)

In the esoteric tradition, it has always been understood that there are "horizontal" and "vertical" causes operating both in individuals and in history. In fact, this distinction might be understood as the *key point* of esotericism. That is, human beings are understood to have somehow "fallen" from a paradisiacal state of radical freedom, in which our orientation is to vertical causes emanating from "above," into a horizontal march through history, characterized by dualism, struggle, conflict, confusion, and worship of and hypnotic enslavement to human institutions. I will not at this point delve deeply into the matter of vertical causes, for that is the subject of Book Four. However, suffice it to say that every human being

> is the product of two heredities—"horizontal heredity" and "vertical heredity," the latter being the imprint of the individuality

> from above and the former being the imprint of the ancestors here below.[99]

Some horizontal causes are fairly well understood, such as genetics, child development, and culture, while vertical causes are not appreciated at all, in fact, not spoken of in polite society. But according to Tomberg, what we experience as history is actually the "whirlpool" created by the opposing streams of history, one horizontal, the other vertical:

> the spiritual-cultural history of mankind is the result on the one hand of the causes which are to be found in space and time, and on the other hand of the causes which are not to be found there, which are of a timeless and spaceless nature.[100]

Similarly, Terence McKenna writes that

> This situation called history is totally unique; it will last only for a moment, it began a moment ago. In that moment there is a tremendous burst of static as the monkey goes to godhood, as the final eschatological object mitigates and transforms the forward flow of entropic circumstance.[101]

In other words, history is the "static" thrown off as primates achieve vertical "liftoff" from merely biological, Darwinian existence. Vertical causes are supersensible and may act from the future, intervening in what what would otherwise be a closed and circular, or merely linear succession of events, without "height" or "depth," and therefore, significance. World history, beginning with the miraculous "cultural explosion" discussed above, is actually full of similar "miracles" which cannot be explained by horizontal historical causes. In fact, a miracle, properly understood, is nothing more than an acausal vertical intervention which bursts through the closed circle of human existence, breaking up the evolutionary impasse and regenerating a spiritually, culturally, politically, or artistically exhausted humanity. Similarly, the "messiah," abstractly understood, is simply a vertical cause personified, one who has descended from outside history to shatter the sclerotic institutional "containers" of man's spirit, which may start off with noble intentions but always end up preventing growth and strangling innovation. Just as a fire is "contained" when it is no longer a threat to the forest, human beings are "contained" when they have wholly given themselves over to the "horizontal" myths, aspirations, superstitions, collective delusions, slogans, desires, and superficial concerns of their culture. The function of the messiah is to help us shatter and slough off all that is "time-conditioned and of merely local or national significance,"[102] which creates a space for re-contact with the ultimate reality that can never really be contained by human institutions.

The messiah always brings down a radical vision of liberty, for only through individual liberty (constrained by the boundary conditions of just law) can history progress and get to where it is going. Without liberty, history would constitute a closed, repetitive system that might produce circular variations on a theme, but no genuine novelty. Just as in an organism, there is no order without hierarchical structure, and there is no hierarchy without telos. Liberty alone leads to chaos, while law alone (for example, in the contemporary Islamic world) leads to rigidity and cessation of growth. Humans evolve only under conditions of liberty constrained by law, oriented toward the true, the good, and the beautiful.

* * *

The nineteenth century historian Jacob Burckhardt wrote that history is "the breach with nature caused by the awakening of consciousness," a statement with which I am in full sympathy. The great twentieth century philosopher Eric Voegelin noted that history is "the process in which man articulates his own nature."[103] Putting these two statements together, I believe that history is a chronicle of our evolutionary sprint from biology to spirit, in which we first climb *down* from the trees of eastern Africa and then *up* the metaphorical Upanishadic tree with its roots aloft, its branches down here below. Thus, we start our evolutionary journey "out on a limb" and soon find ourselves "grounded," but eventually find a "radical" solution to our troubling situation, arriving at the "root" of the cosmos ("radical," of course, comes from the latin word for "root"). This gradual articulation of our nature *requires time,* just as does the articulation of any complex event. But the articulation is ultimately hierarchically controlled "from above." Thus, my ultimate aim in this section is not an historical one but a metahistorical and psycho-spiritual one. Again, this book attempts to draw an ideal line through the whole of creation, from the big bang, through life, mind, history, and beyond, to the the ultimate end of the cosmos. What follows is a historical line drawn from prehistory, through antiquity, and on through to modernity, focusing upon just some of the disturbing "static" thrown off by humans in their unanticipated journey from monkey to God. Obviously, other lines could be drawn—economic lines, military lines, technological lines—but my interest is not so much in proving a historical point as in using historical examples to reveal the ubiquitous presence of a great obstacle to psychological, cultural, and spiritual development: mind parasites. Once you understand the nature of these entities, you will need little convincing that history is littered with their destructive and self-defeating effects. If you don't understand them, then it is unlikely that any amount of argument will suffice, because you are in blissful *denial* of the hostile forces that keep you and most everyone else subdued, tyrannized, and in bondage, doing time behind bars as strong as death (but fortunately, weaker than love).

* * *

Traditionally we have been given only three explanations for the apparent variability of human nature. First, we have the modern scientific belief in a genetically determined, universal human nature that reveals itself in "superficially" different ways in various cultures. Second, there is the religious/romantic view that we have "fallen" from a prior perfection, partly due to the effects of civilization. And third, there is the currently unfashionable Enlightenment/Freudian view that we have evolved up from our barbaric roots by repressing our primitive selves and becoming "civilized."

Here I would like to explore the possibility of a fourth option that combines elements of each of the above: that there is a transcendent realm of universal human nature—a blueprint of our spiritual wholeness, as it were—and that we do deviate ("fall") from it. Nevertheless, our march through history shows an obvious (if sometimes widely vacillating) tendency of progressive evolution, because the passage of time has allowed us to gradually adapt more effectively to the unusual condition of having a self-aware mind. In short, the basic dilemma faced by the human species is that the same situation that allowed us to become self-reflective primates—that is, our neotany and the resultant need to enlist the services of an adult caretaker to organize our otherwise chaotic mental processes—also left us exceedingly vulnerable to self-reproducing "mind parasites" which take up the space where our true self would otherwise be. Another way of putting it is that, because of the mind parasites, the past (our edenic blueprint) has paradoxically not yet been tried. Any observer at any time in history, right through to the present, has been able to look at the human situation and recognize that something is obviously "wrong" with people. Both "conservatives" and "liberals," religious and secular, intuit the divine blueprint, but the former tend to project it onto the past, the latter into the future. However, the divine blueprint exists outside local space and time, and can therefore only be actualized *now.* Both individually and as a species, we become "human" in the degree to which we purge ourselves of the self-serving entities that have no business taking up space in our minds, and which prevent us from claiming our divine birthright.[104]

In 1976, the eminent historian William McNeill published an influential book, *Plagues and Peoples,* which showed "how infectious disease has impacted and altered the course of human history." Specifically, the book revealed a previously hidden, unappreciated side of history, that is, the ongoing struggle between parasites and human beings. Obviously, history from the point of view of a parasite looks considerably different than history from the human point of view, but it is no less real. From the standpoint of these microbes, history has been nothing but a long struggle to find human hosts where they might live and reproduce more viruses who go on to find more hosts. Modern psychology also studies a kind of "microbe," applying the misleading term "internal object" to them. This term, according to Grotstein, "misses the eery, mysterious quality" of the relations between human subjects and these parasitic entities inhabiting a haunted "third world" (a world that is neither subject nor object). Grotstein notes that

> In the dazzling light of the Enlightenment, preternatural spirits, presences, angels, and demons, along with their cosmologies, were bleached into apparent oblivion. These designations waned, and their remains were reminted in the alchemy of a newer "scientific" lexicon. Nevertheless the spirits that occupied their successors (i.e., "internal objects") continued to haunt our minds.[105]

Although evidence of the mind parasites is everywhere present in human history, for example, in the form of ubiquitous demons, evil spirits, witches, and other psychological projections—no one has taken it upon themselves to write a similar book about their historical impact on human affairs, in part because nowadays no one knows just how to regard them:

> These entities seem to occupy a kind of undefined ontological limbo. Whatever their status in the world, their persistence in human experience and folklore is striking. In all times and in all places, with the possible exception of Western Europe for the past two hundred years, a social commerce between human beings and various types of discarnate entities, or non-human intelligences, was taken for granted.[106]

Indeed, if truth were a democracy, each person from the dawn of history getting one vote, the belief in such "spiritual" beings populating the landscape "would unquestionably be the most firmly established truth in man's whole armamentarium."[107] And the problem here is not just that people "believed" (and continue to believe) in these things and left it at that. Rather, the belief in these entities is often prelude to *action*, generally unpleasant. That is, mind parasites are projected into the outside world because they cause internal anxiety. But projecting them outward does not actually eliminate the anxiety. Rather, it simply "mentalizes" the environment, so that the objective world, rather than the subjective world, is experienced as a dangerous, persecutory, and threatening place. What should be a "thought" is instead experienced as a "bad internal object" to be mentally evacuated into the world. As a result,

> the development of an apparatus for thinking is disturbed and instead there takes place a hypertrophic development of the apparatus of projective identification.... The end result is that all thoughts are treated as if they were indistinguishable from bad internal objects; the appropriate machinery is felt to be, not an apparatus for thinking the thoughts, but an apparatus for ridding the psyche of accumulations of bad internal objects.[108]

These "bad objects," or mind parasites, are nearly always projected into other people, which accounts for the historically universal problem of witches, vampires, infidels, anti-Semitism, racism, etc. And the "problem" of demonic others nearly always demands a violent "solution"; that is, the experience of these demonic projections goes hand in hand with the belief that fear and/or violence are the only appropriate responses to them. (In other words, it seems axiomatic that no one who engages in demonic projection regards their projections with indifference.) And it is because of this ubiquitous projective process that

> With pitifully few exceptions, almost all human societies have exercised some form of institutionalized aggression, directing it inward against a group of people within the society or outward against another society.[109]

And the problem does not end there. As Bion explains above, when bearing one's painful thoughts has been replaced by evacuating them, there is no longer a means to actually learn from experience, to reliably discriminate between truth and falsehood, reality and fantasy. Think of it: the mind in this scenario is not interested in truth, but in ridding itself of anxiety; truth is of no concern whatsoever. As expressed in another context by the philosopher Ortega y Gassett, it does not trouble such an individual that his ideas are untrue, because he is only using them "as trenches for the defense of his existence, as scarecrows to frighten away reality."[110]

What happens next is a subtle but nevertheless very important psychic transformation that we will need to understand in order to illuminate one of the most persistent historical patterns in human groups, right down to the present day. That is, when the ordinary mechanism for learning from experience is damaged, it does not simply leave a vacuum in the psyche. Rather, the means for discriminating true and false—for testing reality—is actually replaced by an omniscient, "dictatorial affirmation that one thing is morally right and the other wrong."[111] In short, the domain of learning is hijacked by a specific kind of parasite, an omniscient knower who forbids contradictory knowledge on the grounds that it is not just wrong but immoral. Every perverse but "righteous" social movement throughout history shares this dynamic, from Aztec human sacrifice to Christian inquisitions, from apologists of slavery to Islamic jihads, from the fascist Right to the Marxist Left. What contradicts these movements (to their adherents) is not just wrong, but evil. These movements have a tremendous emotional appeal though, because they provide the parasite-infested individual with "a ready-made drama of self-transcending action and heroic identity. It [is] as simple as that."[112] (Memo to Mr. bin Laden: does this ring a bell?)

## Viral History 101

> The historian of the future… will not compose a history of civilization—that is, the story of technological progress and sociopolitical struggles—but will trace the path of mankind through

> the stages of purification and illumination to its ultimate attainment of perfection.
>
> —Valentin Tomberg, *Covenant of the Heart*

> This was a very nice neighborhood until the monkeys got out of control.
>
> —Terence McKenna, *The Archaic Revival*

For our purposes, we are particularly interested in two forms of disturbed, parasite-driven "thinking" which have plagued mankind from the start, and which may be easily recognized throughout the course of history. One of these involves misperceiving the content of one's own mind in the external world, called projection (or projective identification); the second involves misapprehending aspects of the external world within the self, called introjection. These two processes are intimately connected, in that it is introjection of insecure attachment that leads to fragmented, dysregulated, and dissociated aspects of the self that may be projected outward and acted upon, or defensively kept "inside," where they lead to painful, unpredictable states of deadness, depression, envy, resentment, shame, despair, dread, and anxiety. Both of these processes originate in the earliest phase of infancy, and for obvious reasons. Again, it is during infancy that we experience a relatively boundaryless mental state, with an understandable confusion of inside and outside, and a consequent ability to anxiously project out what we don't like, or to magically import what we do. In their normal operation, these processes are actually essential to the development of a healthy mind, as they are the ground-floor input/output mechanisms that keep the mind an open system, linked with other minds and therefore susceptible to emotional growth and evolution.[113] But in the wake of inadequate, abusive, or neglectful parenting (or even just the "ambient trauma" of a "bad fit" between parent and child), these normal processes may become visibly hypertrophied, leading to very strange results which are *easily* detected in both their personal and historical forms.

One of the reasons for the failure to appreciate mind parasites has to do with their very nature: their most basic "trick," as it were—no different from any virus—is to hijack the machinery of the mind in such a way that the mind does not recognize what has happened. In addition, this early programming is mostly stored in the pre-linguistic, emotional centers of the right brain, making it beyond the reach of language, and therefore all the more likely to be "acted out" in an unconscious manner (indeed, all such "symptoms" are just a more primitive form of communication). Not only that, but once the parasites are hardwired in, they tend to "reproduce" their own dysregulated states, similar to the way that, say, high blood pressure causes kidney damage that in turn leads to higher blood pressure. While it is possible as an adult to develop a psychological "immune system" that can detect and minimize the workings of these parasites, it is impossible to do so as an infant, before we have any idea what is happening to us. Therefore, the most troubling mind parasites are precisely the ones that feel most familiar to us—indeed, that we mistakenly identify as "I." These mechanical patterns, called "samskaras" in Buddhism, "have no awareness of the consequences of their operation. Like parasites that inadvertently kill their host, patterns can and do cause insanity, paralysis, and even death."[114] Thus, until one has systematically identified and eliminated (or at least learned to control) these viral specters of childhood from the mind, one will continue to unwittingly do their bidding, even if it means making oneself miserable in the process.

As a curious psychologist contemplating the past, what really grabs one's attention is how "insane" it so often appears. Indeed, the past provides the psychologist with a veritable cornucopia of seemingly psychopathological ideas and behavior that demand a better explanation than, say, "self interest," "original sin" or "it takes all kinds to make a world." James Joyce's alter ego, Stephen Dedalus, famously regarded history as the nightmare from which we are trying to awaken. In esoteric terms, this is literally true: outward history is only the symbol of inward history, the purpose of which will be made visible at the end, when we fully open our I's and awaken from our "nocturnal immersion" in time. Of course, every once in awhile there is a luminous moment that breaks through the darkness and offers a glimpse of the lighthouse shining from the end of the historical tunnel, but for the most part, wholesale history seems to be, as Gibbon put it, "little more than the register of the crimes, follies and misfortunes of mankind," or to paraphrase H.G. Wells, a race between *emotional health* and catastrophe. In fact, intolerance, self-defeating behavior, cruelty, sadistic violence, lunatic belief systems, collective madness—these are the stock-in-trade of the historian, who, for the most part, simply shrugs them off as inevitable consequences of human nature. But from my standpoint, I would no more attribute, for example, witch hunts, human sacrifice, and cannibalism to human nature than I would attribute the Black Plague to human physiology.

Of course I realize that to call mine a minority view of history is an understatement. But consider it this way. According to Charles Murray, whose book *Human Accomplishment* attempts to quantify human excellence from prehistory to the present, when you assemble the list of people who have contributed the most to art, science, math, philosophy and technology,

> only a few thousand people stand out from the rest. Among them, the people who are indispensable to the story of human accomplishment number in the hundreds. Among those hundreds, a handful stand conspicuously above the rest.[115]

Now, if one takes a dim view of, say, the fourteenth century, the first thing someone will say in response is "Dante," as if such a singular and inexplicable genius represented the *average* mentality of his day (or Aristotle in his, Shakespeare in his, Mozart in his, or Einstein and Joyce in our recent past). The point is that history is already pretty bleak, and you don't have to subtract too many individuals to make it a very dark place indeed. So in the discussion of history that follows, let's try focus more on the anonymous "soil" out of which the few singular geniuses of history have flowered. It is fine to fantasize about living, say, in ancient Athens, or Renaissance Florence, or Shakespeare's London. But as Murray points out, if your socioeconomic status were determined randomly, based upon conditions of the time, just remember that you would likely be a slave, or a feudal serf, or some other type of illiterate common laborer performing mindless, back-breaking work, and subject to frequent wars, plagues, famines, and ill health in general, relieved only by a mercifully brief life.

Although we must guard against generalizing about an historical epoch based upon the very best things to come out of it, I find that this is something that historians habitually do. For example, it may be inspiring to contemplate the construction of the magnificent Great Pyramid, composed of over two million blocks, each weighing more than two tons. Then again, I don't see how we can avoid being disillusioned if we take a moment to empathize with the hundred thousand luckless slaves who spent their lives dragging these blocks around, for what noble end? For the purpose of creating a ridiculously oversized crypt to house the carcass of a dead pharaoh who also had to have his wives and slaves buried alive with him in order to amuse him in the afterlife. It would be as if all of the creativity and ingenuity it took to erect the Empire State Building were expended in order to produce a giant tombstone for Mayor La Guardia. Would we marvel at a magnificent crypt designed by the Nazis for Adolf Hitler, built by Jewish slave labor?

* * *

Despite what may look to us like irrational or harmful behavior, it has become a fashionable dogma in academia that all cultural beliefs, no matter how cruel or preposterous, are beyond any kind of criticism. But because it is almost impossible to see how certain practices—for example, human sacrifice—were adaptive, it is amusing to see how "academically correct" anthropologists invent scenarios to normalize and explain away such behavior. In this regard, anthropologist-apologists are analogous a psychiatrist who tries to "build up his own personal world-view on the basis of what his patients told him."[116] But in my view, these "just so stories" of adaptation become unnecessary if we consider the possibility that all human behavior is indeed adaptive, but not necessarily to the external, "real" world. Rather, the most bizarre human beliefs and practices become perfectly understandable if we look at them as adaptations to the fears and anxieties of the internal, *psychological* world. Again, while this process may not strike you as a particularly elegant solution on the part of nature, this was the best it could come up with to contain and manage the very real anxiety that began afflicting human beings once they awakened to self-consciousness. LaBarre is emphatic that, "To be sure, culture is an adaptation; but it is sometimes adaptive not to outer realities but to inner tensions. That is, a culture is a defense mechanism—partly valid technologically, partly anxiety-allaying magic only…."[117] And, just as when mental illness interferes with an individual's ability to understand reality, cultures may also "know" a "great many things that are not so…. indeed, perhaps the bulk of all human belief is in things that are not only not so but cannot possibly be so."[118]

As a psychologist, I am fascinated not by *ignorance*—which, after all, is perfectly excusable—but by what might be called "motivated stupidity," that is, *knowledge* that cannot possibly be true, and yet persists anyway, often in the face of evidence that plainly contradicts it. Harris writes that "In even the most casual survey of history, one is repeatedly struck by the fact that certain groups do not seem to have the knack for a realistic appraisal" of reality, and instead engage in "a deliberate form of make-believe," which eventually becomes an end in itself.[119] Why should this be the case? In fact, much of what has gone by by the name of culture consists of little more than a grab bag of improvised psychological solutions for the containment of anxiety-provoking mind parasites, handed down from one generation to the next. And just as the disturbed individual defends his fixations in the form of repetition compulsion, rationalization, projection, ritualized behavior, and resistance to change, the cultural group too steels itself against any threat to received tradition for the simple reason that the false cultural beliefs exist to maintain psychological equilibrium, not to actually understand the world or solve a real problem. Cultural historian Eli Sagan agrees that

> The problematic within all moral and psychological advance is that such advance requires the giving up of psychological defenses.... People are racist and sexist in good part because such reduction of other people to objects helps contain anxiety and the tendency to panic. The only manner in which moral and psychological progress is possible is by the creation of new, less primitive, more sublimated mechanisms of defense....[120]

Just as early humans were able to populate the globe by taking their preferred climate with them in the form of clothing and housing, so too were they able, in the form of culture, to recreate psychological micro-environments consisting of defensive fantasies in order to feel psychologically safe and "at home":

> Neurosis, in individuals or groups, is a frightened clinging to the past, and remaining a slave to the forgotten. History and life-history are both in part *events to be recovered from*, through unearthing and re-viewing forgotten premises behind the bitterly defended false answers. History that cannot be understood and neutralized is the neurosis of society.[121]

Thus, for most of human history, culture has proven to be a great barrier to further psychological development. Spiritual schools are virtually unanimous in regarding culture ("the world") as a hydra-headed conspiracy to keep you asleep, a largely repetitious tragicomedy "in which pretentious blind men lead other more modest blind men towards an abyss which will engulf both."[122] In his classic work of political philosophy, *On Liberty*, John Stuart Mill observed that "The greater part of the world, properly speaking has no history, because the despotism of Custom is complete.... Custom is...the final appeal; justice and right mean conformity to custom...."[123] It would be nice if custom always reflected reality, but as Weston LaBarre sardonically put it, "In the symbolic pyramid of culture, very few bricks touch the ground." Remember, before the scientific revolution, just three hundred years ago, there was essentially no cumulative progress in the accuracy of human beliefs about the world: they were almost all nonsense. While this may sound extreme, consider the fact that until just the 1920s or 1930s, the *average* encounter with a physician was wholly ineffective if you were lucky, actually harmful if you were not.[124] Similarly, for millennia—again, until quite recently—human beings struggled to rise above subsistence because of a stubborn inability to recognize how wealth is created. Certainly into the late 18th century, people mistakenly believed that there was simply a fixed amount of wealth in the world, and that it was left to individuals and governments to fight over their share. Not until Adam Smith was it recognized that wealth can grow without limits, but obviously, even now people have a hard time wrapping their minds around this idea. One of the things that makes the creation of wealth possible is the accumulation of surplus capital to invest, but here again, for most of human history this was quite difficult to accomplish because of envious mind parasites that could not tolerate the idea of one person possessing more than another. In a classic work, Schoeck demonstrated that this was one of the *psychological* barriers to *material* development that humans have struggled to overcome. For example, envy is ubiquitous in primitive groups, to such an extent that individuals would rather part with their possessions than live with the anxiety of the envious "evil eye" directed at them by their fellows.[125] These groups are not envious because they are primitive, but primitive because of their envy and paranoia, a finding also borne out by Banfield in another classic study, *The Moral Basis of a Backward Society*.

In fact, what the scientific revolution involved, first and foremost, was the "discovery" of external reality, after countless millennia of confusing it with the content of our own minds. For so long in human history, "Soul flooded the whole of existence and encountered itself in all things. Bare matter, that is, truly inanimate, 'dead' matter, was yet to be discovered...."[126] Thus, only by withdrawing their psychological projections and mentally "keeping themselves to themselves," were humans finally able to rationally deal with the external world. After all, you can't have scientific law in a world governed by capricious (and suspiciously parental or infantile) discarnate entities.

* * *

Were people in the past really no different from us, perhaps a bit more rough around the edges, lacking only a little technical know-how? In order to avoid charges of political incorrectness, let's begin at the very beginning, so that either no one or everyone can be equally offended by my brief tour of the human zoo. Just remember as we sprint through the centuries that I am not concerned with presenting any kind of comprehensive view of history. Rather, I am attempting to make the case that something primarily *psychological* has been interfering with our post-biological evolution over the past 30 or 40,000 years, and that it is the same thing that interferes with our *individual* evolution: mind parasites.

Again, there is a pervasive, highly romanticized notion in academia that the advance of civilization has been the *problem* of human existence, not the solution, and that its distorting effects prevent us from being the lovable, noble savages that we are deep down. One way of testing this hypothesis is to investigate what the first people might have been like, before being "distorted" by civilization. Duane Elgin, in his book *Awakening Earth*, tries to imagine what it might have been like to exist as one of these early humans possessing only a very surface, pre-reflective consciousness with little subjective depth. First of all, realize that your short, nasty and brutish life will only last until about age 30 (if you are lucky), and then pare

> your vocabulary down to a few dozen basic nouns and a handful of verbs. Learn to use facial expressions and bodily gestures to convey much of your meaning.... Except for brief moments of insight, disregard your ability to stand back and observe yourself.... Forget most of your ability to think things through. You have not yet developed the ability to analyze and plan beyond the most rudimentary level.... Put aside any sophisticated emotions, such as romantic love. You do not have a sufficiently distinct sense of yourself or others to support such feelings. Ignore yourself except for your bodily impulses and instincts.... Exclude an extended

> past or future from your awareness. All that is significant is happening *now*.... Everything that happens is the result of invisible and unknown forces. Don't dwell on death. Your experience of loss and grief lasts only for a few hours and then passes into the forgetfulness of present-centered demands.... Don't think about "meaning," because it is not a meaningful concept.[127]

Psychohistorian Lloyd deMause agrees that Paleolithic, tribal personalities experienced such a degree of what we now call "depersonalization," that "they regularly felt themselves breaking into fragmented pieces, switching into dissociated states and going into shamanic trances" in the effort to hold themselves together.[128] Likewise, lives of tribal personalities frequently revolve around dreamtime "spirit possession rituals," group trance hallucinations in which mind parasites are encouraged to completely take over the the host personality, accompanied by a flood of disturbing, unconscious fantasy material centering around the themes of blood, sacrifice, and cannibalistic urges (expressed either directly or symbolically, by ritually eating the animal into whom the parasites have been projected). Through these rituals, the tribal personality is able to temporarily "cleanse" the mind of its parasites, "repair the fragmented self and restore potency."[129]

In his recent book *Constant Battles*, Harvard archaeologist Steven LeBlanc writes that

> The common notion of humankind's blissful past, populated with noble savages living in a pristine and peaceful world [is held only] by those who do not understand our past and who have failed to see the course of human history for what it is.[130]

For hundreds of years, historians and academics have been preoccupied with a sanitized myth of peace and ecological awareness, when the "cruel and ugly" truth is that, in traditional societies, an average of twenty-five percent of the men died from warfare.[131] Likewise, "The oldest known human remains in Europe provide the oldest evidence for cannibalism in Europe,"[132] and infanticide was so common as to be no more troublesome than swatting a mosquito.

In the introduction to his book, *Sick Societies*, anthropologist Robert Edgerton writes that while "All societies are sick… some are sicker than others."[133] Many primitive cultures are dominated by institutions and ideas that not only threaten health, compromise well-being, and imperil survival prospects, but result in "senseless cruelty, needless suffering, and monumental folly in their relations among themselves and with other societies and the physical environment in which they live."[134] Citing just one of countless initiation rituals that various primitive cultures have come up with, Edgerton notes that boys in New Guinea were forced to drink a concoction

> that blistered their mouths and throats, were beaten with stinging nettles, were denied water, had barbed grass pushed up their urethras to cause bleeding, were compelled to swallow bent lengths of cane until vomiting was induced, and were required to fellate older men, who also had anal intercourse with them.[135]

The purpose of such "tribal hazing" is to erase the possibility of individual identity, to inculcate the "obligatory lies" of the group, and to enforce

> Total acceptance of every demand of the elders, no matter how arbitrary or lawless, as proof that you have surrendered your previous identity and are now ready to accept whatever adulthood requires…. By compliance with manifest contradiction the initiate signals his docility and acquiescence. In such cultures the condition of a slave, unresisting submission, is the price a child pays to join the adult world.[136]

In considering these early specimens of humanity, one hearkens back to that same unchanging handaxe they kept cranking out for millennia, generation after generation. With recent attachment research, we now understand that the experience of novelty is central to sustaining brain development in the infant, and that "in the absence of proper stimulation, a brain cell will literally die." Indeed, even neglecting to change the baby's toys frequently enough will cause new brain connections to atrophy as quickly as they form.[137] This suggests that perhaps our Stone Age forebears were not the most stimulating parents, but that they kept psychologically reproducing themselves, trapped in a closed, self-renewing limit-cycle of non-evolution with their children. However, perhaps, as I am suggesting, what needs to be explained is not the evolutionary "rut," for *all* successful species are basically trapped in one—that is how they survive. Rather, what begs for explanation is the uniquely human accomplishment—miracle, really—of having suddenly liberated ourselves from the mindless squirrel cage of Darwinian adaptation some 40,000 years ago.

Oddly enough, the first thing early humans apparently thought to do upon getting off the ape-man treadmill was to conduct a sacrifice, as if to say, "*I* am threatened with death—let us kill plentifully."[138]

> A consensus is emerging that human sacrifice, far from being a cultural oddity, has been a widespread practice among diverse cultures, from small-scale tribes to mighty urban civilizations...and that it has played a role in almost every conceivable form of religious observance...in all cases, to "feed" or appease the gods.[139]

"Sacrificial killing," according to Walter Burkert, "is the basic experience of the sacred" and "the oldest form of religious action."[140] Similarly, Rascovsky writes that child sacrifice "coexists with the origins of most of the mythological or religious processes that formed the beginnings of the sociocultural process," and that with the emergence of agriculture "we find the widespread rite of child sacrifice to ensure a good harvest."[141] Thus, the earliest cultural defense mechanism, the first—and apparently universal—way of coping with the unforeseen awakening of self-awareness was to offer a sacrifice to the "gods." In short, life revolved around anxious obedience to bloodthirsty mind parasites ordering humans to kill other humans for them:

> [A]rchaic religion is humanity's astonishing instrument for turning murder and madness into a sacralized bulwark against madness and murder. More or less refined forms of this same recipe for generating social solidarity and lending it the requisite solemnity have played a part in cultural existence since the dawn of human culture.[142]

The fact that so many diverse cultures in so many different historical settings considered human sacrifice an effective solution to their problems speaks a great truth about the pervasive presence of mind parasites and the urgent need that early humans felt to do something rather dramatic to get rid of them. According to Rascovsky,

> The demand for the killing of the child is portrayed baldly in various myths that signal the beginning of the beliefs at the origins of culture. The demand is often essential for the initiation of harmonious relations between the individual or the society and the deity, or is instead the basis for a pact with the godhead.

In fact, Bailie points out that the Greek word for sacrifice, *pharmakon,* means both "medicine" and "poison," suggesting that sacrifice served as a pharmacological "cure" for the buildup of psychological "toxins" in society. And just like a neurotic compulsion, the sacrifice must be enacted again and again, in order to "recharge" its effectiveness and manage the anxiety that inevitably returns. It is almost as if certain cultures, such as the Aztec, existed only for the sake of mind parasites (rather than *vice versa*), completely revolving around the ritual slaughter of thousands upon thousands of victims (estimates range between 15,000 and 250,000 per year)[143] in order to "feed" a voracious sun that might extinguish at any moment without a continuous supply of human blood. The "voracious sun" is, of course, the angry, demanding parent: "There is no doubt that the tendencies that drive parents to destroy their children" are the result of paranoid anxieties laid down in infancy and reawakened by later stressors.[144] Grotstein notes that

> There is always an abject self within us that seems to be unconsciously chosen to be sacrificed, scapegoated, self-abused, and often projected into others—we believe that, once we attribute malevolent agency to it for all the bad things that happen to us, we can hope to change our fortunes. The first form of justice, after all, involves locating, blaming, and punishing the criminal to eradicate the "pollution" in the community, both social and internal.[145]

The sacrificial victim was often an infant; in fact, "The slaughter of newborn babies may be considered a common event in many cultures," including "the Eskimos, the Polynesians, the Egyptians, the Chinese, the Scandinavians, the Africans, the American Indians, and the Australian aboriginals."[146] Why babies? According to Grotstein, "the sacrifice of human infants was a natural 'curative' remedy for ancient man," because the very "innocence" of the child acts as a sort of psychological *poultice* "to draw and absorb the emotional abscesses" of the community members, spuriously cleansing their "toxins" and restoring them to a state of innocence.[147] (Interestingly, as we will discuss below in Book Four, the Divine does require a certain kind of sacrifice in order to be "nourished," just not in this way. This perversion of an impulse coming from a higher domain exactly parallels the commonplace psychoanalytic observation of normal impulses from lower realms taking on perverse and twisted forms.)

Neumann vividly describes the ghost-ridden world of early humans, who must have felt a "primitive dread" and "constant endangerment" that was "heightened beyond measure when contaminated with what we call the inner world." The projection of mind parasites made for a mysterious landscape haunted

> by the spirits of the dead, by demons and gods, witches and magicians; invisible workings emanate from all these beings, and the reality of these all-pervading effluences shows itself in fears, emotional outbursts... psychic epidemics... murderous impulses, visions, dreams and hallucinations.[148]

In what must be counted as the most profound study of human sacrifice yet written, *Violence Unveiled,* Bailie takes pains to elucidate the logic of human sacrifice, demonstrating not only how it haunted all primitive cultures, but how it continues to play itself out in modern times, albeit in disguised forms—holocausts, jihads, "ethnic cleansing," and other varieties of ritualized scapegoating. In his view, prehistory is characterized by what must have been endless cycles of uncontrollable violence, unchecked by any natural braking system, or legitimate "institutional" violence. What we refer to as "history" is a blood-drenched stage

> during which collective and cathartic acts of violence could be counted on to bring a period of social chaos to an end and, in doing so, to convince its participants and sympathetic observers of the truth of the myth that justified the violence.[149]

Since human sacrifice was practiced so universally, it must have served some purpose that is not obvious to us. Bailie, working with ideas developed by the anthropologist Rene Girard, believes that

> human culture as we know it begins when an act of unanimous violence brings the violence that preceded it to an end in such a breathtaking way that it gives birth to primitive religion. *Myth* remembers this strange event and its dramatic resolution from the point of view of those who derived social benefits from it, namely, those who discovered their first social solidarity when they joined in the common cause of expelling or eliminating their scapegoat. Myth camouflages the violence and recalls it in ways that make it seem valiant and divinely ordained.[150]

Although human sacrifice may certainly appear barbaric to us, Bailie points out that we must try to appreciate how frightening and chaotic it must have been once human aggression was no longer held in check by instinctive mechanisms—as it is for other animals—and instinct began to be overridden by mind parasites:

> imagine what an immense relief it must have been for ancient peoples to discover that a powerful god was now in control of the violence that, as they knew so well, might otherwise rage out of control at any moment. We think of religion as a pious and respectable affair; we are horrified to find that it began in delusion and murder. But we must realize that both its delusions and its murders were vast improvements over the recurring waves of homicidal delirium by which the proto-human world must have been deluged once violence could no longer be controlled instinctively and before collective episodes of it produced the first religions.[151]

Thus began the historically ubiquitous collective psychological defense mechanism for transferring terror and guilt onto a scapegoat and achieving temporary relief by sacrificing the victim.

This doesn't sound like an edenic paradise to me. But if you like perpetual war, senseless violence, ritual sacrifice, systemic abuse and mind-numbing repetition, it was a marvelous time to be alive. Anthropologist Lawrence Keeley, in his taboo-breaking work, *War Before Civilization,* ably documents just how disturbed humans became when they became human. Indeed, an anthropologist from Mars might well have called us *Homo psychosis*: "Whenever modern humans appear on the scene, definitive evidence of homicidal violence becomes more common.... If anything, peace was a scarcer commodity... than for the average citizen of a civilized state."[152] Indeed, the homicide rate of some prehistoric villagers "would have been 1,400 times that of modern Britain or about 70 times that of the United States in 1980!"[153] Although roughly 100 million people died from all war-related causes in the twentieth century, it has been estimated that this number is actually "*twenty times smaller* than the losses that might have resulted if the world's population were still organized into bands, tribes and chiefdoms."[154]

* * *

"Come now," you might protest, "that was before civilization. Can we please have a more recent example, at least a civilized one?" All right then, let's go back to a "golden age," that of the ancient Greek city states. What were they like? Surely the culture of Socrates and Plato wasn't crazy too. Any evidence of mind parasites there? Well, let's begin a little before that, with Homeric man. So fragmented was he by mind parasites that he felt his own impulses were

> not truly part of the self, since they are not within man's conscious control; they are endowed with a life and energy of their own, and so can force a man, as it were from the outside, into conduct foreign to him.[155]

In general, the ancient Greek "felt the experience of passion as something mysterious and frightening, the experience of a force that was in him, possessing him, rather than possessed by him."[156]

In the West, there continues to be an almost absurd idealization of the ancient Greeks, as if they truly were the foundation for our democracy, science, and philosophical tradition. But according to Gress, this idealized view "was not the actual Greece of two thousand five hundred years ago," but a re-creation of "adoring scholars" of the Enlightenment who, either consciously or unconsciously, were attempting to create a replacement for Christianity.[157] But all along, there has been evidence of a distinctively different personality style that has been systematically ignored by starry-eyed historians. In fact, according to the extensive research of deMause, the personalities of antiquity tended to be "exploitive, distrustful, ruthless and lacking in empathy, being preoccupied with fantasies of the power and brilliance of a world filled with arrogant, distant narcissistic heroes and gods and grandiose political leaders upon whom they depended to validate their weak sense of self."[158] And, of course, the rampant pedophilia of ancient Greece speaks to an entrenched, narcissistic psycho-sexual disturbance, with men projecting their mind parasites into vulnerable boys who represented their own sexually damaged selves. This sexual damage was rooted in a profound fear and revulsion toward women, so that the nearly universal practice of homosexual pederasty may be seen as an effort to "rescue" boys "from the perceived dangers of women...."[159] Females were treated especially barbarously in ancient Greece, to such an extent that families rarely raised more than one girl, casually discarding or exposing the rest. The cruel treatment of women and children was not surprising, in that "pity and compassion, to the Greeks, were comprehensible only if they served pride and the drive to fame," and were otherwise regarded as character defects "unworthy of the wise and excusable only in those who have not yet grown up."[160] In fact, "gentleness, kindness, industry, honesty, and integrity were scorned as effeminate and inferior" (and remember, even at the peak of Athenian democracy, less than ten percent of the population had full civil rights; the rest were women, slaves, and children, still subject to infanticide, rape, and abuse of all kinds). Our notion of romantic love simply did not exist, in my opinion because the male psyche was too fragmented by mind parasites with differing agendas, that is, "legitimate wives to beget citizens according to the law, courtesans for pleasure, and concubines for daily use."[161]

Likewise, in the Archaic age of Greece we see strong evidence of the projection of envy, which is one of the most pervasive mind parasites in primitive cultures (and in modern narcissistic personalities):

> [O]ne of the first things that strikes us is the deepened awareness of human insecurity and human helplessness, which has its religious correlate in the feeling of divine hostility [that] forever holds Man down.... the gods resent any success, any happiness.... [T]oo much success incurs a supernatural danger, especially if one brags about it....[162]

This is similar to what we in a more psychologically advanced civilization would experience as guilt coming from the inside, not a supernatural attack from the outside. As Neumann explains it,

> When we speak of a psychic content being projected or introjected, meaning by this that it is experienced as something outside, but is then taken inside, we are postulating a clearly defined structure of personality for which an "outside" and an "inside"

> exist. In reality, however, the psyche began by being exteriorized to a very large extent.[163]

Even Plato maintained that anxiety was caused by demon possession, and that "diagnosis" consisted in identifying the god (that is, parasite) responsible for the problem, so that "he could appease him with the appropriate sacrifices."[164] Here we see how the parasites often have fully formed personalities projected in the form of gods:

> All unconscious contents manifest themselves like partial personalities. Each of these authorities can, as an autonomous complex, obsess the ego and lead to a state of possession, as the psychology of primitives and also of civilized man clearly shows. The psychology of the neuroses teems with such states of possession.[165]

And in offering his prescription for child care, Plato provides a clue as to why the ancient Greeks were so psychologically fragmented and persecuted by mind parasites. Specifically, he advised that disobedient children should be straightened by "threats and blows, like a piece of warped wood."[166] Indeed, in his most famous work, *The Republic,* Plato offhandedly recommends that in his ideal state, any "defective" children—or even just the "offspring of the inferior"—should be quietly "disposed of," so that "no one will know what has become of them." Some have dismissed this as a satirical comment, but psychohistorian Sander Breiner notes that in virtually all Greek cities "the father had the right to kill his child at birth without question," and that "warmth was only expressed toward children when they were asleep, and especially if they died. Children's demands were responded to as unwanted and unnecessary."[167] In Sparta, as soon as the child was born, it was "taken immediately to be inspected by the Elders, who would determine whether the baby should live or die."[168] In Rome, the mother would set the infant on the floor, at which point her husband "would lift the child from the ground, and thereby signal its acceptance to the family, or he could leave it where it lay, indicating that the child was to be abandoned."[169] Sociologist

Norbert Elias agrees that in both ancient Greece and Rome it was exceedingly common for infants to be tossed away

> onto dung heaps or in rivers. Exposing children was part of everyday life. People were used to it.... Public opinion in antiquity regarded the killing of infants or the sale of children—if they were pretty, to brothels, otherwise as slaves—as self-evident.[170]

Bear in mind that it is not just the cruelty involved in actually killing a child; rather, the mere fact that one is emotionally capable of doing this would strongly suggest that parents had severe disturbances in their ability to bond (because of their own emotionally detached parents), so that it would be unlikely that they would be able to relate normally to children who weren't killed.

This understanding of the effect of infanticidal parenting also explains how and why the Greek religious mind was so very different from ours. Whereas the Judeo-Christian God created the cosmos and loved his creatures (in particular, human beings), Greek gods were at best indifferent and unpredictable, at worst downright hostile and sadistic. If they took an interest in human affairs, "it was often to punish rather than to help.... the gods were like judges in a totalitarian state, who might—or might not—mete out punishment to anyone at any time." They were "more like cruel adolescents who delighted in the cunning ways they spread pain and confusion."[171] I don't think it takes any great leap of psychoanalytic insight to point out the similarity of these gods to the cruel and arbitrary parents who might toss a sibling into the river without a moment's hesitation or backward glance. In short, these gods were mind parasites that actually obscured the ability to intuit or recognize the actual God of love. Later, the Romans (who also idealized Greece) regarded Jews and Christians as especially foolish and depraved in their opposition to infanticide and their more humane treatment of women.

It is simply untrue that the presence of an innate "parental love" would prevent atrocities such as infanticide from being expressed toward children. Again, according to Elias,

> a legend has become established which makes it look as if parental love and affection for their children is something more or less natural and, beyond that, an always stable, permanent and life-long feeling. In this case... a social "should" is transformed into the notion of a natural "is."[172]

Parenting is an enterprise that is fraught with emotional ambivalence, and the further back in history we travel, the more that ambivalence is expressed in a direct, untroubled way toward children. In the past, people were more directly influenced by their own feelings rather than their empathic attunement with the child. The slowly evolving attitude of parents toward their children was, as explained by Elias, a huge factor in the "civilizing process" of an otherwise merely genetic *Homo sapiens.*

* * *

So much for the idealized ancient Greeks. Let's fast-forward to Europe, circa 800 A.D. What were those folks like?

> After the extant fragments have been fitted together, the portrait which emerges is a melange of incessant warfare, corruption, lawlessness, obsession with strange myths, and an almost impenetrable mindlessness.[173]

What, no Arthurian legends, no chivalry, no wizards, brave knights, happy villagers? Apparently not. As Neumann explains it, our more-or-less self-conscious state is a "late and uncommon phenomenon," whereas "the unconscious state is the original, basic psychic situation that is everywhere the rule.[174] As a result, the *average* peasant had little sense of a true, individual "self," separate from the collective:

> To them their identity in this life was irrelevant.... [T]here was also no awareness of time.... Generations succeeded one another in a meaningless, timeless blur.... Any innovation was incon-

> ceivable; to suggest the possibility of one would have invited suspicion, and because the accused were guilty until they proved themselves innocent by surviving impossible ordeals—by fire, water, or combat—to be suspect was to be doomed. All knowledge was already known. *And nothing would ever change.*[175]

And so on. Although everyone was "religious," it wasn't in our sense of the term. Rather, it's just that no one was *non*-religious; in fact, "people rarely thought of themselves as 'having' or 'belonging' to a religion.... God and all that pertained to Him was simply *what is,* just as today nobody has 'a physics...'"[176] Again it seems that only with great effort did human beings gradually become aware of the blindly accepted psychic factors that regulated their lives, the mind parasites masquerading as cultural pattern. Indeed, according to Barzun, "the Devil and his minions were as ubiquitous as our viruses," meaning that they were literally everywhere, ready to strike at any time if one's guard should be let down. Only two powers ran the world (itself evidence of severe psychological splitting), the logical outcome being that life revolved around the notion that "the evil one must be fought and the good placated."[177] And even then, "no one doubted in the Middle Ages that the vast majority would be eternally damned"[178] anyway (which, in my opinion, does not speak to the "afterlife," but to the fact that the abused or neglected child grows up with an ineradicable sense of of being "damned," "condemned," and abandoned by providence). It is therefore no coincidence that "Of all the characteristics in which the medieval age differs from the modern, none is so striking as the comparative absence of interest in children," and "on the whole, babies and young children appear to have been left to survive or die without great concern in the first five or six years."[179]

All right then, how about the late middle ages, circa 1500? In his *The Autumn of the Middle Ages,* Huizinga suggests that the dominant passion of men until the fifteenth century was "the thirst for revenge," and that no political considerations could be better comprehended by the masses than the "simple, primitive motives of hatred and revenge."[180] More than the "perverse sickness" of the judicial cruelty of the time, what is most striking to us is "the dull, animal-like enjoyment, the country fair-like amusement" it provided; people "cannot get enough of the spectacle" of suspected criminals "undergoing repeated torture. The people delay executions, which the victims themselves request, for the enjoyment of seeing them subjected to even more sufferings."[181] Cognitively, the typical individual of medieval times was "unable, even for a moment, to do without the crudest of mistaken judgments that… reached an unparalleled degree of viciousness." Huizinga notes that "belief in the reality of imagined facts easily took root among the people," and asks,

> What are we to make of the peculiar rashness that is continuously revealed in the superficiality, inexactness, and credulity of the waning Middle Ages? It is almost as if they had not even the slightest need for real thought, as if the passage of fleeting and dream-like images provided sufficient nourishment for their minds.[182]

A "random probe" into the literature of the time will confirm that most people shared a "dark vision" of "an evil world. The fires of hatred and violence burn fiercely. Evil is powerful, the devil covers a darkened earth with his black wings. And soon the end of the world is expected."[183] Religiously structured mind parasites filled the landscape: "the pressure of the fear of hell and the anxiety about devils and witches, nourished a feeling of general insecurity that tended to paint life's background in dark colors."[184]

Likewise, according to historian Lawrence Stone, people's emotional life had a different structure and character from ours. (Here again, we are not talking about Dante, Leonardo, or Meister Eckhart, but the *average* mentality of the typical illiterate peasant.) Stone concludes that

> social relations from the fifteenth to the seventeenth centuries tended to be cool, even unfriendly. The extraordinary amount of casual inter-personal physical and verbal violence… shows

> clearly that at all levels men and women were extremely short-tempered.... [185]

Not surprisingly, the constant threat of violence seems to have led to what we would consider clinical paranoia, characterized by

> much mutual suspicion and a low general level of emotional interaction and commitment. Alienation and distrust of one's fellow man are the predominant features.... The basic assumption is that no one is to be trusted, since anyone and everyone—wife, servants, children, friends, neighbours, or patrons—are only kept loyal by self-interest, and may, therefore, at any moment turn out to be enemies.[186]

Undoubtedly, this paranoia was rooted (as it almost always is) in childhood trauma. Since children "were often neglected, brutally treated, and even killed," it is not surprising that in sixteenth century English society, "a majority of the individuals who composed it found it very difficult to establish close emotional ties to any person."[187] Likewise, according to Postman, people did not have an emotional attitude to children that we would consider normal or healthy. Indeed, children provoked so much anxiety in adults that a typical parenting manual from 1621 taught that although the child's "body be but small, yet he hath a [wrongdoing] heart, and is altogether inclined to evil." Furthermore, if the child's evil be permitted to continue, "it will rage over and burn down the whole house."[188] The recommended style of parenting, which involved deliberate and brutal breaking of the child's will, resulted in

> a "psychic numbing" which created many adults whose primary responses to others were at best calculating indifference and at worst a mixture of suspicion and hostility, tyranny and submission, alienation and rage.[189]

Thus, for much of history, "Being an adult seems mostly to

consist in having forgotten childhood, and in compensation to indulge in sheer joyously arbitrary power over the child."[190] And the further back in history one travels, the more prevalent this type of attitude toward children seems to be. As we have seen, the more traumatic the childhood, the more "parental cleansing" is required; the more parental cleansing, the more mind parasites; the more mind parasites, the more a culture is erected for the purposes of containing and defending against the parasites. So if our hypothesis is correct, the further back in time we travel, the more incomprehensible the culture will be—the less we will be able to see the "point" of practices that appear to us patently self-defeating or illogical, like child sacrifice, institutionalized pedophilia, crusades, witch hunts, the divine right of kings, the designated hitter, and so on.

* * *

Fortunately we do not need a time machine to see the effect of mind parasites, because in our present world, from the standpoint of psychology, developmental time *is* cultural space,[191] and there are innumerable examples from all around the globe of people inhabiting a certain geographical space who are stuck in an earlier developmental time, both individually and collectively. Bear in mind that in some parts of the world, prehistory only ended thirty five years ago, so that in no way can we say that human beings have "synchronized their calendars." If history is, as Etienne Gilson put it, "the only laboratory we have in which to test the consequences of thought," then we should always be engaged in assessing the "solutions" various cultures have arrived at in confronting the universal problems faced by humans. Perhaps I should reemphasize that I am not coming at his from a political standpoint in order to justify some sort of ethnocentrism. Rather, I am approaching this from a spiritual vantage point, with the idea that culture is one of the things (like ego) that we need to adopt a critical attitude toward in order to transcend. This detached approach actually represents "multiculturalism" in its truest sense, because it doesn't involve blind, wholesale acceptance of any cultural nonsense we encounter (including, of course, our own), but instead forces us to apply a universal standard with which to judge the usefulness of any particular cultural belief or practice. The problem with culture *as such* is that any given culture creates the image of an ideal human as its own end, whereas I am suggesting that what culture should have as its end is the actualization of the human being *as* human being. And the bottom line is that some cultures are better than others at allowing humans to actualize their potential. Or, think of it this way: we are used to the freedom that modern Western civilization grants us in determining who we are, what is important to us, and how best to develop our unique talents. But most cultures down through history have had a very rigid and inflexible conception of what it means to be human, which necessarily results in "a mechanical and tyrannical repression of special qualities."[192] In these cultures, one is only free to express and develop one's humanness in a very narrow range.

Much of the reason for this lack of personal development in pre-modern groups is that they are closed systems (both individually and collectively), whereas only open systems can evolve and adapt. In other words, groups can be more or less open to new ideas, new ways of being, new attitudes, and new inventions, and more or less closed off by taboo, ritual, and obedience to ancestral ways. As explained by anthropologist Roger Sandall, knowledge in closed groups "is irreconcilable with both what we know and how we think today." This is because knowledge in such groups is not *rationally* justified but *culturally* justified, so that everyone is anxiously coerced into believing the same thing, no matter how faulty or implausible:

> All that is needed is for enough people to believe that X is true, and X is true.... What is called tribal "knowledge" usually reflects the needs of group solidarity more than anything else: as such it often represents *culturally justified false belief*....

This leads to the universal principle applicable to all groups, that "*Logical coherence and social solidarity are inversely related.* So the more solidarity you have, the less logic you get, and vice versa."[193]

Indeed, what we would call an individually held "belief" for aboriginal peoples implies "*loyalty to a group* as much as holding a proposition in one's heart as true... or commitment to 'objective' truth."[194] And it is critical to emphasize that these primitive mechanisms do not only operate in primitive groups. The philosopher Karl Popper felt that our evolution from closed to open societies was among the most profound transitions humans had ever made, and that we still struggle with our atavistic desire to subordinate our hard-won individual identity to group harmony.[195] We are—all of us, no matter the culture—asked to believe certain things that cannot possibly be true, to "import" collectively held but erroneous beliefs about reality into our minds, at the risk of being shunned or scapegoated by the group. It is a little disconcerting to realize that we were shaped by natural selection not to know truth, but to subordinate truth to group loyalty, so that the largely *self-willed* paths toward truth and personal individuation are two sides of the same non-Darwinian coin. (Again, our ability to know Truth comes from a non-Darwinian source.) What requires explanation is not tribalism (which comes naturally), but individualism, which is rare, hard-won, and always at odds with countervailing familial and cultural forces.

Although this view certainly doesn't seem controversial to common sense, it is extremely unpopular in the relativistic world of academia, because it posits a universal developmental model for all human beings, and all developmental models imply a proper end point to development. Furthermore, failure to achieve the end point of development is the very definition of pathology (or, at the very least, the end point serves as a way to orient ourselves in transpersonal space, a way to gauge our development). But in the relativistic climate of mainstream anthropology, there can really be no pathology, for every culture is an entity unto itself with no reference to any kind of ideal development beyond its own arbitrary standards. Although this nonjudgmental attitude undoubtedly began with the noble intention of checking the human tendency to deify one's own culture and to denigrate others, the pendulum has swung so far in the other direction that to make any universal value judgments is to risk being branded a racist. And this is why anthropologists strain to normalize such pathologies, perversions and developmental fixations as human sacrifice, foot binding, suttee, genital mutilation, infanticide, torture, ceremonial rape, headhunting, suicide bombers and so on: every culture is regarded as a self-justifying "whole," with no reference to any transcendent realm of values outside itself. But the pervasive notion that culture is an unqualified good represents the worst kind of academic nonsense, and is something that must be actively countered. Indeed, to suggest "that a culture cannot be judged is to say that it has no relation to the realm of value,"[196] a position that starts off merely amoral, but quickly becomes immoral, because it grants approval to what is patently bad or destructive toward the end of becoming more human. To say that all cultures are not only good, but equally good, is no more valid than to suggest that all families are equally good with respect to the goal of creating healthy and happy children, a statement most of us know to be insupportable. And yet, the vast majority of anthropologists continue to say it.

I will cite just one out of thousands of examples, the recent discovery in the mountains of Chile of three children who had been ritually sacrificed 500 years ago.[197] Lest you think there was anything horrifying or barbaric about this practice, these children were actually the benefactors of "the highest honor the Inca civilization could bestow: becoming a human gift to the mountain gods." In fact, one of them had even had her head placed in a vice from birth, so that she would have the distinction of her skull growing "into the shape of a mountain peak," thus resembling the god to whom she would be sacrificed. Although they were buried alive, we are assured that the children "exude an air of tranquility," and that "this was not a time of terror and horror but of peace and worship." And with this fortuitous archaeological find, researchers are hoping the little ones "prove as valuable to science as they were precious to their people." Here we see a fine example of complete moral inversion, in what amounts to the glorification "of collective intimidation, humiliation, and thought control, with all its... potential for unhinged sadism,.... which elevates solidarity above truth."[198]

An anthropologist is often someone who sees beauty in every culture but his own. But in order to become an anthropologist, you must first attempt, in so far as it is possible, to step outside of culture *per se*, to divest yourself of the distorting cultural myths that bar one from freely investigating and apprehending reality. On the one hand, this psychological independence from cultural programming is regarded by anthropologists as an obvious virtue, and yet, the same standard is not applied to people in other cultures who are still under the hypnotic spell of their own personal and cultural mind parasites. Fortunately, many scholars in undeveloped countries are beginning to turn the tables on our academically correct anthropologists. That is, they are rejecting the condescending glorification—magnanimously conferred by western anthropologists—of cultural traits that are plainly maladaptive repositories of mind parasites, and appreciating the unique beauty of Enlightenment values. According to Pinker, "Preserving cultural diversity is considered a supreme virtue today, but the members of the diverse cultures don't always see it that way.... no one can fail to notice that some cultures can accomplish things that all people want (like health and comfort) better than others."[199] He approvingly quotes Thomas Sowell, who notes that "Cultures do not exist as simply static 'differences' to be celebrated but compete with one another as better or worse ways of getting things done...."[200] For example, one African scholar describes the cultural traits that help shackle development in present-day Africa, the chronic anxiety produced by malevolent spirits

> hidden in the folds of the clothes of every African chief.... [J]ealousy dominates all interpersonal relations, which is less the desire to obtain what others possess than to prevent any change in social status.... African thought avoids skepticism, another virus carried by the individual.... As soon as ancestral beliefs are threatened, the only possible choice is between established order and chaos....[201]

In eloquently summarizing the negative effect of mind parasites on cultural and psychological development, Etounga-Manguelle notes that "A society in which magic and witchcraft flourish today is a sick society ruled by tension, fear, and moral disorder.... Witchcraft is for us a psychological refuge in which all our ignorance finds its answers and our wildest fantasies become realities."[202] And the immobilizing belief in witchcraft is by no means a minor problem; rather, the extent and intensity of these fears are said to be "startling. As recently as [2001], at least 1,000 alleged witches were hacked to death in a single 'purge' in the Democratic Republic of the Congo."[203] Not only is the fear of witches *not* declining, but it continues to be a "primary social fear" in places like South Africa. It is obviously difficult to develop rational thought where mind-parasites predominate, for it means that "there is always a world beyond the veil of appearances, and it is the task of supernatural explanation to search in that world for malignant motives."[204] Similarly, in such a paranoid world, "there is no such thing as an innocent injurious act. Accidents don't just happen. But if they do, someone is held responsible and must pay a price."[205] Freedom to think and speculate is curtailed, because this kind of world is dominated by taboos and "magical tribal institutions which can never become objects of critical consideration."[206]

The daily news often comes down to an epidemiological report of mind parasites, that is, the incidence, distribution, and control of these psychopathogens. Especially in today's climate of parasite-driven religious terror, examples are far too numerous to mention, but you may find it a very useful spiritual exercise to dispassionately read your newspaper with an eye toward detecting mind parasites, rather than in the conventional way, as if the the news were actually a chronicle of logical actions by rational agents. (In order to avoid being sidetracked by charges of insensitivity, I will omit mention of the particular cultures involved; our sole interest is in detecting the presence of mind parasites, not in being provocative or politically incorrect. Just pretend you are a Martian who is studying human beings and trying to figure out why they do some of the things they do.)

A newspaper report states that in one region, there is a widespread belief that raping a prepubescent virgin gives one a "dose of purity" that "brings mystical powers" which can prevent and cure

AIDS.[207] Oddly, this behavior is attributed by the writer of the piece to mere "ignorance"—that is, a lack of information—as opposed to the active presence of something in the mind that causes it to believe something that cannot not possibly be true, that is, that by raping someone, you are "consuming their spirit." Indeed, it is the learned "spiritual practitioners" of this land who help fuel the problem "by prescribing pedophilia as a remedy for everything from money woes to AIDS" to "ancestral transgressions" to "ridding a family of evil spirits" (that is, mind parasites).

In another geographical area, it is common to slash away the clitoris and labia of adolescent girls, using a razor blade or piece of broken glass, and suturing the wound with an opening the size of a matchstick for the passage of urine and menstrual blood. The alleged "purpose" of this mutilation is to protect "female purity" and family honor, because (they say) the clitoris is "dirty" and "poisonous," and "can cause a voracious appetite for promiscuous sex" which "might render men impotent."[208] In other words, purity, honor, and male potency are under attack from mind parasites intent on causing them intolerable shame and humiliation. In fact, in a nearby area, a recent newspaper story reports that a mother who gave birth to a child out of wedlock will be punished by burying her alive up to the chest, so that she may be conveniently stoned to death.[209] However, in a fit of mercy, the state will wait until the mother weans her baby to carry out the punishment. Here again we see the outright terror induced in parasite-infested men over the idea of unbridled female sexuality. In other words, something is being projected into women to make them unbearably frightening, to such an extent that they must undergo sadistic medical procedures or gruesome punishments, anything to appease the parasites.

Ah yes, but parents everywhere love their children and want what's best for them, right? Well, I suppose it depends on what you mean by "love." In this culture, fathers love their daughters so much that they will murder them if they are seen in the company of the wrong man, say, a Christian. In one case, some brothers raped their sister and subsequently murdered her because she had "dishonored" the family by being raped. You see, daughters here are not regarded as *persons,* but as *property* over which the father has the absolute right to dispose of as he pleases. Of course, you cannot murder your daughter for just any reason, any more than you can burn down your house or business. However, "once that murder has been determined to be merely a result of an 'honor killing,' no criminal investigation by the police ensues."[210] Perhaps it is an understatement to point out that this pervasive cultural attitude represents a deep "fear and hatred of female sexuality."[211] Indeed, another nearby country has banned Barbie dolls as a threat to sexual morality. As their Committee for the Propagation of Virtue and Prevention of Vice put it, "Jewish Barbie dolls, with their revealing clothes and shameful postures, accessories and tools are a symbol of decadence to the perverted West. Let us beware of her dangers and be careful."[212]

In another country, there was a recent epidemic of terror around the presence of a "literal" parasite, an imaginary goat-sucking vampire.[213] There was a "wave of panic across the state" as mothers "quit sending their children to schools for fear they would be attacked on the way," and groups "armed with torches have been attacking caves… to burn out the bats." Although, as in one of the cases mentioned above, "ignorance" is cited as the reason for the hysteria, this is not the type of ignorance that is susceptible to being corrected by obtaining the facts (as is true of mental illness in general). Although federal experts intervened and announced results of autopsies showing that the supposed animal victims of the vampire died of natural causes, "science couldn't dent the goat-sucking rumor," because of the "ocean of superstition and suspicion" among the people.

One can usually detect the presence of mind parasites because again, as indicated above, they nearly always cohere around issues of projected aggressive or sexual impulses. For example, in some places, women are forced to wear dark veils covering their eyes, because it is felt that the eyes transmit a "dangerous" sexual impulse into men. In another country, attacking women with sulfuric acid has become "a cheap, convenient and horrible" way for men to "take feelings of powerlessness out on wives and girlfriends."[214] These disfiguring attacks coincide with a rising tide of male frustration leading to a backlash "directed at curtailing women's choices." There is envy of women because of a belief that they receive "privileges because of their beauty.... By destroying her looks, [the attackers] think they have destroyed her life," thus mitigating their envy. And lest you should think that the fear and envy of femininity is merely harbored by an embittered fringe of this society, note that women are so filled with dangerous sexual projections that the majority of prepubescent girls here still must undergo genital mutilation in order "to curb their sexual urges." And "crimes of honor" such as a jilted lover disfiguring his girlfriend's face with acid—are "all but condoned" in this society. (And just to emphasize that the women of this country are no more free of mind parasites than the men, the above-referenced article refers to a recent survey there, finding that 86 percent of female respondents felt that husbands were justified in beating wives, for example, if they "talk back" or "refuse sex." This is a classic example of the "identification with the aggressor" parasite.)

* * *

> [I]f an outside observer had been able to monitor the developments in human societies over the 500 years up to about 1700, he or she would not have been optimistic.... Mankind seemed to be caught on a treadmill.... Basically, almost all the trends of the last 2,000 years had to be reversed.
>
> —Alan Macfarlane, *The Riddle of the Modern World*

There is a wide range of scholars, including Charles Taylor, Eli Sagan, Weston LaBarre, Lawrence Stone, Sri Aurobindo, Jean Gebser, and Norbert Elias, who have recognized that human nature is not a universal "essence" that has remained unchanged throughout the course of history, and that it has only been quite recently—mostly in the past three hundred years (with notable exceptions, of course)—that our notion of the modern self has become the norm. While they all have their own definitions of the modern self, all of them are consistent with my thesis that the true self is only able to flourish when we purge our psyche of mind parasites, and increasingly experience our selves as emanating from a unified center within, unfragmented by a sense of persecution and duty from "above" (the superego, often externalized in the form of societal coercion) or disturbing drives and impulses from "below" (the id). For example, according to Taylor, by 1700 or so,

> something recognizably like the modern self is in process of constitution.... *Thought and feeling*—the psychological—*are now confined to minds.* This follows our disengagement from the world, its "disenchantment".... [215]

Likewise, according to historian Jerry Muller, the eighteenth century witnessed the emergence of a "new mode of self-understanding" which derived not merely from social position and the imitation of an externally given cultural norm, but

> from an individual identity carved out for oneself. The new ideal was the cultivation of a multifaceted individuality, expressed in philosophy and literature, in theater, in music, and in the visual arts.... Reading became a means of developing one's mind, and of interacting with other minds on the written page.... Art, released from its liturgical and ornamental functions, came to be prized as a value in itself.[216]

Finally, after thousands of years of confusion between outside and inside, mind and world, there is a new kind of polarity between subject and object, whereby the subject is not only able to more objectively apprehend the object, but to recognize a new range of *inward* phenomena, including everything from neurotic conflict and multiple "subselves," to the infinite nature of knowledge, meaning, and consciousness itself: "Indeed, we could say that the very notions of subject and object in their modern sense come to be within this new localization.... [T]his way of seeing things [had preveiously] made no sense."[217] Coinciding with this new understanding of the self was "the discovery of Nature, which became no longer a repository of allegories but commanded attention in its own right."[218] The withdrawal of psychological projections leads to the liberating "disenchantment" of the world and, with it, a decline of magic, which represents the hypnotic condition of being held in thrall by the externalized content of one's own fragmented mind. Schuon describes this kind of stifling psychic imprisonment as follows:

> As we exteriorize ourselves, we create a world in the image of our dream, and the dream thus objectified flows back upon us, and so on and so on, until we are enclosed in a tissue, sometimes intractable, of dreams exteriorized or materialized and materializations interiorized.[219]

Thus, the emergence of the modern self—both historically and personally—represents the hope for a literal escape, a release from imprisonment "in uncanny external forces," and a new found "self-possession" which is the very opposite of our former possession by mind parasites. Human beings had to first escape the gravitational pull of family and culture before any further spiritual progress could be accomplished. This is still not easy, as we are first a group animal before an individual one, and the price we all pay to be "socially sane" is to share the bulk of our "group-insanities."[220] As one writer recently put it, commenting upon how unfulfilled his life would have been if he had not escaped his traditional culture,

> I probably would have lived my entire existence within a five-mile radius of where I was born. I would undoubtedly have married a woman of my identical religious and socioeconomic background. I would have faced relentless pressure to become an engineer, a doctor or a computer programmer. My socialization would have been almost entirely within my ethnic community. I would have a whole set of opinions that could be predicted in advance. *In sum, my destiny would to a large degree have been given to me.*[221]

* * *

Philosopher Charles Taylor agrees that a "new, modern notion of objectivity" was "correlative to the new subjectivity."[222] That is, only with the achievement of our ability to reliably discriminate between subject and object was the scientific revolution possible—the study of the world of exteriors, of the actual properties of matter, if you will—a systematic method to differentiate what we have been told from what we have learned, and to stop the dead hands of our cultural past from stifling the living. And likewise, only then was there an equally sound basis for a science of pure consciousness, unconflated with the external world. Only now can it be seen that we are

> mistaken to treat the "world of mind" as if it were merely a metaphor, or a dim reflection of the physical world. It is *another country*, and we all have passports to cross into it.... It is a realm in itself, an interior universe in the most literal sense.[223]

Our individuation from the cultural group mind represented an historical achievement of the first magnitude. In fact, the culmination of the third singularity—itself a singularity hardly less unique and unanticipated than the others—occurs when we differentiate from the "we" of the cultural herd and actually become ourselves, a novel, singular, unrepeatable "I" of the cosmos. Although the blueprint of this unique self is present at birth, it must be *actualized* in life, and there are, as we have only touched on above, any number of cultural, familial, and historical factors that are invariably arrayed against the individual who, more often than not, dies before he is born, swallowed back into the collective. This was the conclusion of the historian of technology, Lewis Mumford, who agreed that human inventiveness could only begin

> to improve the quality of life when human beings began to think of themselves as *separate* individuals, rather than as identical with their community. Persons diverging from accepted norms,

> including pioneering inventors and thinkers, have been since antiquity (and in some parts of the world are still even now) persecuted or expelled from their tribes as being possessed by evil spirits.[224]

"Every culture," writes LaBarre, "is a bar to the exercise of free rationality."[225] As such, before you allow a culture to pull you into its vortex, you had better develop a way to gauge its potential virulence and assess what you are giving up in order to enjoy the advantages of membership. In fact, there are some clear-cut criteria one may use in judging the health or pathology of any given culture: the extent to which the culture in question permits *integration* of our psyches and *actualization* of our potential. If you apply these simple criteria, you will quickly come to the realization that for 99 percent of human history, most cultures have actively stifled the expression of any unique potential, while at the same time erecting preposterous world views encouraging psychological fragmentation in the form of bizarre rituals, scapegoating, belief in strange gods, paranoia between the sexes, racial hatred, institutionalized violence, pointless taboos, and abuse of children. This is why, with regard to history, my specific recommendation is the same as it would be for anyone involved in an abusive relationship: get out.[226]

The great but relatively unknown occult philosopher Dane Rudhyar arrived at a very similar conclusion, writing that a prerequisite of post-biological human evolution and liberation (or "moksha," as it is called in Hindu metaphysics) involves "reaching a state of inner freedom from bondage to the outer patterns" placed upon us by culture. Spiritual advance must begin with differentiation "from the collective power of society, religion, and culture." In this regard, "yoga" is simply a generic term that refers to all methods that assist us in transcending "the collective patterns imposed by society and culture upon every newborn human being."[227] In the final analysis, human history will be seen as a transitional state from "a biological level given characteristically human features through a series of local and exclusive cultures," to a "spiritual integration" which promotes the "actualization of powers and faculties latent in present-day human beings."[228] And although the attainment of individuality is a "conquest" of monumental import, "once you have realized within you something like a personal, independent, and conscious being, then what you have to do is break the form and go farther."[229]

The very possibility of evolving the software of the human mind depends, as Eli Sagan has observed, on our being rescued from past cultural patterns, because cultures always have a component of coercion that tries to get all of its members "on the same page," so to speak:

> Individuality has its genesis in negation and dissent; individualism results from a separating-out from the group, from society as a whole.... [M]emory of childhood is necessary for the creation of individuality.[230]

The operative word here is *memory* of childhood, because remembering our childhood represents the polar opposite of unconsciously acting out its conflicts and secret attachments. This is true both individually and collectively, because primitive groups without a written history

> lack sufficient "communication" with their own intellectual history to be able to have much perspective or moral sophistication about their problems—just as a child lacks experience of a life-history, which might help him to get bearings on himself and his predicaments.[231]

Put another way, the unconscious is actually *the past in the present;* it is that portion of the past that we were unable to psychologically metabolize when it occurred, so that it is continually projected onto current situations and relationships, resulting in the past being thoroughly conflated with the present, interior self with external world. None of us, I should hasten to add, ever completely escapes from the projection of mental phenomena into the external world; nor would we want to, for that would lead to entrapment in an absolutely sterile, mechanical, and non-renewable experience of existence. What we are referring to are rigid, forced, maladaptive conceptions of reality stemming from a fragmented mind futilely attempting to escape from itself, the present-day residue of the unmetabolized past. We must each of us, in our own way, fight for the cultural circumstances that make intellectual, emotional, and spiritual growth possible, because most cultural circumstances actively suppress our growth as human beings. Cultures are *particular*, whereas civilization implies a *universal* standard of development. In reality, a healthy culture promotes the development of *persons,* "insofar as a person is defined as an autonomous being existing essentially to achieve self-development and self-actualization."[232] And the extent to which a culture is able to do this is its only moral claim to power; but since each person is unique, it is not possible for a culture to define the exact endpoint of development, as this would impede the free discovery of one's own essence—both words must be emphasized, for one's essence must be *freely* (without compulsion) discovered and freely *discovered* (not "given" by some external model or teaching).

But then it must be surrendered to something higher.

* * *

Swept along by the crosscurrents and undertows of history's insane "kaleiderescape,"[233] the fatal dis-ease of life became only more acute for human beings. Stumbling and bumbling down the darkness of centuries, our self-awareness only ratcheted up the tension, the dilemma of precarious being floating aimlessly over, but still firmly tied down to, a somehow familiar and yet alien material sea with no apparent destination.[234] If this be existence, then humans were nothing more than a "useless passion," declared Sartre, a "chance deposit on the surface of the world," according to Becker, "carelessly thrown up"

> by the same forces that rust iron and ripen corn, a sentient organism endowed by some happy or unhappy accident with intelligence indeed, but with an intelligence that is conditioned by the very forces which it seeks to understand and control....

> What is man that the electron should be mindful of him! Man is but a foundling in the cosmos, abandoned by the forces that created him. Unparented, unassisted..., he must fend for himself, and with the aid of his limited intelligence find his way about in an indifferent universe.[235]

As soon as a fragile and anxious loophole in biological necessity, the ego, was discovered, there were really only two choices—with life, stasis is not an option—either be pulled back and dissolve into the body or collective mind, or move forward and explore further upward into this new dimension beyond the boundaries of the senses.

As a consequence of their apparently separate, death-bound little selves, human beings began envisioning and longing for the whole, for an ideal existence located somewhere in the past, an eden, or in the future, a heaven, where all tensions are resolved, the circle is unbroken, and we are returned to the source from whence we came. But is there really any way out of our chronically "unfulfilled passion for wholeness"?[236] Can the extended surface of the mind ever encompass so much that it is able to loop back and envelop the whole? Is there a four-storied wholeness (matter-life-mind-spirit) located in the future, not just a single-level, factitious wholeness located in the material past, before life even existed? Is it possible to evolve beyond our present impasse of a mere mental life in which, no matter how far we explore, anything we can prove has already been disproven, and the sum total of all our actions inevitably adds up to a futile zero, like my tax returns?

Are we nothing more than cosmic squatters who must repay our borrowed being at the end of our days, or do we have an option to purchase a piece of prime eternal real estate?

Evidently so. From the moment human beings understood enough to grasp their tenuous condition, they have been frantically trying to locate the escape hatch, to pick the lock, to find a rabbit hole out of the decaying world of transient form, a way ashore from the unrelenting riptide of horizontal time. After having wrested individuality from conformity, only to find a roomier prison pod, human beings sought to escape from individuality and become universal, a "mode of the infinite." As one mad genius enthusiastically put it,

> Wherever we turn we find man running around in circles as if trapped and searching for the exit in vain and in desperation.
>
> *It IS possible to get out of a trap.* However, in order to break out of a prison, one first must confess to *being in a prison. The trap is man's emotional structure, his character structure....*
>
> The first thing to do is to find the exit out of the trap.
>
> The nature of the trap has no interest whatsoever beyond this one crucial point: WHERE IS THE EXIT OUT OF THE TRAP?....WHERE IS THE EXIT INTO THE ENDLESS OPEN SPACE?
>
> It turns out that the trouble is not with the trap or even with finding the exit. The trouble is WITHIN THE TRAPPED ONES.[237]

To paraphrase Reich, some of the trapped ones developed philosophy, in order to wonder about the nature of the trap, or to argue over how to live a proper life within the trap. Later ones developed science for the purpose of studying the walls of the trap. Some became artists, in order to decorate the trap, while some became physicians, so as to help secure a long life within the trap. And institutionalized religions, of course, prayed for delivery from the trap and promised an eternal life outside the trap after death. But a few of the trapped ones, by following a newly discovered current of being through to its non-local source upstream, far away from the terminal moraine of the outward-turned senses, did eventually identify a passage hidden in plain sight, through which lay yet another altogether surprising but felicitous discovery: a Mighty Strange Attractor at the...

*Venturing across the great divide separating man from the incorruptible sphere of the gods, our inward explorers found themselves pulled into the orbit of the Great Attractor.*

# BOOK FOUR

## COSMOTHEOSIS:

## *It's a Onederful Life*

The law of gravitation formulated in physics by Isaac Newton also has its soul-spiritual counterpart in the inner life of man, which is placed in equilibrium between the heavenly and earthly gravitational fields. Both forces of attraction reach into the inner life of man, where they function as urges and yearnings.

—Valentin Tomberg, *Covenant of the Heart*

Is it not reasonable to to suspect that a singularity must emerge near the end of the complexification process, rather than at its beginning? When we reverse our preconceptions about the flow of cause and effect, we get a great attractor that pulls all organization and structure toward itself over several billion years.

—Terence McKenna, *Chaos, Creativity, and Cosmic Consciousness*

The divine totality is, like its analogue the biological organism, implicit in every one of its parts and phases.... Because of this implicit presence in every finite being, every finite proclaims the existence of God.

—Errol Harris, *Revelation Through Reason*

... end of history—*Woo hoo!!!*—the One True Being ontologically prior to existence and from Whom existence itself was derived. By merely fooling around with the software of their own minds, these inward explorers—eccentric psychonauts mostly unfit for conventional existence or simply unwilling to accept the slave wages of normality—identified a trap door into a vertical dimension, and found there a return-route to the forgotten country from which humans had set out Before the Beginning. Venturing across the great divide separating man from the incorruptible sphere of the gods, our virtual adventurers then found themselves pulled into the orbit of the Great Attractor, the very ground and goal of existence, the unseparate Source of all being, a mostly uninhabited region at the outskirts of consciousness, the Final, Absolute Reality where cosmos flowers into deity and Bang! you're divine.

According to the anonymous author of one of the classic texts of esoteric Christianity, Meditations on the Tarot,

> The "good news" of religion is that the world is not a closed circle, that it is not an eternal prison, that it has an exit and an entrance.... "Perdition" is to be caught up in the eternal circulation of the world of the closed circle...[whereas] "salvation" is life in the world of the open circle, or spiral, where there is both exit and entrance.[1]

All religions profess to have located this escape hatch, a cosmic loophole in the closed circle of existence, to such an extent that any given religion may be thought of as the codification of at least one person's escape—from self, from contingency, from suffering, from sin, from death, from the tangled labyrinth of time itself. But all too often, one person's escape has become another group's prison, as the mind parasites continued to wage battle for their piece of the human psyche, moving quickly to put out the fire of spiritual experience wherever it threatened to spread. It is largely because of personal and impersonal mind parasites that the search for Truth is always opposed by formidable, antievolutionary forces, and "cannot take place outside the war in the imagination between competing perceptions of reality."[2]

In the esoteric tradition, the material world is considered only the "outer crust" or "epidermis" of the great cosmic organism.[3] But importantly, as emphasized by Smoley, the esoteric understanding of "matter" does not pertain to "physical substance alone." Rather, "even a thought or emotion is 'matter.'"[4] And it is not so much matter that is the problem, but the materialistic mode of thought: in order to know reality, we must be cured of a disease (or pneumapathology) called "Materialitis," or perhaps "Reductionosis." That is, given the limiting belief that matter is ultimate, there is nowhere you can go in the world that is not already at the farthest outward reach of the cosmos, and nowhere you can go that will make it any roomier. (Imagine a two-dimensional being trying to "get away from it all" by going on vacation somewhere in Flatland; anywhere he goes, he will still be restricted to a cramped planar existence, and never experience the comparatively infinite freedom of the third dimension, even though that dimension is equally available from any point in Flatland.)

However, there appears to be widespread agreement among spiritual cosmonauts that "the human state is a gate of exit," even "the only gate for the terrestrial world," and that human beings may act as the very portal "through which all of creation can pass on its return to God."[5] In fact, based on the testimony of countless saints and mystics from time immemorial, this "secret passage" is always here, merely awaiting our unwavering decision to pass through it. In so doing, we may compress the time it would otherwise take to collectively reach that cosmic fulfillment toward "which the human race as a whole, advancing at an almost imperceptible rate of progress, will reach only after aeons of time."[6] In Orthodox Christianity that ultimate fulfillment is known as *theosis,* or direct awakening to the divine-cosmic drama.

It is often because of antievolutionary mind parasites that religion, which has the goal of liberation, freedom, mind-expansion, and openness to reality, is just as likely to be identified with repression, narrow-mindedness, bigotry, and frankly weird beliefs. This is the conventional, "exoteric" religiosity with which most people are familiar. But there is another form of religion—a slender thread of esoteric beliefs and practices stretching back through antiquity, and preserved by an elite corps of resistance fighters experimenting with death-defying techniques of karmannihilation and egobliteration—whose goal is nothing less than "moksha," or release from the mindless, closed and repetitive wheel of conventional life—the low grade sensate/emotional/intellectual joys of the hedonic treadmill.[7] Riding the long coattails of these cosmic frontiersmen and omsteaders, we may—if their unsane testimony is to be believed—attain our true destiny, that is, the union of our local human soul with the nonlocal, transcendent, and metacosmic existence. According to Sri Aurobindo, the purpose of yoga—perhaps the most generic, universal form of applied theognosis—is to lay open "a gate of escape out of the vicious circle of our ordinary human existence."[8] Evidently, the only way out is *in,* from "consciousness of the outward and apparent to the consciousness of the inner and real."[9]

Well, we might as well get an early start. All of us will return to this realm sooner if not later, most of us "feet first" by way of suffering and struggling against the inevitable tide of disillusionment, loss, and physical disintegration, a few of us "heart first," through the discovery of a perennial Truth, a hidden Way, and an eternal Life. But either way, SOME DISASSEMBLY IS REQUIRED.

* * *

Who is the first soul on record as having finished the human race, broken through to the other side, and awakened to the Invisible One without a second? The earliest definitive documentation of the actual existence of the ultimate singularity is in the Vedic literature, especially the Upanishads, which were probably composed between 1,000 and 600 B.C. Although human beings had certainly set up "diplomatic relations" with the divine prior to this, we are making a sharp distinction between the objective discovery of God, a mental/conceptual understanding which belongs to the higher mental realm, and the radical awakening to, and identification with, the ultimate, non-local ground of Being, which defines the truly mystical. Like all other world spaces, the spiritual world has an inside and an outside (*nirguna* and *saguna brahman,* or God with and without attributes), and dualistic mental images of God, no matter how sublime, still fall within the conventional symbolic, subject-object realm of psychological space—which is why mere knowledge of any kind can never be "ultimate." This is in contrast to genuine recognition and realization of the Absolute, the supreme Self, which is an entirely different, transcendent form of knowing: knowledge through acquaintance or identification, the same way one knows one is alive, has sensory perceptions, or has a mind. It is actually the end of the first, second, and third singularities. Or is it the beginning?

## 4.1 Unknowing and How to Communicate It: The Hazards of Talking Pure Nonsense

> It is the Eternal Wisdom underlying the teachings of all religions, the *actual facts*, of which we can never have more than interpretations unless we ourselves gain experience of them.
>
> —Sri Krishna Prem, *Man, The Measure of All Things*

> You are going, not indeed in search of the New World, like Columbus and his adventurers, nor yet an *other* world that is to come, but in search of the other world that *now is*, and ever has been, tho' undreamt of by the Many, and by the greater part even of the Few.
>
> —Samuel Taylor Coleridge, *On Logic and Learning*

### *1. The Problem of Knowing What Cannot Be Known*

Few of us have the means or resources to carry out original research in physics, biology, or neurology. However, each of us has the equivalent of our own particle accelerator with which to carry out the most sophisticated psycho-spiritual research. None of us need rely solely upon the revelations of others, of "second hand" spirituality gleaned from texts, commentary, authority, or threats from men in funny hats. Nevertheless, it is safe to say that for most people, little of their knowledge of spirit is first hand, any more than their knowledge of physics or medicine is first hand. Of course it is fine to defer to experts in matters of science, medicine, and plumbing repair. But in matters of our deepest concern, such as our spiritual nature, it is possible for us to use derivative, second-hand knowledge as a defense against experience, so as to foster the comforting delusion that we know what we actually do not know. Heschel cites the apocryphal example of the yeshivah student who was asked whether he could swim, to which he responded, "I do not know how to swim, but I understand swimming."[10]

To be blunt, most of what goes by the name of religion consists of superimposing a grid of religious "knowledge" over the domain of Spirit, thus foreclosing the possibility of actually "discovering" its truth. "The answer," wrote Maurice Blanchot, "is the disease that kills curiosity." As any innovative scientist can tell you, since much of scientific advance consists of making more interesting errors, "creative blundering" is one of the important pathways to truth. Similarly, spiritual growth requires bringing to bear a certain degree of higher bewilderment, learned ignorance, and strategic unknowing, as we turn our gaze away from the outward world of sense experience and toward the inner Self. This may seem like a small thing, but it is actually of monumental importance, because most people, despite their best intentions, simply "hear" and "see" what they already know. But in order to clear a space for genuine spiritual knowledge, we must begin by *not* knowing. Only then will we be in a position to have an experience of the Ultimate Principle that is *beyond doubt*, because all merely mental conceptualizations of anything are open to doubt and logical refutation.

### *2. Escaping the Prismhouse of Language*

A related problem is the matter of language. One of the difficulties we run into when we even attempt to describe Spirit with language, is that it will take on all sorts of attributes that are an underlying property of language *per se,* not Spirit as such, causing us therefore to mistake "a deficiency in language for a key to truth."[11] This is actually one of the main reasons why there are so many divergent and seemingly irreconcilable theologies, because any smooth-talking rascal with a little charisma and a storehouse of colorful religious terms can easily superimpose a compelling verbal grid over something as subtle as Spirit (hallelujah, can I get a witness?), just as a clever blind person could construct a convincing theory of colors by analyzing the mathematical relationships between different light frequencies, but have no idea why you shouldn't wear brown shoes with a tux.[12] Therefore, we should always bear in mind that "The only way to get past religious words and concepts is to seek, without compromise and self-pity, the Reality behind them.[13] And the only way to do this is to avoid "pastorized" milk and drink directly from the sacred cow, as we shall see in the following section.

## *3. Sense & Nonsense: The Problem of Facts and Experience*

Now that we don't know anything about Spirit (or how to say it), let us begin with the self-evident premise that all genuine spiritual knowledge must be grounded in experience. It seems almost facile to say so, but it needs to be emphasized that any claims about Spirit must in the final analysis emanate from (at least *someone's*) spiritual experience, not from spiritual belief, hearsay, rumors, dogma, tradition, faith, or authority. Quite simply, there is no theory, no scripture, no doctrine, no revelation, however luminous, that can replace *experience.* And the experience must be of spiritual reality—the actual "facts," relatively uncontaminated by personal and cultural noise (mind parasites), unverifiable beliefs, local interpretations, secondary ideologies, and idiosyncratic artifacts of our evolved nervous system. Ultimately, knowledge of these facts cannot be conveyed in the same way ordinary empirical or rational knowledge may be directly passed from brain to brain. Rather, what can be taught is the truth about the *ways to realize* knowledge of these facts; the knowledge we are seeking cannot ultimately be taught but it can be *discovered*. And, for reasons that will be discussed later, it generally must be discovered again and again, unlike conventional (i.e., logical or empirical) knowledge which, once discovered, stays that way (assuming the discoverer has publicized his or her discovery).

While it may seem presumptuous to refer to spiritual "facts," all esoteric traditions—from the early desert fathers of the Christian Way, to the Vedic seers, to Tibetan Buddhist monks—speak of a trans-empirical realm corresponding to our inner spiritual intuition that is as real as the empirical realm that answers to our five outward senses. Spiritual research is *scientific* to the extent that, according to Sri Aurobindo, "it proceeds by subjective experiment and bases all its findings on experience"[14] of these facts. While there are, of course, different scriptures and theologies, these must be understood as multiple views of a hyper-dimensional, trans-human manifold irreducible to a single *exterior* formula. Again, Aurobindo:

> It is a fact that yogic experience runs everywhere on the same lines.... admittedly, we are dealing with a many-sided Infinite to which there are and must be many ways of approach; but yet the broad lines are the same everywhere and the intuitions, experiences, phenomena are the same in ages and countries far apart from each other and systems practised quite independently from each other.... That would seem to show that there is something there identical, universal and presumably true—however the colour of the translation may differ because of the difference of mental language.[15]

Aurobindo's neo-Vedantic perspective would appear to be exactly mirrored in orthodox Judaism; according to Heschel, it is clear "that men's opinions about God throughout history do not show a greater variety than, for example, their opinions about the nature of the world."[16] Likewise, practitioners of inner, mystical Christianity generally have more in common with esotericists from other faiths than they do with members of their own religion who have only an outer, exoteric view.[17] Another way of expressing this is to say that religions "are the *product* of Religion, but they are not Religion itself."[18] It has only been quite recently—certainly within the last two hundred years or less—that human beings have actually been in a position to begin constructing a "critical religiosity," in which we are sufficiently acquainted with other faiths to separate the essential and eternally valid from the accidental, transient, local, customary and purely superstitious. Before that, nobody "had" a religion *per se,* any more than they "had" a culture. People were simply embedded in an unquestioned culture and religion, and did their best to imitate "the ways of the ancestors."

### *4. Do You Read Me?*<br>*The Problem of Revealed Scripture*

Although spiritual experience is ultimately "self evident," there is no doubt that scripture and other sacred texts can, among other things, "be a corrective in helping [us] distinguish between truth and deception in [our] own experience."[19] But just as you wouldn't trust someone who had only studied surgical textbooks to perform an operation on you, it is probably unwise to trust spiritual advisors who cite a text as their only authority. Without question texts can be helpful, but not as a replacement for experience. An Orthodox Christian monk put it thus: "Without the experience and testimony of the saints about the reality of God, the Bible would be an empty letter."[20] As expressed by Shankara, a disease cannot cured by repeating the word "medicine," but only by taking it. Even in Judaism, the great Rabbi Abraham Heschel warned that dogmas can only "point to the mysteries of God," and "mark a way not an end.... Dogmas are obstacles unless they serve as humble signposts on the way."[21] A text may be taken as a road map or tour guide, or perhaps provide us with a resonant language to employ in order to think about Spirit, which is otherwise "unthinkable." Radhakrishnan uses a good analogy here, noting that, in science,

> we accept what the greatest investigators in those departments declare for truth; in music we attend to what the accredited great composers have written, and endeavor thereby to improve our natural appreciation of musical beauty. In matters of religious truth we should listen with respect to what the great religious geniuses, who strove by faith and devotion to attain their spiritual eminence, have given out.[22]

But here again we must be very careful not to allow the "word" to replace the experience, only to help us name and store it. And even then, the word must be susceptible to an accumulation of experiential meaning, that is, it must be "unsaturated." As expressed by Plotinus, language should be cautiously employed

> only to give direction, to urge towards that vision beyond discourse, to point out the road to one desirous of seeing. Instruction goes only so far as showing the road and the direction. To obtain the vision is solely the work of him who desires to obtain it.[23]

Even if we assume that scripture is a revelation of God, it seems axiomatic that it still has to be revealed *to* someone, and that the meaning of the particular revelation varies widely from person to person, depending upon their capacity to receive it. Therefore, just as "A hundred texts cannot make fire cold," scripture that is not grounded in experience "is mere sound without sense."[24] In the final analysis, "conclusions of the scriptures… must be experienced by the aspirant himself," or not at all.[25]

The most problematic spiritual words are those that are already so saturated with meaning that they are no longer useful as "containers" for the accumulation of meaning through experience.[26] For example, in the world of ancient Rome, where power was venerated above all, to suggest that a lowborn peasant and common laborer was the "Son of God" was about the most shocking thing one could say. But with time, as words and ideas become saturated, they lose their capacity to vault us out of our habitual mental orbit. Nowadays, in order to have the same shocking, counterintuitive impact, you might have to say that the Son of God was a personal injury lawyer or television executive. (This, by the way, is one of the reasons people are understandably attracted to religions from outside their own culture—because they are cast in unfamiliar terms, they retain some of their original linguistic potency.)

Undoubtedly the most saturated word in all of religious discourse is "God." In fact, this word is already so overloaded with cultural, historical, and idiosyncratic personal meanings that its use for communication with others is extremely problematic. Not only that, but if you already "know" what God is, then there is no space left for the word to accumulate meaning through experience: the word has become completely saturated and is therefore functionally dead. Judaism attempted to address this issue by preventing the word from even being uttered, assigning "G-d" an unpronounceable name. According to Heschel, the greatest obstacle to spiritual knowledge

> is our adjustment to conventional notions, to mental clichés. Wonder or radical amazement, the state of maladjustment to words and notions, is, therefore, a prerequisite for an authentic awareness of that which is.[27]

Likewise, according to the traditions of the desert fathers of Orthodox Christianity, before beginning the spiritual journey, serious seekers must first "renounce our own images of God," for the simple reason that the ultimate "is beyond all images, thoughts, and concepts."[28] Real faith, according to the Buddhist teacher McLeod,

> is the willingness to open to the mystery of experience. It contrasts with belief, which is the attempt to interpret experience to conform with habituated patterns that are already in place, including those from your culture and upbringing.[29]

It is all too easy to confuse our thoughts about god with God, which is why so many theologians are in reality "theodoxians," dispensing not knowledge of God, but opinions (*doxa*) about God.

Even if you were to rely upon a textual authority for the acquisition of spiritual knowledge, it still seems obvious that the text's authority is only there by virtue of its ability to facilitate some experience of Truth and that, unless you have access to a detector of Truth within your own being, the text is useless (one person becomes a Sufi mystic, another straps on a suicide belt, one meditates to realize the Brahman, another finds justification for the caste system, and so on). A valid spiritual practice is designed in part to help identify, engage, and develop the internal spiritual faculty that allows us to recognize Spirit in the first place. This is really not any more mysterious than, say, the process of becoming a wine connoisseur. In that case, the connoisseur starts out like everyone else, with an initially crude sense of taste that becomes increasingly refined and able to make more subtle discriminations with development, so that the identical wine will be experienced in dramatically different ways, depending on one's capacity of discrimination.

In reality, authentic scripture cannot even be understood without the operation of a noetic faculty that transforms mere language into something beyond language. In some mysterious way, scripture "contains" not only the spiritual knowledge it wishes to convey, but also the "luxicon" that unlocks itself, somewhat like DNA, which contains the "map" of the genome, but also the means to read and carry out its own instructions. Without this self-generated noetic light, scripture is no different than any other sophisticated, high-minded, philosophical blah-blah that can be understood by the "normal," spiritually undeveloped personality.

## *5. Fallacies of Religion and Scientism*

If we are to develop an appropriate research program to investigate spiritual reality, the first thing we must do is, in some sense, create a "composite portrait" based on our thus far fleeting glimpses of the immaterial suspect we are pursuing. This is difficult to do at the outset, because we do not want to presuppose too much about it. As formulated by Huxley, "too much working hypothesis means finding only what you already know to be there and ignoring the rest."[30] And this is especially problematic in the realm of Spirit, where people have a decided tendency to think what is thinkable and a strong motivation to "discover" what is desirable, not what is true. We might call the problem of "too much hypothesis" the "fallacy of religion." (This fallacy is not, of course, limited to religion, but is pervasively present in political, cultural, and psychological thought, in fact, the humanities in general, which are overrun with pseudo-religions masquerading as theories and ideologies. These parasitic pseudo-religions form closed systems that distort and obscure reality through the prismhouse of ideological I-glosses.)

Conversely, Huxley points out that "no working hypothesis means no motive for research, no reason for making one experiment rather than another, no way of bringing sense or order into the observed facts."[31] This problem of "no hypothesis" we shall refer to as the "fallacy of scientism." Instead of enlarging our thought so that it fits the phenomena, this fallacy reduces, ignores, or excises the phenomena to fit the theory, often leaving a universe too impoverished even to sustain the original phenomena. This is why, strictly speaking, science has no "theory of spirit"—as put by the philosopher Eric Voegelin, it is philosophically "closed" and "logophobic"—because it does not acknowledge the existence of the divine or transcendent ground in the first place. Trying to use science to track Spirit places us in the position of E. F. Schumacher, who, while visiting communist Moscow, became lost and was attempting to find his way by consulting a map of the city. He became confused because, although he was standing outside a large Russian Orthodox cathedral, he could not locate it on the map, only to later realize that the communist government had removed all churches from the map. The "logophobia" or "pneumapathology" of science is actually a spiritual disorder whose symptoms include "refusal to engage in the search for the truth of existence,"[32] closure of the soul and resultant estrangement from the transcendent ground of being, adherence to rigid ideological and methodological preconceptions, the substitution of "secondary realities" for the primary One, and the inevitable worship of false gods in the form of intellectual "graven images."[33] It leaves our world in the now familiar position of being "turned backwards and upside down, with its face toward darkness and nonentity and its back to the sun of truth and the source of being."[34]

### *6. Saying More With Less: The Problem of Conceptual Abstractness and Concreteness*

The esteemed western mystic Franklin Merrell-Wolff made the sad but commonplace observation that "the record of traditionalistic religion is one of essential failure."[35] Unfortunately, exoteric religion often doesn't seem to actually *do* much of anything, or to help us *achieve* something beyond mere assent to one seemingly arbitrary creed or another. According to Joseph Chilton Pearce, if we judge religious institutions by the actual fruit they bear rather than the beautiful creeds they enshrine, we shall be disappointed to discover not only that "spiritual transcendence and religion have little in common," but that historically they have been "fundamental antagonists."[36] Ironically, while the founders of great religions have (evidently) successfully made their own crossing to the heart of immortal being, they have generally "left poor bridges for others. It is this bridge-building that is the really important work" of spirituality.[37] Thus, while conventional religions all have a bridge to sell us, the questions are, will the bridge hold up for our own psychic exodeus, and where will it actually take us?

Let me emphasize that by no means do I intend to convey any disrespect toward those for whom their religion is "working." However, it is genuinely difficult for many people in the modern world to experience conventional (or *exo*teric) religion as much more than a carrot-and stick enterprise, offering special post-mortem consideration in exchange for compliance on earth with a sometimes opaque list of do's and don'ts. In fact, one of the purposes of this book is to demonstrate that this is not the case, and that religion, if properly understood and practiced, is not only reconcilable with the modern world, but that it is the key to understanding reality and the *cure* for various spiritual diseases—pneumapathologies—of modernity.

One of the problems that has limited the effectiveness of conventional religion is that it is both too abstract *and* too concrete, with respect to both theory and practice. The excessive concreteness of religion accounts for the tendency of religious experiences to be invested with a rigid meaning which in turn leads to *ad hoc* theologizing, because there is no way to logically relate all the disparate individual experiences to one another. This has been especially problematic in Western religions of the Judeo-Christian tradition, which have often tended to ignore the construction of a credible, intellectually respectable metaphysic in favor of highlighting certain historo-spiritual "facts" that can never be proven, but which are regarded as the essence of the religion: a miracle here, a divine intervention there, big trouble up ahead with a beast rising out of the earth.[38] While these "facts" are understood to be of great spiritual significance, there is hardly any effort to fit them into a general epistemological or ontological framework that respects everything else we know to be true of the world. Spiritual experience is first theologized, then theology is historicized, and finally history is concretized, reducing religion to a required belief that certain seemingly unlikely historical events actually occurred in a completely literal sense, say, humans being banished from the Garden of Eden, or God creating the world in six days. As a result, the historical element in the Bible "has been unduly emphasized, while books that are purely allegorical and mystical have been construed as history."[39]

"Religions," according to Schuon, "are cut off from one another by barriers of mutual incomprehension."[40] That is, people tend to forget that religion points beyond itself, to something that is *not religion,* just as reality is surely independent of the words we use to describe it. But spiritual experience is generally inflected through a certain predigested belief system, so that people tend to "think that a different system with a different terminology is representing a different reality."[41] As expressed by philosopher Bryan Magee,

> only if concepts are detached from association with the uniquely particular can they perform the tasks for which they exist, namely, storage and communication. There is, and there has to be, less information about reality contained in empirical concepts than in the experiences from which they derive.[42]

But because religions "accumulate a lot of local and communal historical traditions" with the passage of time, they "tend to become credal and formal, and are left incapable of universal acceptance."[43] Early Desert Fathers of Christianity such as Origen railed against this kind of concrete thinking, in that "to take the language of the Bible 'literally' was for him to empty it of all transcendent reference, to confine it to the 'corporeal' world. Allegory was required to give the biblical text appropriate depth and density of meaning."[44] Harris points out that what religion promulgates in its early, concrete form is likely "a representation at some more or less undeveloped stage, of what emerges under criticism as a metaphysical concept."[45] Ironically, both religious "fundamentalists" and spiritually bereft secularists are identical in approaching scripture in such an unsophisticated, concrete, and literal manner. In both cases, as Young puts it, the "factuality" of scripture is the focus of critical attention, rather than its "pointing beyond itself."[46]

But irrespective of whether or not something actually "happened" in an historical sense, the historical (or horizontal) perspective of any scripture is only useful insofar as it helps to illuminate a non-historical or "vertical" dimension operating outside chronological time. Both religious and scientific fundamentalists attempt to locate in historical time what can only be found in metaphysical space, and mistakenly regard conventional history as more "real" than the deeper or higher truth from which it is a declension. To cite just one example, one may well believe that Moses led the enslaved Israelites out of the death-cult of Egypt and into freedom. But what relevance does this have for us today, unless it is still possible, with divine assistance, to escape the spiritual death-cult of our own psychic Egypt and be led toward the higher Light and Life? Likewise, if we consider some of the words used by Jesus—bread, water, blood, vine, birth, father, son—each of these has a literal sense, an abstract sense, and a highly resonant spiritual/experiential sense. In fact, one could almost define scripture as a special kind of language that operates in a top-down fashion, containing material from every stage and dimension of reality, from the mystical, noetic, and spiritual, to the moral and psychological, to the mythic and allegorical, to the concrete, material and historical. And this is precisely why it is so easy for billions of people to get caught up in the most concrete and literal aspect of scripture, oblivious to the higher and more subtle meanings it contains, for "they have ears, but hear not."

* * *

We have been dwelling on the excessive concreteness of religious communication, but we must also take care to avoid the excessive abstractness of religion, which makes it difficult to relate religious communication to actual spiritual experience, to "realize" what the communicant is talking about. This is a problem that afflicts intellectuals in general and theologians in particular. That is, the more educated one is, the more one tends to have a storehouse of concepts that are taken over as "finished products," without any encounter with the concrete reality from which the abstractions were taken. This kind of defective learning eventually causes a rupture between the ideal and the real. That is, the disembodied ideal is passed on from generation to generation of theologians, to the point that the actual experience to which it applies has been lost.[47] Religious talk necessarily begins to lose its relevance if we can no longer "feel" what it is referring to. In short, as Hegel emphasized, the *ideal* must be comprehended in its *incarnation*, which, ironically, really just emphasizes the original metaphysical innovation introduced to the world through Christianity—that is, that the ultimate *abstraction* (or logos) "dwelt among us" in a *particular* human being.[48] (You might say that the ultimate "real" is neither ethereal nor earthly, but earthereal.)

If we rely only on the concrete, then we lose ourselves in a world of particulars, of "brute facts" that cannot be generalized, thought about, and effectively communicated. But if we go too far in the other direction, toward excessive abstraction, we generate a whole new range of problems. That is, abstract concepts are only useful "in so far as they derive from experience and can be cashed back into it." Otherwise, our conceptions "are not rooted in anything we ourselves have ever observed, experienced, felt, or thought. Even when these are accurate they are still not fully authentic, for they are not truly *ours*."[49] More ominously, one can readily understand how the "fanaticism of abstract thought" may lead to inquisitions, jihads, and witch hunts. That is, no abstract idea, concept, or symbol can actually "contain" spiritual reality. Nevertheless, the ideal may dictate that only one kind of religious experience is true or possible, but this does not stop people from continuing to have concretely real encounters with the Divine. This frustrates the intellectual/theologian, who cannot understand that "it is our abstract ideas that fall short of reality, not reality that falls short of our abstract ideas."[50] It is only one small step further to rationalize the persecution of others, who are regarded as defective forms of the abstract, sacred Ought.[51] The list of great mystics who have been persecuted for having the "wrong" type of religious experience is too long to catalog here.

* * *

In order to overcome the above problems and fallacies of religious thought, several developments are needed. Mainly, we must understand the dialectic between the abstract and concrete: the abstract must be embodied in the concrete, but at the same time, the concrete must be seen as the instantiation of the ideal. Practically speaking, we need to have more of a two-way relationship between theory and practice, beginning with a theory (or metaphysic) that is not so abstract or concrete that it prevents us from personally investigating its truth value. Without question we need to have generalized final truths, but these truths must be exemplified in particular instances that are readily realizable by anyone who sincerely takes the time and effort to discover them (or, more likely, to "become" them; theoretical "know-how" must be combined with spiritual "be-who" in an onto-noetic fusion). Dogma that cannot be verified in the "school of experience" devolves into mere idolatry—secondary and derivative graven images no less primitive than the toenail clippings of an exalted saint. In addition to a theory that can map the area under investigation, we need a practice that allows us to actually have experiences that may confirm, refute, or modify the theory. And third, we need to develop a more abstract, "unsaturated" language to communicate our findings with one another, not just with those who are suggestible or predisposed in some other way to believe.

Therefore, a working metatheology will illuminate and organize the particular spiritual "facts" of our experience, while our realization of spiritual facts should be able to lead to a metatheology flexible enough to explain and account for the spiritual facts of our experience. If these facts are to be universal, then they must be attainable by most anyone; if they are special instances attainable by no one else, then we cannot build any general theory based on them. In short, the experience, and not its formulation, must be entirely concrete, whereas the formulation must be abstract and yet capable of concrete realization. And, just as in any other scientific endeavor, we must be in possession of a theory to illuminate and organize spiritual facts, but at the same time be prepared to alter our theory if and when new facts warrant it. In so doing, we will have a living system that can encompass all genuine theologies *and* all authentic encounters with the Ultimate. Furthermore, we will not be in the fallacious position of attempting to derive spiritual knowledge from *a priori* spiritual concepts, but rather, employing symbols and concepts to store and retrieve spiritual knowledge and experience.

Where does this leave traditional religion? In fact, we should have no objection to the great established religions, so long as they are understood to be self-contained symbol systems capable of the storage *and retrieval* of primordial experiences with transcendent reality. That is, the Truth of any religious symbol above all lies in its "effective power of illumination and not in its literalness."[52] And Truth, if it is actually Truth, is beyond any single expression of it, and yet present in each of its expressions. If something is true, it is universal, and compels acceptance. Radhakrishnan emphasizes that

> There is no such thing as a private truth, any more than a private sun or a private science. Truth has an intrinsic and universal character, which depends on no individual, not even God. The process of apprehending reality may be private or singular, *but not the object apprehended.*[53]

In point of fact, Truth is *inexhaustible*, flowing as it does from the direction of the Absolute (which is beyond image and form) into the relativity of formal language, and no single religious system, no matter how expansive, can ever contain it. That is why absolute Truth is ultimately *concrete* and not symbolic, in fact, the most concrete experience available to mortals. Absent the light of this antecedent Truth, religious forms are analogous to using a crystal to "light up a dark place." A crystal is, by its very nature, "luminous, but its properties of purity, transparence, and power to condense luminous rays are inoperative without the presence of light."[54] Or, to use a more prosaic image, they are like "the reflector lights on the back of automobiles whose only ability to radiate light" emanates from another source.[54] Religious texts are beautiful crystals that fail to enlighten unless illuminated by the light of primordial Truth.

Having pointed out the dangers of taking scripture too literally, the fact remains that most any spiritual tradition asks us to believe things that may at first seem implausible. However some degree of "belief in the unbelievable" may actually be a necessary component to deconditioning ourselves to the narrow and restricted consensus reality of our particular culture. Many modern sophisticates shun religion because their misuse of reason informs them that God cannot possibly exist, when the very point of a serious spiritual practice is to discover for oneself whether or not God exists, not through means designed to know other realities, but by utilizing the proper, time-honored methods.[56] Employing our usual cognitive categories to "pierce the mystery" of God "is like trying to bite a wall."[57] According to Smith, what may strike a modern rationalist as "categorically unbelievable" is just the thing that might "serve as a bridge that leads beyond the phenomenal realm," beyond the world of appearances.[58] In other words, we need to somehow "bypass" our habitual, saturated way of thinking, and one way of doing this is to properly immerse ourselves in the highly resonant, mythopoetic language of religion. That language must be presented in such a manner that the knowledge it conveys cannot be reduced to, or evaluated in terms of, our mundane, worldly understanding of reality.

A fine example of the approach I am advocating is in a book entitled *The Beginning of Wisdom,* by Leon Kass. Kass approaches the first five books of the Bible—the Torah—in the same manner as he would any venerable work of philosophy, steering a middle course between excessive piety (the fallacy of religion) and modern skepticism (the fallacy of scientism). Remarkably, what he discovers is an astonishingly deep, thoughtful and astute treatise on our universal human nature, both in our "fallen state," unaided by divine wisdom, and in our attempt to accord more fully with our higher nature, or divine image. As such, although the Torah is outwardly "about" a few particular Jewish tribes in the distant past, it is really about "trans-historical and universal wisdom" that applies to everyone, at all times. It is an attempt to teach us "not what happened (once) but what *always* happens, what is always the case."[59] Indeed, according to Mouravieff, any scripture ultimately exists only "to tell us about *ourselves,* and not for any other reason."[60] As it so happens, the Torah *is* universal (or at the very least contains an extraordinary amount of universal wisdom applicable to anyone, at any time), which tends to support the claim that its source must be trans-human. It comprehends us more thoroughly than we could ever comprehend it.

But alas, "Although the spirituality of the Western religions contains a profound knowledge of the self, these traditions have on the whole been unable to communicate this knowledge in a language and under conditions that can be accepted by the contemporary secularized seeker."[61] The very real problem for most of us in the postmodern world is that once we have stepped outside the tent of traditional religion, it is very difficult to get back in, recover our innocence, and experience the symbol system as an adequate representation of reality. What makes matters worse is the fact that most religious models are generally introduced in childhood, which frequently stunts the religious imagination; many individuals who fall away from religion spend their lives in rebellion against an immature or dysfunctional conception of God internalized in childhood. This practice is no different than if we were to provide impressionable children with defective, overly abstract or reified models of anything, say, behaviorism, Marxist economics, or deconstructionist literary theory.

* * *

In the following section we will attempt to address all of the above problems by formulating a language of interrelated symbols that "map" religion in the most abstract way possible, while at the same time leaving the symbols relatively "empty," so that they may accumulate meaning through experience. Among other things, the system describes what you are actually trying to *do* when you do religion—any religion—and why religion "works" when it works. It is not intended to replace any single religion, but to help *realize* what any given religion conveys in more vague or mythological terms.

And although we are seeking the Religion underlying all religiosity, let me emphasize that we are explicitly rejecting a shallow religious syncretism, in which we would take outward beliefs from all traditions, and arbitrarily throw them together in some sort of new-age spiritual gumbo. First, that would be ignoring the proposition that there are readily verifiable facts of spiritual experience available to anyone sufficiently motivated—that is, an emotionally stable, virtuous, and humble person with pure intent and sincere aspiration—to find them. And secondly, such an agglomeration would include not only the secondary interpretations, but also the frank errors of others, who may not necessarily have approached the endeavor with the proper attitude and appropriate safeguards. In particular, just as is true in any line of research, it is important to "cleanse," calibrate, and stabilize the instruments of research, to make sure that the facts are not contaminated by noise, bias, and other errors. In spiritual research, the instrument that must be "sanetized" (sic) is nothing less than the researcher, the self, which is the focus of chapter 4.3.

## 4.2 Building a Better Logos: Insert Your Deity Here

> The progress of knowledge is a single process, and it is at once the progress of science and religion.
>
> —Errol Harris, *Revelation Through Reason*

> Among other things, religion is also research. Research into, leading to theories about and action in light of, nonsensuous, nonpsychic, purely spiritual experience.
>
> —Aldous Huxley, *The Minimum Working Hypothesis*

So what should the "minimum working hypothesis" of our spiritual inquiry be?[62] At this point in our mythadventure, based on what we have learned about the wholeness and non-locality of our cosmos, we can certainly say that we have sufficient evidence to affirm the possibility of an unmanifest ground of being without claiming to know just what it is, what are its exact characteristics. Let us call this O, standing for the ultimate, unchanging, unqualified, non-dual ground and source of our being. This may also be the appropriate time to introduce a second symbol, Ø, which stands for, among other things, dualism, the bifurcation of subject and object, god with attributes, maya-vidya, the phenomenal universe, and ignorance. (Again, please feel free to fill in any of these symbols, or "pneumaticons" [as opposed to emoticons] with your own content; one of the purposes of these symbols is to create an unsaturated spiritual language through which each individual may "realize" and "discover" their meaning. The total meaning of each symbol transcends any of the hints I may provide; in fact, the symbols should be regarded as empty and unsaturated containers to be filled with *experience*.)

* * *

Given the irreducible wholeness of our cosmos, it makes sense to begin with the proposition that O may be conceptualized as being both transcendent (the whole) and immanent (co-present in all parts of the cosmos). Thus, we may also affirm with a high degree of confidence that it may be possible to realize O (since we are parts of the whole, and the whole is therefore present in us). But this knowledge would have to be of a special kind, that is, from the inside, *through identity*, not from the outside, in the more typical subject/object mode of cognition. The facts we will be dealing with will not be objective and exterior but subjective and interior, suffused with *being*. These two modes of knowing (empirical/rational vs. noetic/esoteric) are as different as seeing a written musical score versus actually hearing (and deeply understanding) the musical performance encoded in the score. For our purposes, it is the difference between mere ideas about Reality versus the formation of an experiential relationship with it, or a textbook definition of "life" versus the feeling of what it is like to be alive. O is the interior beheld unity that all religions, in their outward multiplicity, are converging upon.

* * *

Here we will introduce several more symbols. The world we shall symbolize as ) (, the local human ego as (•), ordinary knowledge of )( as (k). Those without any spiritual practice assume they understand spirituality, just because they have some familiarity with its outward (exoteric) content, (k). However, (n) represents a realm of facts that is inaccessible to (•). Moreover, unlike (k), which can be passed like an object from mind to mind, (n) can only be known subjectively, that is, it must be *realized* anew by each individual in order to become *understanding.* (Again, we can know without understanding, but cannot understand without knowing. Interestingly, only by understanding O can one know with certainty of its existence. This is why most intellectuals *know* that O does not exist.)

Genuine (n) involves the realization and assimilation of spiritual facts within a *transformational* space between between two subjective centers, or beings, whereas (k) involves the conformity between a subjective center and an external part or surface.[63] For this reason, genuine religion may be thought of as the science of the ultimate subject (or Being), whereas science is the religion of the ultimate object (matter writ large). For similar reasons, Truth (with a capital T) is a function of conformity with O, while truth (which is still a kind of truth) represents conformity with **Ø**. To quote the outstanding esotericist Mouravieff on this point,

> Starting from the centre, positive science extends, specializes, and so diverges towards the periphery. At the limit each point forms a separate discipline. Esoteric science begins from the multiplicity and variety observed on the periphery accessible to our senses, and moves towards the centre.[64]

The center is O.

Just as our personal self comes into being in the space between brain neurology and empathic (or unempathic) others (see chapter 3.2), (n) arises in the space between us and O. According to Pearce, a neural network that evokes a particular state (including a spiritual state) is in reality a field distributed in an infinitely complex way throughout the brain and nervous system. However, (n) cannot be reduced to a mere neural network, any more than love, beauty, or morality can be dismissed by pointing to the places in the brain that light up when we are experiencing them. Rather, evoking the network gives us access to a matching field of resonant phenomena vibrating at the same frequency.

Although the activation of a neural network is a local phenomenon, it resonates with nonlocal dimensions, as can be seen in the creation of art. For example, the great jazz musician John Coltrane, although engaging in a form of radical improvisation, was able to create a spiritually charged musical world space that paradoxically preceded his entry into it. The same is true of the improvisational paintings of Kandinsky. Apparently, this is possible because O "requires" some local frame of reference or system of symbols in order to realize itself in the world, be it through painting, music, or ecstatic poetry. Evidently, the universe is filled with such "empty" fields of pure logos awaiting a nervous system sophisticated enough to evoke them. In other words, O, which exists outside time and space, may actually require a time-bound nervous system to manifest locally. Thus, according to Pearce, "Man's mind is a mirror of a universe—which in turn mirrors man's mind to some indeterminable and unknowable extent," so that "we must allow our heart and spirit to build the neural machinery necessary to translate and display" what we are calling O.[65]

This is exactly how Ken Wilber conceptualizes the ontology of these higher fields. The realm of (n) may be thought of as a "morphogenetic field," "evolutionary groove," or "developmental space" that exists as potential rather than a "fully actualized reality." These potentials, which "exert an undeniable attraction" on human development,

> are in many ways still plastic, still open to being formed as more and more people coevolve into them.... As these higher potentials become actualized, they will be given more form and content, and thus increasingly become everyday realities.[66]

While we all start out more or less determined by the genetic, cultural and familial circumstances that shape (•), as we begin detaching ourselves from its karmic patterns of samskaras, we find ourselves pulled into the phase space of O and coming under its influence.

* * *

So let us define the object of our spiritual research as follows: "the ultimate, unchanging, unqualified, non-dual ground and source of our being." And let us define our research program as the attempt to know this principle not in any exterior, intellectual, or theoretical way, but to know it experientially. Therefore, our ultimate goal is nothing less than "the ultimate, unchanging, unqualified, non-dual ground and source of our being, realized experientially," or O—>(n). We have no real interest in (k)—>O, as this is the realm of conventional churchianity, God-talk, or pneuma-babble. It produces the watered-down theology of those imprisoned in the intellect, a spirituality "by the (•), for the (•)." True, living spirituality is designed to facilitate experiences in O, but unfortunately, often devolves into mere (k), or worse, erroneous, reified ideas about O, that is, (-k)—>O.

In fact, using (k) to reason about O inevitably generates (-k), because (k) knows only surfaces, exteriors, and particulars, but elevates them to the ultimate. No matter how many layers of )))((( it peels away, there is always another layer of ) ( underneath. This peeling-away process is often confused with the achievement of *depth,* but it is a peculiar kind of depth, because deep down it is really quite shallow—just more ) (. Therefore, to study O with (k) is to misunderstand it; as it pertains to metaphysics, (k) is ultimately empty and indistinguishable from ignorance. Nevertheless, (k) seems to have an almost addictive, even hypnotic hold on certain (•)'s, and especially serves as a kind of opiate, or ersatz religion, for the intellectual class. But like all addictions, (k) has only a temporary effect on the person who chases after it, who will remain as expanded or contracted, happy or unhappy, evolved or unevolved, as he was before, no matter how much of it he acquires. The (k) thinker is analogous to a "lawyer who argues in favor of the person who pays him," so that if one is honest with oneself, one must eventually conclude that the accumulation of (k) can only end in rational agnosticism, or certainty of one's own uncertainty.[67] This is because (k), in the final analysis, follows from the false promise, "ye shall be as gods," thus further isolating and enclosing (•) in its own little derivative world, and foreclosing the possibility of evolution or upward escape through communion with O. (n), on the other hand, has a transformative effect on the person who understands it, as it raises and expands the level of being, which in turn "makes room" for more (n).

* * *

Of course, we live today in a world that has largely lost contact with (n), in an intellectual climate that considers only (k) about ) ( to be real; in fact, even (k)—>Ø is considered too metaphysical for modern philosophical tastes. However, regardless of what is at the other end of (n)—whether or not, for example, the thing called God actually exists—human beings undeniably possess an innate metaphysical need, an "oming instinct," an inborn "pneumaphilic" (spirit-seeking) tendency, just as if spirit did exist. While you may find it odd that human beings come equipped with a built-in way to intuit super-sensible dimensions, this is really no more problematic than our inexplicable ability to perceive beauty in music. No one who loves music allows the experience of enjoying it to be diminished by the mystery of why we have a love of music. Likewise, unless you are one of the unfortunate few who is truly spiritually "tone deaf," incapable of intuiting O, you needn't worry at this juncture about how or why you have the capacity to do so. Merely trust that this latent capacity exists, and that therefore "there must, surely, correspond a field or world, of other dimensions no doubt, answering to that capacity."[68]

In fact, spiritual teachers from all traditions are unanimous in their assurance that human beings possess an instrument of knowledge that can know O, an "eye of the soul," even though this faculty goes undeveloped in most people. In contrast to (•), we will symbolize this entity (¶). Just as our sense of vision is designed to transduce light waves into visual representations, or our sense of hearing to transduce air vibrations into sound patterns, (¶) is able to transform another kind of "vibration" into (n). Indeed, not only does (¶) have a form of perception analogous to "seeing," but it can also "hear" (at least in those who have ears) and intuitively "touch" the eternal. Thus we may say that, just as (•) obtains (k) of ) ( or Ø, (¶) is able to realize (n) as it pertains to O.

(¶) may also be fruitfully thought of as a kind of spiritual "placenta" which mediates metabolic exchanges and transmits life-giving nutrients, almost as if in preparation for some sort of "second birth." It is both the way *out* and the way *in,* the way *up* and the way *across.*

* * *

Knowledge is partly a function of the knower, so in order to perceive (n) you will have to close one "I" and open another. All spiritual traditions maintain that our two natures—(•) and (¶)—are oriented in distinctly different directions and supported by two different "environments," and that (•) and its opaque field of (k) form a sort of barrier between "us" and O. Before we begin the spiritual path, most of us are fully identified with the transient, deathbound (•), which is mostly a creature of heredity and environment, composed of both temporary and semi-permanent emotions, thoughts, memories, habits, desires, and fixations. But (¶) is oriented on a vertical plane that is said to be outside "the world" and "perpendicular" (so to speak) to time. Like a mirror-image of the Freudian unconscious, it often exerts a silent influence from behind or "above," creating its own preferences, traits, and capacities in us that cannot be explained by any experiences (•) has ever had.

If we compare the consciousness associated with (•) to a two-dimensional field, it is as if there are numerous unmarked "springs" dotting ) ( that bubble forth influences from a third dimension. These springs may be encountered or stumbled upon in a variety of ways, but must be followed back to the non-local source from which they originate. That source may only be accessed *here* and *now,* not amidst time's flow, but through something analogous to *memory* operating on a vertical plane. In order to become aware of vertical memory, you must *get a clue* and *take a hint*: That is, life is a dense network of interconnected signs, auguries, hints, clues and helpful tips. As we approach O, this will become more apparent, taking the form of falling coincidences and bursts of synchronicity that point to a hidden unity behind the temporal particularity of outward events. As part of our general orientation toward O, it is important to pay close attention to this phenomenon.

* * *

From the standpoint of (¶), (•) has no ontological reality. It is no more real than our dreams, not so much an illusion as a temporary condition that ends with death. It is "nothing but a complex mass of mental, nervous and physical habits held together by a few ruling ideas, desires and associations—an amalgam of of many small self-repeating forces with a few major vibrations."[69] Because it is an insubstantial, ever changing, and factitious entity with no real being, (•) is plagued by an incessant, existential separation anxiety, a feeling of "wrongness" that causes most (•)'s to run for comfort, distraction and affirmation in the direction of the god[s] that created it. (•) responds to the very narrow band of vibrations that brought it into being, mostly in the sphere of repetitive emotional dramas and pleasurable and unpleasurable physical sensations. Most (•)'s will spend their entire lives turning round and round, tethered to a vibrational core that is awakened by external situations that resonate at the same bass (or base) frequency.

Indeed, a frequent preliminary step that propels one into a serious spiritual practice is the realization that (•) is actually a sort of self-imposed prison that cuts us off from the renewing, vivifying powers of our source in O, and provides only a sort of theoretical, partial, and ultimately false and misleading view of reality. Alone among the animals, it is "unnatural" for human beings to be in their "natural" state. This is the idea of "the fall," which, esoterically understood, means that, although we are born an alienated (•) in a fallen ) (, our true station is really (¶) in communion with O. At every step along the spiritual path, it is our task to choose between living in reaction to, and as an extension of, ) (, or to be in alignment with O. To put it in Biblical terms, it is the difference between eating from the tree of knowledge versus eating from the Tree of Life. Indiscriminately obtaining all our psychic nourishment from the (k) tree effectively exiles us from our Oedenic birthplace and leads to various forms of spiritual malnutrition.

* * *

While some come to spiritual practice through the painful discovery that (•) is a form of solitary confinement between two dark, meaningless slabs of eternity, others come by way of ecstasy, rapture, and wonderment. In fact, it is not infrequent for even the most impacted (•) to have occasional glimpses of O, symbolized (?!). These "peak experiences" of authentic being are those rare and sudden moments when the cosmic veil has been lifted and we have been "touched by the eternal," when the world has opened up and we have been granted a foreshadow of our true inheritance in O. (Thus, they are also "peek" experiences that burst the "seems" of appearances.)

(?!) often comes in the form of a generally spontaneous experience in O. According to Sri Aurobindo, the "affirmation of something essentially superior to his present self is the basis of the divine life in the human being."[70] In fact, it is said that "an experience of cosmic consciousness is vouchsafed to everyone at least once in a lifetime, however fleetingly,"[71] and that even the most stubbornly secular among us will experience sneak-previews of O, only to ignore, forget, or explain them away. Others may become aware of a long string of mysterious "clues": special problems, unexplainable quirks, strange affinities and capacities, bizarre synchronicities that have opened up a whole new path or vista in your life. This often comes down to a process of retrospectively uncovering past choices based on a spiritual journey you did not even know you were on, and thereby discovering a hidden identity that has been nourished all along by small but persistent signs of sacred luck and holy happenstance (and often what appeared to be *bad* luck at the time). This in itself can begin to open one up to a universe that operates on distinctly different principles than the ones enunciated by the usual scientific models.

However, once identified with (•), most people will experience only rare moments of (?!). In reviewing your past life, it may be possible to remember those moments when the transpersonal broadcast broke through your habitual programming loud and clear, when the eternal signal came in and preempted your usual boring "reruns." Our goal, of course, is to be in a mild state of (?!) at all times; for in truth, while we mistakenly attribute (?!) to various circumstances, the phenomenon itself is actually unconditional. It is a matter of removing obstacles to its reception, not setting up elaborate, complicated, or expensive situations to trick (•) into relaxing its grip for awhile. (It is helpful if you have had many (?!) at random times, so that you can see how irrelevant the external situation generally was to its presence or absence.)

All of us can, with even unschooled intuition, receive these transitory, partial, and mixed messages from O, the flotsam and jetsam that washes up from the farther shore. But without any spiritual frame of reference, most people don't know what to do with (?!). Some simply forget about them, while others attempt to frantically chase after and recreate them through emotional excitement and hedonic distraction. Such Dionysian characters often attempt to terminate (•) with extreme prejudice. Although it would be misleading and sanctimonious to dismiss this approach as fruitless, it doesn't present itself as a sustainable lifestyle, nor may it be consistent with the relatively long life required to achieve a stable (¶). For other, more sober types, these tantalizing flashes of an alternative reality may become the initial motivation for a more methodical spiritual practice that attempts to follow (?!) back upstream to their source in O. Only through spiritual development can these metaphysical freebies evolve into a more conscious relationship to something that is felt as a continuous presence.

* * *

In the esoteric tradition, it has always been understood that "thought-forms" "have a powerful and quasi-independent existence once they are generated,"[72] and that "as abstract as these entities may seem to us, they also in their way wish to live and grow and reproduce."[73] If our goal is liberation from (•), these entities pose a daunting obstacle, for "to be free is to be capable of thinking one's own thoughts—not the thoughts merely of the body, or of society, but thoughts generated by one's deepest, most original, most essential and spiritual self, one's individuality."[74]

By way of analogy, consider your back yard. Upon closer inspection, you will immediately discover its ownership is more ambiguous. "Your" back yard is in all likelihood inhabited by birds and other small animals, trees, plants, weeds, insects, microorganisms, fungi; and furthermore, all of these will still be there long after you are gone. Likewise, you can no more claim absolute sovereignty over your mind than you can over your back yard, in that it is inhabited by a variety of entities from different planes of consciousness, each with a will all its own. As described by Sri Krishna Prem,

> If we make an effort to isolate our selfhood from the phenomena of sense, one of the things we see is that, apart from the conventions of ownership, we do not possess anything, not even our bodies. We are usually in the position of observers, often against our will, of a flow of "external" or "internal" events... [75]

Although most people will never realize it, the truth of the matter is that they are victims of identity theft. The majority of what we blandly accept as "thoughts" may be more accurately described as thoughts in search of a thinker who will allow them in and give them harbor.[76] Once that happens, they may take over the machinery of thinking, in the identical way that a virus takes over the machinery of a cell in order to reproduce itself. This is why the "thinking" of most people is so disappointingly circular, repetitive, and unimaginative: it isn't really thinking at all, just thoughts that have taken over the apparatus of the mind, a boring and predictable replay of prerecorded tapes.

As such, it is a mistake to assume that everyone begins with a relatively unified (•). Rather, most people, because of the fragmentation produced by mind parasites, are actually inhabited by numerous "partial I's," symbolized (•••). Not only that, but because these fragments of subjectivity tend to be externalized, the average person is •••(•)•••, with no stable awareness of, or contact with, (¶), much less O. These people have not yet become Masters of their Domain, and are divided and conflicted, often acting out their psychodramas with ) ( and with other •••(•)•••'s. This is why a guiding principle of any serious spiritual practice is to begin observing the thoughts passing through (•)—to cease believing everything you think, and begin to open a "gap" between you and them. All who wish to develop along the spiritual path must

> separate the two parts of the mind, the active part which is a factory of thoughts and the quiet masterful part which is at once a Witness and a Will, observing them, judging, rejecting, eliminating, accepting, ordering corrections and changes....[77]

This is by no means an easy task. As described by McLeod, it is akin to "hand-to-hand combat without hands," in a mortal battle "over who or what is going to live your life—you or your patterns. As in combat, one or the other has to die."[78]

Given the problem of parasites and multiple selves, it makes sense that the ongoing practice of the spiritual life must involve a deconditioning of (•), accompanied by the systematic strengthening and development of (¶). McLeod, coming at it from a Buddhist perspective, writes that "All spiritual work is essentially destructive in nature." This is because

> The purpose of spiritual work is to return to original mind, to reclaim our lives from the confusion and distortions of conditioning and wake up to what we are and what this experience we call life is. No matter what or how we think of the sources of conditioning—karma, environment, family background, genetic structure, evolutionary inheritances, cultural values—we are deeply conditioned. Habituated patterns of reaction and behavior run much of our lives. They create suffering for us, create suffering for others, and cut all of us off from the mystery of being.[79]

Likewise, "all Yoga," according to Aurobindo,

> is in its nature a new birth; it is a birth out of the ordinary, the mentalised material life of man into a higher spiritual conscious-

> ness and a greater and diviner being. No Yoga can be successfully undertaken and followed unless there is a strong awakening to the necessity of that larger spiritual existence.[80]

This awakening must be followed by a conscious (and repeated) decision of the will, involving an "upward orientation in the being, an illumination, a turning or conversion seized on by the will and the heart's aspiration," an act "which contains as in seed all the results that the Yoga has to give."[81]

* * *

Just as the external world would be an utterly obscure, featureless, unknowable void without our physical senses, the spiritual world is nonexistent to us without the senses to intuit it. Moreover, "Just as a muscle grows only through abnormal demands placed upon it, so, in a similar manner, do our inner faculties as well."[82] All of the esoteric traditions agree that there are certain techniques and practices required to strengthen (¶) and facilitate the transition (•)—>(¶), thereby allowing O—>(n). Ultimately, whatever else they do, all religions attempt in more or less intelligible ways to discern "between the Real and illusory" and provide some means, however effective, to open the trans-dimensional doorway and align ourselves with "the Permanent or to the Real."[83] That is why all of the traditions also agree that we cannot "serve two masters," that is, both (•) and (¶). Rather, one of them generally has to go: either (•) obscures and prevents (n), or we strengthen (¶) and transcend (•). But how? This is what virtually all spiritual practices are designed to accomplish.

Assuming a stable (•), the first step in any spiritual program involves a gradual disidentification from (•), beginning with a turning toward, and opening up to, the presence of O. According to Bruteau, "The most important thing in initiating a contemplative attitude toward life is being still and open."[84] That is, mental silence "is the indispensable climate for all revelation; noise renders it absolutely impossible."[85] The symbol (o) stands for such things as faith, surrender, renunciation, purification, self-offering, and openness to being, while (—) stands for silence, stillness, tranquility, peace, and shanti.

The primary aim of meditation, for example, is to achieve (—), or as enunciated in Patanjali's classical system of yoga, to "silence the oscillations of the mental substance." In fact, it is a safe generalization that "practically all techniques of prayer and meditation are aimed at stilling the mind (—) so that the Absolute can be made manifest in us."[86] Just as nature abhors a vacuum, (n) "has a horror of fullness."[87] That is why the practice of Yoga essentially involves "a preparation for perfect spiritual receptivity,"[88] virtually identical to the Bible's advice to "be still and know that I am" (*Psalms* 46:10).

Although one aspect of (o) involves "faith," it is not in the sense that this word is usually used, that is, a sort of required belief in some arbitrarily crazy or preposterous notion. In other words, "blind and misconceived belief is not real faith," for the very reason that "it cannot blossom into knowledge," or (n).[89] Rather, (o) is a *functional* faith, a willing suspension of disbelief, not necessarily an active acceptance of the patently unbelievable. It is more of a child-like (not childish) openness to reality, and a concomitant trust that (o) will be rewarded by a benign response from We-Know-Not-Whom. Although outwardly a simple thing, (o) is a prerequisite to the acquisition of (n), and is the esoteric meaning of such phrases as "the meek in spirit shall inherit the earth" in the Bible, or "If you want to become full, let yourself be empty" in the Tao Te Ching.

Importantly, if the effortless concentration of (—) is not at the same time practiced with some form of (o), it may simply lead to a very relaxed (•), a slightly roomier egoic prison pod. There is no higher purpose to mere relaxation, liberation, or "flow," unless these things are achieved for the purpose of *ascending.* Steinsaltz points out that while we must indeed liberate ourselves from the "alien influences" of ) ( and "break free of the chains, the limitations, and the restrictions imposed by environment and education," if this is pursued in an aimless fashion with no clear transcendent goal or vector, it will not only result in failure to discover the true self, but a sort of impotent "spiritual exhaustion."[90]

On the other hand, (o) without true (—) can simply loosen one's psychological boundaries or open one to all sorts of "sneak attacks" from ubiquitous adverse influences (symbolized >(¶)<), not just the helpful non-local operators that are always standing by. Evidently, these "adverse influences" are "built into the system," so to speak, and are there for the general protection of all. Think of your magnificent human form, which evolved all on its own, without any conscious assistance on your part. Mother evolution is generally content to meander at her own pace, and there are consequences for those who attempt to seize its tiller without the proper attitude and preparation. Evolution was doing fine before you arrived on the scene and will continue to flourish in your absence, and those who are not mindful of that fact are likely to be brought to heel in unpleasant ways. A word to the wise: if you are trying to be an exception to the slow but effective law of General Evolution, you had best conduct yourself exceptionally. You can't say you haven't been forewarned, for these admonitions are plastered everywhere in scripture, such as in the Upanishads:

> The Self cannot be known by anyone
> Who desists not from unrighteous ways,
> Controls not his senses, stills not his mind,
> And practices not meditation.[91]

Or as Bob Dylan once sang, "to live outside the law you must be honest."

* * *

"Real contact with the spiritual world," according to Tomberg, "always engenders the influx of forces."[92] As described by Aurobindo, as soon as we set out on the spiritual path, our

> old predetermined destiny begins to recede. There comes in a new factor, a Divine Grace, the help of a higher Divine Force other than the force of Karma, which can lift the sadhak beyond the present possibilities of his nature.[93]

That is to say, while (•) is situated on a "horizontal" plane, and grows through interactions with ) ( and other (•)'s, (¶) is located on a "vertical" plane, and draws its energies from another source, which we will symbolize (↓). This ubiquitous and free-flowing (↓)—recognized by virtually all spiritual traditions—is the two-way link between part and whole, Father and Son, divine and human, but to take advantage of it, we must prepare ourselves:

> [G]race falls like rain on everyone but, also like rain, it can only be received by a vessel properly prepared to catch it. The preparation involves a change of readiness brought about through spiritual discipline and self-purification. Without preparation we are merely rough stones on which the rain of grace slides off.... The entire process is a paradoxical mixture of effort and effortlessness. The effort is spiritual practice, our own ascent toward heaven; the effortlessness is grace, which perpetually descends from heaven for our benefit.[94]

Much of your task, as you embark on the spiritual path, is to begin "amplifying" (↓), instead of drowning it out with worldly distractions. At first (↓) will be inconsistent and wavering, like a distant radio station that comes in and out. But with persistence, (↓) begins to feel more like a presence, a pleasant electrical current descending from above, at various times felt at the top or back of the head, in the throat region, in the heart or belly, in the hands, or elsewhere. Only by maintaining (o) and (—) can we keep from drowning out this resonant current with the coarse thoughts and sensations of (•) and distractions of ) (.

Ideally, (↓) should matched by our own energy, (↑), symbolizing such things as aspiration, repentance, metanoia, prayer, or any other practice that activates our desire for union with O. The emergence of (¶) is characterized by, among other things, the above-noted subtle physical sensations that accompany (↓) and (↑). Here it is almost as if a "second body" is being born, a more subtle vehicle that corresponds with (¶) in the same way that our gross body is thoroughly suffused with (•). At the same time, (o) and (—) go from being frustratingly transient states to relatively permanent traits of (¶). In addition to this profound shift in the "location" of consciousness, there is a dramatic change in the content of consciousness as well; that is to say, (¶) leads directly to (+n), a deepened ability to understand esoteric knowledge, and perhaps even to amaze your pharisaical friends by spontaneously producing it, that is, "speaking as one who knows." As described by Smoley, you may feel as though

> your whole body and soul are merely a sort of telescope through which something much larger and wiser and more powerful is peering out at the world. As such realization grows and deepens, you may increasingly sense that you know certain things without knowing *how* you know them. You begin to have access to the knowledge that is common to the whole human race.[95]

As (↓) grows in strength, it brings with it a sort of nourishment that fosters an expansion of psychological space and a "lightness" of of being. This is the result of being an *open system* on the spiritual level; just as we take in food to sustain our body or truth to nourish the mind, this is a kind of metaphysical "daily bread" that feeds our "body of light." Other traits follow (or more generally, reappear), such as innocence, transparency, spontaneity, simplicity, and the automatic ability to distinguish truth from falsehood in areas of great depth, about which (k) thinkers necessarily live in permanent uncertainty. (This is the famous "B.S. detector" for discerning Bogus Spirituality from the Real Thing.) The birth of (¶) is truly a "new beginning," the "creation of a new person, who is as unique as the original creation of the world out of nothing."[96]

A primary purpose of (o) and (—) is to establish a "polarized" relationship between (¶) and O in order to heighten the "current" that courses between them. Under normal circumstances, a sort of metaphysical "gravitation" binds (•) to the objects of the senses and lower emotions. However, as we begin severing our habitual ties to (•), we may begin to find ourselves within the field of another attractor, which Merrell-Wolff associates with a feeling of spiritual "levitation."

Elsewhere he compares the process to that of a magnetic bar, which has the same amount of energy as an unmagnetized bar, except for the fact that in a magnet the energy is polarized between positive and negative, rather than dispersed equally throughout the bar. (•) is analogous to the unmagnetized bar, which forms a closed system, shut off from the higher field. Much of conventional religious ritual, as opaque as it may outwardly appear, is designed to "re-polarize" our otherwise dissipated spiritual magnet, so that we may become aware of the "current" that flows from O. Likewise, the cultivation of *humility* (because you are not *full* of your*self)* acts as as an attractor of (↓).

Being that we are made "in the image of O," perhaps it is no surprise that we have our own "magnetic center," that is, "an internal faculty that is drawn like a magnet toward inner truth." Not only can this "take the form of uncanny synchronicities and meetings with mysterious helpers at just the right time" but it can also "produce major tensions and upheavals in the soul" when its higher needs are not acknowledged.[97] I believe this is because, in a Hegelian sense, O is "infinitely restless," ceaselessly acting in and through us, generating dialectical tensions and upheavals that spur self-realization through the creation of higher unities. This creative destruction

> manifests itself perpetually in forms or aspects of itself which are only partial and provisional.... At the same time, nothing less than the self-complete whole can render the partial phase or provisional moment intelligible, for the truth is the whole; and it is this truth, immanent in the partial phase, which reveals its limited and finite character. It is this, likewise, that generates the internal contradiction in the finite, drives it into its opposite (what it lacks and excludes, what negates it) and forces it to unite with its other to produce a more complete representation of the whole in which the less adequate manifestations are sublated.[97]

* * *

Just as with physical birth, the birth of (¶) can and usually does bring complications and trials (not to mention the fact that the "birth" of a new mode of being necessarily involves the painful "death" of an old one). For example, once you begin to examine (•) in the light of day, you may be shocked to discover that the expensive formal education you secured for yourself was analogous to "burning" someone else's CD and using it to operate your own hard drive, filling you with a sort of stale, conventional understanding that blankets reality and dulls imaginative engagement with the world. At the same time, this may be accompanied by a feeling of fragmentation or empty anxiety, a sort of void zone, "no man's land," or nameless dread that will persist until a new kind of mental activity begins to replace what had previously been taken as thinking. The problem commonly encountered at this juncture is that, as (•) begins dying to ) (, the world will begin to lose much of its former allure, with nothing yet to replace it. This is because there appears to be a transitional "zone of equilibrium," or ( ), that persists after we have overcome the gravitational pull of ) (, but before we are drawn into the Divine Attractor, O. Schuon says that we inevitably come to a point where we are "no longer completely of this world, nor yet of the other," causing us to "call into question all the existential categories of which we were so to speak woven."[99] According to Damascene, a priest-monk of the mystical Eastern Orthodox tradition, "We know that our metanoia is genuine—that is, that a Divine change has really occurred in us—when we have a revulsion for what before appeared sweet to us."[100] From this perspective, ) ( may begin to look like a false, ugly, mindless, absurd and even "satanic" wilderness, an utterly ephemeral and counterfeit pseudo-reality of distractions and enticements (or "temptations").

In dealing with the arid bewilderness of ( ) and attempting to move beyond it, one is commonly confronted with a lengthy phase of trials, temptations, and problems emanating from the lower, "infrahuman" planes of consciousness. In the effort to alleviate what amounts to sense of a "hollowness," devoid of all meaning, it is easy to "jump start" (•) and obtain a spurious sense of life and meaning by pursuing these temptations, which are either of a hard-wired, sub-human physical and emotional nature, or compulsive little activities, goals, and wishes left over from our past life. Remember, even if you were to forcefully yank on the brake of the Karmic Express, its sheer momentum will continue to carry it down the tracks for a while, so that you shouldn't be surprised at the persistent weeds that continue to appear in your spiritual garden. These are the result of the karmic "seeds" you have mindlessly deposited throughout your life, each with a different life cycle (many seeds take years to sprout). They will continue to sprout up long after you have stopped being naughty, just as the good seeds you are currently planting will take some time to germinate and yield their sound fruit.

As such, this "bitter harvest" can also serve as a very useful phase of ongoing "purification," as you will be confronted with certain psychic patterns that had served as compulsive generators of spurious meaning and factitious being for (•). As a "consolation prize" for the absence of real freedom or truth in their lives, most people find themselves addicted to these counterfeit forms of power, freedom, love and truth, such as redundant wealth, sexual conquest, fame, worldly success, intellectualism, etc. Again, most of the activities (•)'s spend their lives passionately pursuing are ludicrously devoid of real meaning, significance, or satisfaction, and in the long run simply further entangle them in the mortal abyss of ) (. While most (•)'s are pestered by occasional glimpses of this blunt existential fact (-?!), one generally does not confront it head on until one has begun disentangling oneself from (•) and ) ( and begun looking at them in an objective, dispassionate way.

Not so much a no-man's land as "no-God land," what happens during ( ) is that aspects of ) ( will continue to resonate with anything inside of you that remains responsive and sympathetic to them. This provides you with an ideal opportunity to illuminate some of the sub-human affinities, formations, and parasites taking up space in your psyche. As a matter of fact, the ongoing effort to integrate these "abysses of truth"[101] will form much of the basis ("work") of your spiritual life. Unfortunately, it appears to be a truism that you will only be able to *stably* ascend as far as you have descended in the psyche, for the very reason that increased efforts "to spiritualize our nature call up from the depths of the subconscious a corresponding opposition, bringing to the surface slumbering and unsuspected atavisms of our lower animal nature and attachments."[102] Without question you may have peak experiences, blissful sensations and moments of illumination, but unless these higher contacts are harmoniously integrated with the rest of the psyche, they will be no more enduring than a weekend psilocybin adventure. Think of your mind as extending into infinity in both directions, so that you cannot colonize the space in one direction without colonizing the space on the opposite end. You may even have the frustrating experience of confronting the same basic problem again and again, but on each occasion of its appearance, having the opportunity to resolve it at a deeper level of the psyche. Here the process is really not that different from conventional psychotherapy, except that the spiritual "working through" process takes place in the space between you and a transcendent Subject instead of between you and a therapist.

One of the benefits of (—) is that it provides a technique for responding to these external vibrations with an internal silence instead of sympathetic resonance. With the development of (—), we may train ourselves to "underreact" to the ubiquitous pull of the world (what Christian mystics call *apatheia*), thereby depriving (•) of the emotional drama and other falsehoods it requires to maintain itself and remain metaphysically asleep. Perhaps it should be emphasized that this is not so much the absence of passion as its displacement toward a higher purpose: "The degree of passion for Truth is directly proportionate to the degree of dispassion for anything that stands in the way of realizing Truth."[103] It is not the same as "emptying the mind" and trying to have no thoughts, but raising awareness to a plane which is above the level where ordinary thought takes place. In so doing, we may "recognize that the thoughts are *not who we are,* and are not even our own, but are a foreign element, as it were."[104] Indeed, with persistence, we may begin to experience the ego and its desires as *external,* to such an extent that "what formerly seemed to be one's own thoughts or feelings start to seem more like the arguments of noisy neighbors...."[105]

* * *

History records many examples of avatars or "god men" who break into temporal history, and are said to be direct manifestations of O. As von Bruck writes, "Every authentic religious tradition reflects such a breakthrough in history."[106] Without getting into specific cases, we will symbolize these "I-Ammisaries" ⌽. Genuine ⌽'s are relatively few and far between, and are often the founders of great and not-so-great religions. While psychologists only diagnose individuals, ⌽'s generally diagnose *all of mankind,* and each of them offers a slightly different treatment for the pneumapathology they see. ⌽'s can act as intermediaries between O and (¶) through a sort of sympathetic resonance that attracts us to them (≈), thus amplifying our own (n). Not just "word made flesh," ⌽'s may also be thought of as the "end made middle" or "eternal made temporal." That is, they are the perfected end toward which history is flowing, made manifest in time. These "urgent telograms" from the office of the eschaton are dropped from on high, like spiritual depth-charges "into the ocean of history, in such a way that [their] waves ripple outward in time,"affecting us (and world events) even today.[107] Although their literal words may at times be contradictory or ambiguous, they themselves are the Truth.

Almost as helpful as ⌽'s are the authentic spiritual masters, ⦽'s, who have ascended the ladder of consciousness from our side of manifestation, and can therefore show us the the hidden passageway that leads out of ) (. These "fleshlights" also have a very powerful (≈) that can shatter (•), give (?!) and (-?!), or activate (¶). Being that ⦽'s are "instructed by O," only ⦽'s (among rank-and file humans) are "qualified to teach." That is, ⦽'s have an effect that transcends space and time, to such an extent that even meditating upon their written words can cause strong (?!) if we are properly (o) to them. Merrell-Wolff calls this phenomenon "induction," whereby contemplating or being in the presence of an ⌽ tends to arouse a corresponding level of consciousness, the repetition of which tends to "produce a condition such that the latent and indigenous Inner Light of the individual is aroused sympathetically into pulsation and thus, ultimately, 'catches on,' as it were, for Itself."[108] Needless to say, we should "seize every opportunity available to come within the sphere of Those who can serve as such Centers of induction."[109]

For one thing, as we progress along the path, we will be faced with tests, pop quizzes, hostile forces, sneak attacks, and a final exam. Again, strange as it may seem, your spiritual progress will arouse the attention of forces that wish to thwart you and maintain the cosmic status quo. Certainly you can "go it alone" if you choose to, but it can be of incalculable assistance to establish a relationship with someone "dead" or alive who has trod the narrow path, passed the tests, overcome the pressure of the world, and vanquished the demons. They will be more than happy to help you do the same if only you ask them. It's not as if they're busy doing something else.

* * *

To summarize: with persistent exercise of (+o) and (+ —), you should begin to sense a gravitational shift in your being, away from (•) and toward (¶). Once in a more stable relationship to O, the existence of a sort of dynamic, synergetic, spiritual metabolism becomes apparent, symbolized (↑↓). Whereas (•) is in open relationship with ) ( and other (•)'s, growth of (¶) takes place on a non-local vertical plane, creating an open system with O. The difference between <—(•)—> and (↑↓) may be thought of as the difference between a repetitive and recycled mind versus one that is ceaselessly renewed and refreshed by a hidden source of vitality—it is what the Bible refers to where it is written, "do not be conformed to this world, but be transformed by the renewing of your mind."[110] In the words of Sufi scholar, Sayyed Nasr, "The truth descends upon the mind like an eagle landing upon a mountain top or it gushes forth and inundates the mind like a deep well which has suddenly burst forth into a spring."[111]

In addition to feeling "lighter" and more transparent, (¶) has other attributes and qualities that can be easily detected, such as calmness, a sense of expanding psychological space, a quiet sort of unconditional joy that has nothing to do with mere physical pleasure, a newfound depth in everyday matters of living, and spontaneous tears that may communicate gratitude or just the "sweetness" of life. The world becomes impossibly rich, in that there is a sense of living from the inside-out, such that nothing is trivial; intrinsic meaning is constantly being spontaneously and effortlessly generated from within:

> there is only wonder, the realization that the world is too incredible, too meaningful for us. The existence of the world is the most unlikely, the most unbelievable fact.... In our unmitigated wonder, we are like spirits who have never been conscious of outside reality, and to whom the knowledge of the existence of the universe has been brought for the first time.[112]

This reversal and realignment of the self, as the center of our being shifts inward, is so distinct and transformative that it is referred to as conversion, illumination, or being "born again." It is a "totally new beginning... the creation of a new person, who is as unique as the original creation of the world out of nothing,"[113] the emergence "from a smaller limited world of existence into a larger world of being," from the individual to the cosmic.[114]

Once you have reached this point, you will have a literal "hunger" or yearning for O, so much so that life is felt to be meaningless in the absence of its vivifying presence. This is where the image of the spiritual renunciate comes from, the individual who looks like he is engaging in all kinds of austerities in exchange for a touch of the divine presence. In actuality the reverse is true—that is,

> the real Sage is anything but ascetic, however much He may appear to be so to the sensual man.... the Sage in his withdrawn life is not imposing hardship upon himself. Actually He faces more hardship moving in public places, administering large affairs, attending the ordinary amusements of men, etc., for in all this there is a distraction that makes the deeper enjoyment difficult....[115]

* * *

Ultimately, of course, (¶) is not our final spiritual destination, but rather, merely the "vehicle" we use to arrive there. In the end, it is another temporary identification that we will have to abandon on the way to a non-dual understanding of O. Here there are several grades lying between (¶) and O that needn't concern us at this point, at least not until we have established a beachhead in the world directly above ours. It is enough to say that, in the end, we discover that all along we were really ⊙, and that ⊙ and O are not-two.

## 4.3 Self-Directed Theognosis: Commanishads and Upanishalts for Extreme Seekers

> The ten commandments signify much more than simply a moral code of daily life. They signify, further.... the method and the conditions of fructification of the spiritual life, including all forms and degrees of practical esotericism.
>
> —Anonymous, *Meditations on the Tarot*

Perhaps it is difficult today for us to think of the Ten Commandments as state-of-the-art spiritual advice (rather than a somewhat antiquated list of coercive and inflexible rules). However, according to Bruteau, the Commandments are equally "statements of revelation and empowerment. They tell us what we need to do to fulfill ourselves....[116] Like all scripture, they have an exoteric as well as esoteric meaning. In the following section, we will analyze them from an esoteric standpoint, in order to demonstrate their contemporary relevance for extreme seekers and off-road aspirants. Rather than focusing on their excellent moral content, we will treat them more as "commanishads" or perhaps "upanishalts" that deal with the different ways we can either align with or separate ourselves from O.

By way of a preliminary discussion, note that the commandments were only revealed to Moses after he had achieved liberation from the bondage of Egypt, or ) (. This was followed by years of wandering in the desert, or a period of ( ). Moses then ascended (↑) Mount Sinai, where he had an encounter with O. Interestingly, Moses was only able to approach O through a sort of thick darkness, achieved through (o) and (—). (That is, (o) and (—) "darken" the lower realm in order to access the higher, just as the darkness of night is required to view the starry sky.) Finally, (n) was "distilled" from the "cloud of unknowing" that Moses had entered, and "became translated or concretized into human, earthly language" in the form of the Decalogue.[117] Thus, God's deuspensation begins with the uber-Commandment, "I am the Lord your God, who brought you out of the land of Egypt, out of the house of bondage" (*Exodus* 20:1). This statement has universal significance, for it is the promise of all religion: that we are not orphaned in the horizontal wasteland of material existence, and that faith in O can bring us out of ) ( and (•), into the open circle of a higher life.

*You shall have no other gods before O*

> In the heart of all things, of whatever there is in the universe, dwells the Lord.
>
> —Isha Upanishad[118]

The first commandment is prior to all the others, both literally and figuratively. In other words, there can be no gods before O, for the simple reason that O is the prior condition of there being anything at all: it is the Whole of which everything else, including us, is a part. However, if this is not recognized, humans will inevitably turn to a "false god" by default.

It is a truism that we cannot avoid worshipping something. Whether or not you believe you are religious, in point of fact, you must regard something as "ultimate," whether it be matter, mathematics, truth, love, or even your own mind. Nor can humans live without faith. The secular humanist, for example, has an inexplicable faith in human beings despite, say, the 100 million people killed and murdered as a result of human-derived secular ideologies in the twentieth century.

But spiritual energies can only reliably descend into a life that is theocentric. That is, only by orienting our selves to O may we "see through" the ever-changing world of appearances presented to our senses, and "Know that the Name of God is the Name of the Unity of All Being"[119] The first commandment is by no means "a prohibition against thinking and researching, but a command and a summons to orientate thought and research towards divine truth."[120] The truly radical idea of the unity of Reality is not a kind of dogmatic knowledge to be "possessed" like any other (k), but "a star in the heaven of eternal Being which shines, ever-radiating and inexhaustible, into the world of temporal existence."[121] Spiritual progress is only possible if we navigate our lives by the Light of our transcendent source and goal that abides in its Oneness outside space and time.

*Accept no substitutes: You shall not deify Ø and (k)*

> He alone is the reality. Wherefore, renouncing vain appearances, rejoice in him.
>
> —Isha Upanishad

In order to actually know O, we must renounce all forms of idolatry, not just as it pertains to material icons and relics, but with respect to our own thoughts and images. Behind all idolatry is a persistent (and ultimately parasitic) materialism that reduces O to some tangibly manifest idea or object that can be thought about in the ordinary way. However, we must rid ourselves of the graven thought-forms etched into our own neural networks and achieve a kind of "emptiness" in order to clear a space for (n). We must always bear in mind that the "leaves and branches" down here below have only sprouted from the Tree of Life whose invisible trunk and roots are aloft (otherwise, you become the existential sap).

Of course, mind parasites can "think," and it is easy to confuse our thoughts with theirs, whether they arise from within or have "washed ashore" from the alternatively noxious or vacuous tide of cultural/academic/media sheepthink. Therefore, do not put out a welcome mat for them, for they require your tacit cooperation to take up residence in your mind. The field of parasitic thought constitutes a sort of "screen" or barrier between you and O. In truth, it is the spiritual battlefront where most of the action in your practice will take place. Once parasitic thoughts take root, it is as if a needle

> full of poison, penetrates you and spreads the deadly substance throughout your body. Your spiritual world becomes contaminated and you are affected on a very deep, fundamental level.[121]

While the words "contamination" and "poison" may sound like polemic or hyperbole, there is no doubt that everything you allow into your mind has a psychic effect—TV, movies, music, news, friendships, and so on, and that there is an ongoing competition in your mind over whose thoughts you are going to think. (In fact, if you cannot smell the soul pollution in the airwaves with your "third noustril" (-?!), you may have more preliminary work to do in identifying (¶)). To avoid this kind of contamination, it is critical to consume the proper spiritual "food" and cut back on the graven mass media images that draw you down into the "tempest of the day." By and large, the major news media operate from what Aurobindo called the "vital mind," a narrow and restricted cognitive world with little intellectual, much less spiritual, content. They too "resonate" at a certain frequency that will awaken a sympathetic response in you if you are not vigilant. Once you begin observing the phenomenon, you will easily recognize it. It is especially pervasive in today's media climate, where multiple cable stations attempt to cram fifteen minutes of news into twenty-four hours of programming, thereby combining emotionalism and repetition to induce hypnosis and spiritual capitulation.

Therefore, you should "wean yourself from the momentary" (Kierkegaard) and make sure you give yourself each day your daily transubstantial bread. That is, instead of poring over the "news," which reinforces the mass hypnosis that binds you to the false and ephemeral, it is a good idea to make contact with O, to "wake" upon awakening each morning by reading the "eternals"—that is, timeless and perennial wisdom that has no expiration date. Doing so helps maintain the link to O, so that supernatural telograms and vertical recollections may be downloaded. (By all means avoid mass-market, pop-religion, self-help books by self-proclaimed teachers, as their graven thoughts, words and images will only lift [or lower] you to the dimension the writer inhabits.)

*You shall not use the names of O in vain*

> OM is Brahman. OM is all. He who meditates on OM attains to Brahman.
>
> —Taittiriya Upanishad

O has actually revealed Its name to human beings, in fact, several names, and each of these possesses a peculiar sort of power that should not be abused or allowed to become saturated. Among God's names are the "I AM" revealed to Moses, which is identical to the *OM tat sat* ("Brahman alone is") or *so ham* ("I am that") of Vedanta. "I AM" can only be uttered in the first person—in other words, only an "I" can affirm that "I AM."[123] In order to avoid saying the "I AM" in vain—that is, to no purpose—we must understand that this special name refers to the realm of eternal being (or Brahman), as in Jesus' paradoxical statement, "Before Abraham was, I am." Interestingly, God instructed Moses that the "I AM" was to stand "forever," as a way for all subsequent generations to remember Him (*Exodus* 3:15). Why "remember" and why "forever?" Because by meditating on the eternal "I AM," we are attempting vertical recollection of the divine-cosmic Self, which is outside the field of time—it is forever and always, the "axis Iamundi."

There are other ways to take the name of God in vain. One of the dictionary definitions of "vain" is "having no likelihood of fulfillment." As discussed in chapter 4.1, the very use of the word God can be problematic, as for most people it is so saturated with meaning that there is no space for it to be filled with experiential content. When the language of spirit is denatured in this manner, it makes it all the more difficult for us to "fulfill" our spiritual destiny.

And in truth, dear reader, the humble purpose of this book was to communicate a way to think about God and religion that would not be vain: the Word made fresh. Although the book may at times appear irreverent or perhaps even blasphemous, I have the highest regard for the traditional revelations of Christianity, Judaism, and Vedanta, but worry that their message will become increasingly "vain" if not reconciled with modernity and presented in such a way that their deep meaning can be appreciated by contemporary minds. Thus, although some may think I have "taken the name of the Lord in vain," quite the opposite is true.

*You shall observe the sabbath speed limit*

> When all the senses are stilled, when the mind is at rest, when the intellect wavers not—that, say the wise, is the highest state.
>
> —Katha Upanishad

If "observing the sabbath" meant nothing more than taking it easy on Saturday or Sunday, it would hardly have much spiritual significance. However, remembering the sabbath has to do with vertical recollection, and cultivating the leisure necessary to achieve it. Esoterically speaking, the sabbath refers to the OMnipresent "hole" in creation that allows for (↓) and (↑) to enter and leave the "kingdom of man." The hole is accessed (among other ways) through meditation, prayer, and contemplation, each of which involves a turning toward what is "behind" and "above" the external world and its nihilocracy of urgent nonsense. The restrictions and constraints associated with the sabbath are actually meant to achieve this purpose. One does not have to be an observant Jew to understand this principle. Since every day (indeed, every moment) is a microcosm of the whole "week" of creation, your daily meditation or prayer is a remembrance of the sabbath, an attempt to slow down, turn away from the lower world, and relax your way into the higher consciousness.

Keeping the sabbath holy is also etymologically linked to the idea of "wholeness" and healing. In our normal consciousness we are caught up in the stream of time, where the unity of reality is broken up into memories, hopes, regrets, goals, plans, wishes, an so on. But "sabbath consciousness" restores both our wholeness and the wholeness of creation. In truth, it is a "memoir of the future," a "return" to the unmanifest paradise of Eden. From this perspective, the world does not need to be "worked on," but is perfect as it is. It simply needs to be enjoyed.

In order to find one's way into this higher consciousness, it is necessary to observe the sabbath speed limit. While everyday life runs at its own jagged rhythm, the rhythm of eternity is much slower and more uniform, corresponding approximately to the rhythm of relaxed breathing. Take the rhythm of in-spiration and ex-piration literally, one as a gift of the higher Life, the other as an offering of the lower one. Let each inhalation infuse you with the divine substance, and let each exhalation be a surrender of (•), so that you may "dilate time" and live more in harmony with the leisurely and even blissful pace of eternity. (Someone once said that enlightenment is as simple as a completely relaxed and open body.)

Ultimately, the sabbath must be internalized, so that one has access to it at all times—so that the very real and tangible pressure of the world cannot sink its teeth into you and remake you in its image. This does not so much involve a suppression or mortification of the self as the creation of a "zone of silence" between self and world, like a portable monastery, so that you may be in but not of the world. Without this interior monastery, it is simply too difficult to maintain one's spiritual equilibrium when "coming down" into the world. A fruitful spiritual life is not consistent with an overly hurried, rushed, or frenzied lifestyle in which we are fully caught up in the world. Try to practice under-reacting to things, to create a buffer zone, a realm of inner space that is unaffected by the shifting fortunes and constant distractions of mundane existence that pull you *down* and *out*. In practicing this, you will eventually be able to feel when your reactions not only chain you to the world below, but you will be able to observe the local, conditioned "entity" that is summoned into being through your habitual responses. You will able to sense the wholeness conferred from above, and the fragmentation that is engendered below.

The paradox at the heart of the sabbath is that you must live your life as if you already abide in the eternal, because you do, but aspire to get there as if your life depended on it, because it does. The former is more difficult than the latter, because your worries, anxieties, plans and conventional aspirations trick you into thinking there is another way out. And if you believe that, you are doing the adversary's heavy lifting for him.

*You shall honor your supernatural father and mother*

> Never fail in respect to the sages.
> See the divine in your mother, father, [and] teacher...
>
> —Taittiriya Upanishad[124]

Here again, this directive makes little sense as a "commanishad" if taken too literally. Its real meaning is that, to the extent that our parents are worthy of honor, it is because the archetypes of our otherworldly Mother and Father are revealed to us through them. It also means not rebelling against the divine order in an adolescent manner, as so many jaded adult sophisticates do. Parents are deputized by the divine to act as transpersonal evolutionary agents on earth (which is why it is so tragic that so many parents fail to fulfill their primary obligation—to shepherd children to the real Parent—and even usurp God's power, becoming "bad gods" and "lording it over" the child—see below.) As discussed in chapter 3.2, it is now well understood that the growing mind of the young child is indistinguishable from the parental environment in which it is immersed, and that the love we receive in those early years will sustain us throughout the remainder of our lives. Once that love is established within us, it is our task to spread it horizontally, into the world, and vertically, back toward our eternal Parent.

Just because we have left our worldly parents, it doesn't mean that we require no additional spiritual parenting. Therefore, this commandment also applies to (↓)'s and (↑)'s, to the avatars and spiritual teachers whom we should respect and honor for the sometimes incredible sacrifices they have made for our benefit, and for the truly priceless wisdom and guidance, even salvation, they provide. Thanks to their hard work, the hole (and Whole) in creation is always accessible.

*You shall not murder truth, beauty or goodness*

> Worlds there are without suns, covered up with darkness. To these after death go the ignorant, slayers of the Self.
>
> —Isha Upanishad

On the one hand the commandment against murder is obvious, but it nevertheless has esoteric meaning. Murder involves the taking of innocent human life, but Tomberg relates it more generally to maintaining "a constructive attitude, which is essential to the spiritual life...."[125] Indeed, as discussed in chapter 3.1, true artistic creativity (which involves a kind of spiritual "fertility") is surely one of the hallmarks of the presence of Divine influence on the human mind, and we should take every opportunity to honor, preserve, and enjoy the inexhaustible storehouse of transcendental beauty—music, poetry, painting, literature—that has been bequeathed to us through this Divine-human partnership and fusion.

There are many ways to murder a soul without taking a life, and most soul murders are undoubtedly committed by those who are so spiritually damaged as to be functionally dead. Most psychic deadness occurs as a result of childhood trauma, and those whose souls have been murdered in childhood are probably responsible for most of the real trouble in the world. They constitute a kind of "walking dead" who are often compelled to "convert" others (including, of course, their own children) to their way of non-being. As described by Bollas, these vampiric individuals seem to go on "living" by

> transforming other selves into similarly killed ones, establishing a companionship of the dead.... [A] new being emerges, identified with the killing of what is good, the destruction of trust, love and reparation.

Bollas goes on to say that the individual who has endured such a psychic death attempts to overcome and "transcend" it by killing, "by sacrificing to the malignant gods that overlooked his childhood."[126]

If you are remotely sensitive, you can actually "feel" an undead individual draw the life out of you, not just "in person," but in the news media, movies, magazines, music. The sensation is roughly the reverse of (≈). At times you may be aware of a sense of psychological "jamming" (as in a disrupted radio broadcast), of "sucking" (as you feel your life force ebb away), projective identification (so that you feel either fragmented or unwillingly drawn into someone else's drama), or "flatlining" (so that you simply feel "dead" in their presence).

In addition to enjoining murder, the commandment implicitly proclaims the importance of promoting Life in everything we do, not just limiting ourselves to innocent human life, but to the Good, the True and the Beautiful as reflected in the human sphere. There is a culture of Life and a culture of death, and the cultural necropolis can only maintain itself by an increasingly brazen assault on Truth (as well as beauty and decency). It is therefore also a cult of hypnotic enslavement, for only the Truth can liberate us from this zone of illusion. In your day-to-day life, you must refrain from activities that advance the infrahuman tide of ugliness, barbarism, and falsehood in our endarkened world.

*You shall be faithful to your highest ideal*

> Let the truth of Brahman be taught only to those who... are devoted to him, and who are pure in heart.
>
> —Mundaka Upanishad

This upanishalt deals more abstractly with the concept of fidelity to one's highest ideals and aspirations, of keeping promises to our better self. Tomberg sees adultery more generally as another form of soul-murder, "of separating soul and body, whose union is the archetype of marriage."[127] Soul and body form a harmonious union, and separation of the two in any sphere of activity is the equivalent of murder, since the higher life is not possible without their union. In adhering to the soul in all we do, we remain "faithful" to the Good, the True, and the Beautiful. Interestingly, the Latin root of adultery is *adulterare,* meaning "corrupt." If we transfer our loyalty to that which corrupts us, we will soon discover that it clings to us as much as we adhere to it. Therefore, we must make a daily commitment to our transcendent purpose, turning away from "soulless" activities, interests, and relationships, and toward those things that enrich and deepen our being. (Again, depth itself is a dimension of soul, so that achieving it is a pathway toward recognition of the soul's existence. In the absence of the soul, the world has no depth—everything is of equal importance, or else simply has the importance our feelings attach to it.)

It is important to understand that this comanishalt is by no means urging some sort of dry, austere, or self-denying approach to life, or that it is somehow condemning pleasure. Quite the opposite. In fact, in Jewish tradition, it is said that the the first thing God will ask you upon your death is why you did not partake of all the permitted pleasures He so generously bestowed for your enjoyment. Similarly, for reasons we cannot explicate here, the real purpose of yoga became corrupted centuries ago, leading to a radical disjunction between the world of Spirit and the world of the senses. In actuality, it clearly states in the Upanishads that "In dark night live those for whom" the external world is the sole reality, and "Darker still for whom the world within alone is real." Again, O is both immanent (fully in the world) and transcendent (fully beyond it), and it is our task to be the image of That. In other words, the point is to "achieve immortality" in the world, not through mortification and withdrawal, but by the more difficult path of engagement with the world. We mustn't "ascend the mountain" with only our soul, nor should we descend into the world with only our body. For it is written, "those who combine action with meditation cross the sea of death through action and enter into immortality,"[128] that is, through the sacred union of soul and body, spirit and matter, God and Darwin, Adam and Evolution, Papurusha and Mamamaya.[129]

*You shall not lie, especially to yourself*

> This calm of the senses and the mind has been defined as yoga. He who attains it is freed from delusion.
>
> —Katha Upanishad

What mainly prevents O from working more productively in us is that (•)'s are habitual liars who constantly use the left brain to superficially "patch up" discontinuities in being. Until relatively recently, it was assumed that our deepest "humanness" must be located in the left brain, because that is where language and formal logic reside. But in fact, the flimsy veil of language is superimposed on a right brain that plays host to our deepest, truest sense of self, which extends into our limbic system, heart center, and other chakras. It is only half-ironic to suggest that "language was given to man to conceal his thoughts."[130]

Although we are constantly being "destabilized" by O as it catabolizes partial expressions of itself and spurs us to greater unities, language is quick to explain away these little "birthquakes," creating factitious wholes and spinning a false continuity. One cannot overestimate the importance of constructing a true autobiography, in which we are unified and balanced not just in psychic space, but in developmental time.[131] Again, the unconscious is the past in the present; to the extent that it is not recognized, remembered and integrated, we will be haunted, rebuked, vexed, thwarted and enticed by its split off, subterranean promptings. We all begin the spiritual path with an abundance of alibis, self-flattery, justification, psychic holes and envelopes, temporal discontinuities, and spatial disconnections. In order to become one with reality we must first become one with ourselves, which is further discussed in the context of the following section on desire, envy, and covetousness.

### *You can't get enough of what you don't really need*

When all the desires that surge in the heart
Are renounced, the mortal becomes immortal.

—Brihadaranyaka Upanishad[132]

The Buddha was correct in emphasizing that a major source of human suffering emanates from attachment to the phantom-forms known as our desires. That is, most people are mechanically pushed and pulled around by their passing desires, impulses, and passions. However we are not necessarily aware of our bondage, because when one of these false desires is being gratified, a transient sense of "freedom" is experienced (when in actuality, ungoverned desire is the opposite of freedom). Moreover, we soon fall under the influence of what Aurobindo called the "desiring mind," which serves to rationalize and justify our desires, as if indulging them will lead to any lasting peace or fulfillment. "Job one" of the desiring mind is to foster a kind of amnesia, so that we repeatedly fool ourselves into believing that fulfilling the next desire will finally break the cycle and bring us real contentment. Like the referred pain of a back injury felt in the knee or ankle, it serves to misinterpret the "pain" of separation from O and "refer" it to the outside world.[133]

An important step on the spiritual path is to discover the falsity of the desire-mode of being, and how it hypnotically roots us in the ephemeral. Here it is important to make a distinction between destructive and unnatural desires that have their source outside ourselves, and "appetite," which arises from the natural self. Spiritual impasses do not necessarily arise from "normal enjoyments and pleasures," but from "those things, peculiar to each one of us, which rule us and not we them...."[134] As Heschel put it, "We usually fail to discern between authentic and artificial needs," to such an extent that "more people die in the epidemics of needs than in the epidemics of disease."[135]

A rule of thumb with regard to distinguishing a healthy from a destructive desire is that, in the case of the latter, we inevitably attempt to get more pleasure out of its satisfaction than there really is in it. Natural appetites are fine, but trouble awaits those who try to wring more pleasure out of food, or sex, or money, or possessions, than there is in them. Natural appetites can be satiated, but the gods of abstract metaphysical desire require constant tribute. Here again one must bear in mind the limitlessness of the human imagination. Just as it opens out to infinity vertically, so too can envy and covetousness extend "horizontally" in a boundless way. Being that we are creatures of imagination, no matter how much we already possess, we can always imagine something more or better, which can cause endlessly unfulfilled striving and grasping on the horizontal plane.

The cultivation of humility and gratitude work to oppose covetousness and envy. This is why (¶)'s who feel least worthy of it receive the most (↓) (and vice versa). The Divine needs some elbow room to operate, and humility actually creates a psychic space that is as large as your ego, which is pretty large. Both humility and gratitude counteract unhinged desire, in that they cultivate an attitude of thankfulness for what we have, rather than preoccupation with what we don't even really need.

In short, to paraphrase Mouravieff, the spiritual life involves making the transition from mindlessly willing for that which we uncritically yearn, to consciously yearning for that which we actually want (which is enlightenment and liberation). In making this transition, it may appear as if our conventionally understood "horizontal" freedom is diminishing, which is true. However, the point is to exchange it for a more expansive "vertical" freedom that is relatively unconstrained by material circumstance, so that the old freedom is eventually regarded as a comparative enslavement. Once this begins to happen, our New World is so compelling that we simply no longer have the inclination to "keep up appearances" in the old world of appearances. Thus, the transcendence of envy and covetousness is better understood as a reward than an Ultimatum.

* * *

> For the more one discovers of God, the more one finds one has to learn. Every step in advance is a return to the beginning, and we shall not really know him as he is, until we have returned to our beginning, and learned to know him both as the beginning and end of our journey.
>
> —Bede Griffiths, *The Golden String*

> Everything is organically connected to everything else in such a way that nothing is irretrievably and only a thing. Everything is part of a single organism. And each part "remembers" how once it, too, was part of a great unity that had no parts.
>
> —Lawrence Kushner, *The River of Light*

Zzzzzz.... Nothing. BANG! Good God.... What, on earth?.... It's alive! Boo! Parasites! War, famine, plague, war, famine, plague.... Get out. Get in. Relax and float downstream. A hole in the river. Only drowning men can see it. Slipping away, softly now. Beneath the waves, ocean of being. Shhh, peaceful. So quiet in here. Don't touch that dial. BANG!

Sensei, you are tripping! Come back and finish book!

Right. Where were we? Ah yes, leaving the phenomenal world behind and rising into the gravitational field of our ultimate resting place.

Because we have two eyes that view the world from slightly different angles, we are able to perceive depth in our field of vision. But there is another, more subtle "eye" above those two, and when it becomes functional, we are able to envision an altogether more profound and spiritualized depth in our field of Being, not with the senses, but with the imagination that transcends them. In a way, everything looks the same. And yet everything is completely different, like an inverse image. But instead of a reversal of left and right, as when looking into a mirror, this is a reversal of top and bottom, inside and out, consciousness and matter, time and eternity: One Cosmos Under God, Indivisible, with Liberation and Joyousness for All.

Umm, care to elaborate?

In Book Two we discovered that Life is the meaning of matter, that to which matter points and converges upon. Similarly, in Book Three we found that Mind is the meaning of Life, that to which it points. And now we realize the meaning of our very existence, that to which it has always been pointing and converging upon: the Unity of Reality. Once again by turning the cosmos upside down, ultimate meaning is found not at its material base but its immaterial summit: "The [physical] universe is the final effect, but it is utterly dependent for its existence upon this base or foundation of Meaning," so that "the world of space and time, as it appears to our senses, is nothing but a sign and a symbol of a mystery which infinitely transcends it."[136] Instead of an unbridgeable gap between us and our Source, we now live in a transformational space, or plenitude, where order is prior to disorder, where the Whole confers significance on the part, and where Meaning is antecedent to all of Creation.

Just as biology was a loophole in material necessity, and the local self an escape from biological necessity, we discover in the non-local Self a commutation of our egoic death sentence, and with it a newfound realm of gratuitous freedom lying in a dimension of bottomless depth rather than in mere external liberty. Here again the experience is analogous to the stereoscopic images discussed above in Book Two. At once the scattered four-dimensional markings constituting our world dematerialize and "merge into one at a point beyond the horizon of ordinary thinking and experiencing."[137] As the local self is absorbed into the hyper-dimensional realm of Spirit, the "parts" of our being converge on the greater and more comprehensive entity that is their meaning, endowing us with an "integral knowledge in which the whole is known in every part and every part is seen to mirror the whole."[138] Only then do we find out what we are made of—a Divine substance that has returned to itSelf, even though it never really left in the first place.

The pneumapathology that caused us to impose our projections onto Reality and absolutize the finite is cured in the only way it can be, by realizing the non-local Whole which transcends the empirical world and, in a complementary way, by seeing that local appearance is nothing more than a mode of the infinite: "The Absolute is the relative, and the relative is the Absolute.... not two sides of one thing, but different standpoints, aspects, i.e., cognitive positions from which reality can be regarded."[139] We have overcome our endarkenment and achieved Cosmotheosis, the transcendence of the local self and union with the living God. This blessedly mixed marriage is not an undifferentiated oneness, nor a static twoness, but a dynamic twoness in Oneness experienced both outwardly and inwardly, in an ecstatic union of finite and Infinite. This is the Origin, or "cosmic center" that orders the world and confers its coherence, meaning, and direction (which are three aspects of the same phenomenon). As we "cross over to the other side" and our being rises close to the Origin, we

> do not see a sum of multiple truths nor a countless number of truths added to one another.... it is the whole that you see first; the whole presents itself in its entirety, in its wholeness, without division.... you have the simultaneous vision a whole that exists as a unity.[140]

Thus, in our properly oriented, right-side-up universe, its unity and coherence are experienced from the top-down, in light of our source and destiny in the non-local singularity at the end of the cosmic journey: the Self contains the universe, not vice versa. Swami Abhishiktananda, one of the first to recognize that traditional Christianity and Vedanta represented two views of the identical Truth, writes that

> There is no doubt that it is by becoming more and more aware of the Divine Presence in the secret place of our hearts that we become more and more aware of that same Divine Presence surrounding us on all sides.... Truly speaking there is no outside and no inside, no without and no within, in the mystery of God and in the Divine Presence.[141]

Similarly, Teilhard de Chardin, writes of a concretely experienced presence, "the consciousness of a deep-running, ontological, total current which embraced the whole universe in which I moved; and this consciousness continued to grow until it filled the whole horizon of my inner being." And Rabbi Lawrence Kushner proclaims that "the end is seeing for even one moment that the apparent multiplicity is in reality a unity," and that "all that is necessary to unify the worlds is to be aware that it is only by an illusion that they seem to be separate at all."[142]

In the end, we are no longer a scattered, fragmented multiplicity in futile pursuit of an ever-receding unity, but a Unity that comprehends and transcends the multiplicity of the cosmos. The universe, human history, and consciousness itself all achieve their fulfillment when any being passes into this Unity. Thus "the end of our spiritual destiny is really an origin...a return to the beginning, a veritable re-ascent of time back to its non-temporal source."[143] We are Ones again back by oursoph before the beginning, before old nobodaddy committed wholly matterimany and exhaled himself into a world of sorrow and ignorance. Back upin a timeless with the wonderfully weird Light with which everything was made, a Light no longer dispersed and refracted through so many banged-up and thunder-sundered images of the One. Back at the still point between the vertical and horizontal, where eternity pierces the present moment and we are unborn again. For the Latin word for end, *finis,* also means goal, while a uni-verse is "one turn," and with the realization of our nonlocal, trans-temporal Being, we have made one full turn and rearrived at the celestial resting place from which we set out, finding our serene and solitary Self in perhaps the last place we would have looked, just as we left it. The twice-born human being, after a difficult conception, long gestation, and painful delivery, at long last stands upon the empyrean shore expecting to take his place among the immortals, when, of all things, floating over the credenza, a little cherub with a nasty sword asks us to.... [144]

*Cloud-hidden, floating alongside the ancient celestial trail, bathed in the white radiance of ecstasy central. On your left is the dazzling abode of immortality, on your right is the shimmering gate of infinity.*

# AFTER THE END: *Cosmobliteration*

When a man attains to the stage of self-annihilation he can thus be said to have reached the world of the divine Nothingness. Emptied of selfhood his soul has now become attached to the true reality,the divine Nothingness.

—Lous Jacobs, *Hasidic Prayer*

I saw that genuine Recognition is simply a realization of Nothing, but a Nothing that is absolutely substantial and identical with the SELF.... From the relative point of view, the final step may be likened to a leap into Nothing. At once, that Nothing was resolved into utter Fullness, which in turn gave the relative world a dreamlike quality of utter unreality.

—Franklin Merrell-Wolff, *Experience and Philosophy*

Seamless, unnamable,
it returns to the realm of nothing....
Approach it and there is no beginning;
follow it and there is no end.

—Stephen Mitchell [Tr.], *Tao te Ching*

...leave our alter egos on the ego altar and surrender three forms of identification: I me mine.[1] Just follow your nous and you'll make amends meet in the muddle of the mount.[2] No kali-waiting though, either pay your deus or be nilled to a blank.[3] I am a jealous landlord, and the rend is now redeemable on your mirromortal garment.[4] So you want a luxury corps at pentecost?[5] What lieability has my only begotten sonofabang![6] Ahriman is his own

---

1. **Surrender** of ego identification is perhaps the key to spiritual development. It is an active offering, or sacrifice, not a passive acquiescence or subjection. "In point of fact, initiation is similar to death. It is the human being's return to his origin. To be initiated means learning how to die, i.e., how to reascend to the light." Magnien, in Tomberg, 1992, p. 236. "It is fantastic, this light which empties, annihilates, fulfills you; and how true the *Upanishads* are! But to discover them is a mortal blow, because you only discover them in yourself, on the other side of death! Abhishiktananda, 1989, p. 303.

2. Recall from the introduction that we are boring through the cosmic mountain from two sides, and trying to meet in the middle. But words can get muddled as we mount our ascent and our familiar "am" ends.

3. ***Kali:*** Hindu goddess of death. **Nilled to a blank:** "In the New Testament allegory there are two crucifixions: one relating to the soul's descent into matter, the generation of the physical form, and the other to it's ascent to spirit, or regeneration in the solar body." Pryse, 1965, p. 36. The second crucifixion mystically takes place in the brain, or "in the place called *Golgotha,* the skull." op cit, p. 86.

4. "Worn-out **garments** are shed by the body; Worn-out bodies are shed by the dweller within the body." Isherwood, 1987, p. 40. While we are the image of the divine, we also carry the image of our past deeds. This latter mirror "reflects clearly," so that "lying and subterfuge will be to no avail." When your case is called, "Be not frightened, tell no lies, face truth fearlessly." Leary, et al, p. 87.

5. ***Lux:*** light. ***Corps:*** body. According to the esoteric tradition, our material body is embedded in a subtle body of light, and one of the milestones of spiritual growth occurs when we begin to perceive or intuit this luxury corps. **Pentecost** refers to the descent of the Holy Spirit into Jesus' disciples after his Ascension, with the aim of completing the Incarnation.

6. **Liability:** "At the center of our being is a point of nothingness which... belongs

worst enemy![7] If your powers of deception were cleansed, then nothing would appear as it isn't. No body crosses the phoenix line lest it be repossessed and amortized. Some by fire, some by flood, but all buy the farm & bury the form.[8] No budget bardos here, but you can still have the tome of your life.[9] Just passover the deeds of your propriety and be a zetalight in its obit.[10] Yes, we accept ego death, so vacate your premises, abandon your conclusions, and cash in your chimps.[11] Eloha, that's a good bye for the Love that removes

---

entirely to God…" Merton, in Ware, 1977, p. 55. **Lie:** According to the esoteric tradition, man is an inveterate liar, both to himself and to others, mainly in order to create a factitious continuity in being. "We live in a world which is immersed in lies and moved by lies." Since spiritual growth involves the evolution toward truth and consciousness, we must at the very least try to give up our addiction to self-deception. Mouravieff, 1989, pp. 28-30. **Sonofabang:** "… the Son of God did not become a man, as one too often hears. He became man, with the result that our human nature as such has been infused… with the very nature of God." Cutsinger, 2003, p. xviii.

7. ***Ahriman:*** in Zoroastrianism,the spirit of darkness which is at war with the light. It is the spiritual task of humans to prevail over Ahriman, both within and without.

8. Suffering "is due to ignorance, because ignorance blocks the vision of Reality and causes… attachment to names and forms." Adiswarananda, 2003, p. 55

9. ***Bardo:*** the after-death (or ego-death) planes referred to in the *Tibetan Book of the Dead,* or *Bardo Thodol.* Passage through them is not always easy, and the experience is not necessarily purchased cheaply: "Strange sounds, weird sights and disturbed visions may occur. These can awe, frighten and terrify unless one is prepared." Leary, et al, p. 47. Making it through to the Clear Light may require "ecstatic self-sacrifice." op cit, p. 66.

10. **Tome, Obit:** "And another book was opened, which is the Book of Life. And the dead were judged according to their works, by things which were written in the books." *Revelation* 20:12. Esoterically understood, the Book of Life "contains only what is of eternal value, i.e., that which is worthy of living eternally—*that which is worthy of resurrection.*" Powell, 2002, p. 565. It is a sort of "spiritual double-entry accounting," in which the "sorting of the eternal from the transitory will take place." Smoley, 2002, pp. 70, 71.

11. **Ego death:** "You have to pay with whatever you have available as a preliminary

the sin and other scars (speaking allegheirically).[12]

Your Man in Nirvana reporting from the serene of the climb.[13] Before caterpultering your buddhafly, lotus pray: last rung in's a written gag, so your seenill grammar and gravidad be not be malapropriate for my laughty revelation.[14] Don't worry, it's just aphasia go through before the noesis in your head becomes real.[15] Ascent you a son, amen for a child's job![16] That's the New Man, we're just putting him on.[17] When you reach a ribald age, you can

---

to the total ego-annihilation that will be demanded. The Lord pays cash; but his currency does not go to the credit of any worldly bank account." Ashish, in Ginsburg, 2001, p. 100. According to Mouravieff, one generally must reach a state of "moral bankruptcy" before one can truly understand the false and factitious nature of the ego, and thereby begin to reorient oneself toward the Real.

12. ***Eloha*** is the singular of Elohim, one of the Hebrew names of God. Say **goodbye** to your ego and say hello to redemption. "The Love that moves the sun and other stars." Dante, *Paradiso.*

13. **Climb:** "Esoterically understood, the ladder is… the cosmic system whereby God, the One and transcendent, manifests as the many and the immanent, and the many return to God again." Smoley, 2002, p. 156.

14. "We must awaken the Kundalini, then slowly raise it from one **lotus** to another till the brain is reached." Vivekananda, in Adiswarananda, 2003, p. 185. "The ladder that leads to the Kingdom is hidden within you, and is found in your own soul. Dive into yourself and in your soul you will discover the **rungs** by which to ascend." St. Isaac the Syrian, quoted in Chariton, 1966, p. 164.

15. **Aphasia:** loss or impairment of the ability to use words. In this case, the loss is only temporary, as we develop our *noesis* and grow in our ability to describe what is beyond language.

16. "Whoever does not receive the kingdom of God like a **child** shall not enter it." "The little child does not 'work'—he plays. But how serious he is, i.e., concentrated, when he plays! His attention is still, complete and undivided… " Powell, 2002, p. 20.

17. We must "put off the old man with his deeds, and have to put on the **new man** who is renewed in knowledge according to the image of Him who created him…" *Colossians* 3:9.

grasp the wheel of this broken-down trancebardation. The experdition is nonsensuous (a punway round trip), so prepare for nonsense and theidiocy.[18] A theosaurus will help you circumnavigate, but you'll need a plastic exejesus for the darshan your vehicle, that's the crux of the master.[19]

Sheol is out, summa vacation in the pneumatosphere.[20] Freedom from freudom guaranteed, no ids, angst or lust. Unknowculate your brain, make your resurrections in advance, and don't forget your peaceport.[21] Allahboard! Blestoff from the errport and leave your apprehensions behind.[22] Kant take 'em with you, not on these

---

18. **Theodicy:** defense of God's essential goodness in view of the existence of evil.

19. Considerable **exegetical** plasticity is recommended to unpack all of the meanings in this text. ***Darshan:*** sanskrit for "seeing God."

20. The hebrew ***sheol*** refers to the underworld or abode of the dead who will presumably be resurrected at the end of time. If the main body of this book was an oppressive *summa,* then this part is the joyful vacation.

21. "The true knowledge of God appears then as an **unknowing,** because it takes place beyond the frontiers of any human capacity to understand or rationalize…. " Clement, 1993, p. 231. Unknowing is much more difficult to attain than knowing, because it is associated with the sacrifice and death of ego. "It is by unknowing that one may know Him who is above every possible object of knowledge." Lossky, 2002, p. 25. The gnostic gospel of Phillip avers that "Those who say they will die first and then rise are in error," and that disciples must "receive the **resurrection** while they live." Pagels, 1981, p. 14. The "coming to life of the nobler elements of man's nature, which were suppressed and slain during his earthly sojourn, is called 'the first resurrection.'" Pryse, 1965, p. 63. "Resurrection begins already here below…. The truest moments of our life, those lived in the invisible, have a resurrection flavour. Resurrection begins every time that a person, breaking free from conditionings, transfigures them." Clement, 1993, p. 268.

22. "Thoughts are like airplanes flying in the air. If you ignore them, there is no problem. If you pay attention to them, you create an **airport** inside your head and permit them to land." Elder Paisius, quoted in Damascene, 1999, p. 318.

preadamite planes and not beyond the necropolis of nine gates (what a give-up-the-ghost town!).[23] De-part and be-wholed like in them seers' dialogues of old, then aim your eros for the heart of the world.[24] In lama land, there's a wise old man, and he'll goose your nous for you.[25] If you chela you ego, you'll be una without a saguna in no time flat (that's spanskrit for adios).[26]

Cap'n Huxley speaking: here & now, boys, here & now.[27] Reverse worldward descent and cross the bridge of darkness to the father shore; on your left is the dazzling abode of immortality, on your right is the shimmering gate of infinity. Return your soul to its upright position and extinguish all (me)mories, we're in for a promised

---

23. ***Kant,*** of course, mistakenly believed that we had access only to the phenomena apprehended by our senses, not the noumenon, or ultimate reality, beyond them. "In meditation we gain spiritual altitude by rising to the higher **planes**," planes which are actually anterior to human consciousness. Adiswarananda, 2003, p. 15. In the Bhagavad Gita, the human body is referred to as the "city of **nine gates**," that is, eyes, ears, mouth, etc.

24. The Upanishads essentially consist of **dialogues** between seer and disciple. "Affix to the Upanishad, the bow incomparable, the sharp arrow of devotional worship; then, with mind absorbed and heart melted in love, draw the arrow and hit the mark—the imperishable Brahman." Isherwood, 1987, p. 64.

25. As you know by now, the ***nous*** is the divine faculty in humans.

26. ***Chela*** (pronounced key-la): spiritual disciple. ***Saguna*** brahman is God with attributes. **Adios:** "go with God."

27. Those familiar with Aldous Huxley's *Island* remember the birds who populated the island and reminded inhabitants to be "**here and now boys**, here and now."

28. Union with ultimate reality goes by different names in different traditions, including *nirvana,* knowledge of brahman, attaining the Kingdom of Heaven, obtaining the pearl of great price, and entering the **promised land**.

landing.[28] Touching down in shantitown, reset your chronescapes and preprayer for arrisall. Ananda chance to sat down at the last resort and enjoy a little moksha (or maybe some bhakti) at somarise.[29] Sorry, menyou have only one taste.[30] Whoops, where'd ego?[31]

O Death, you old mahahasamadhi, show us your secret mannascrypt, your Divine Cosmodeity.[32] Take us before & beyond this womentary maninfestation, reveal not the horizontal but our inmost upmost vertical bigending. Floating upstream alongside the ancient celestial trail, out from under the toilsome tablets of time, cast your I on the meager image below. So long. So short! Whoosh! there

---

29. ***Shanti*** is the spiritual "peace that passeth understanding." ***Ananda*** is the divine bliss and ***sat*** the pure Being associated with ***moksha,*** or spiritual liberation. ***Bhakti*** is heartfelt devotion to the personal god. ***Soma*** is a mysterious substance referred to in the Vedas that confers immortality upon those who drink it.

30. "This is the experience of **One Taste**, where every single thing and event in the Kosmos, high or low, sacred or profane, has the same taste, the same flavor, and the flavor is Divine." Wilber, 1999, p. 82.

31. The **ego** can only abide in the realm of duality, of "I not-I."

32. Non-dual experience of ultimate reality is called *samadhi,*" while ***mahasamadhi*** refers to "death," the "great *samadhi.*" "... [S]o-called 'natural' death is fundamentally a natural ecstasy—notably, a natural *samadhi,* where the transcendent Self accomplishes union with the personal self, in withdrawing it from the body and uniting with it" Powell, 2002, p. 289. "This is the meaning of **death:** the ultimate self-dedication to the divine.... For the pious man it is a privilege to die." Heschel, 1966, p. 296. Ma**haha**samadhi, **secret mannascrypt:** "Under the guise of a science of death," the Tibetan Book of the Dead "reveals the secret of life..." Govinda, quoted in Leary, et al, p. 30. "Like laughter, *satori* [enlightenment] is something that happens suddenly..." Watts, 1994, p. 170. Self-realization is in fact the punch line of the cosmic joke.

went your life.[33] Returning to the Oneself, borne again to the mysterious mamamatrix of our birthdeath, our winding binding river of light empties to the sea.[34] Cured of plurality, highdegger zen die velt, Ancient of Dasein: as it was in the beginning, same as it ever was... same as it ever was... same as it ever was.[35]

Holy creation, shabbatman, time to rejewvenate (oy!).[36] Off to see the River Man, starry-eyed and laugh-

---

33. **Floating upstream:** The discipline by which one realizes the inmost Self "may be compared to the turning back of the downward course of a swift river." Nikhilananda, Vol 1, p. 159. This is a stream that bears the disciple "irresistibly in one direction," where "the heavenly forces of attraction predominate and earthly gravitation works in him ever more weakly." Tomberg, 1992, p. 72. **Meager image:** "... there is, attainable to us, a consciousness...transcendent not only of ego, but of the Cosmos itself—against which the universe seems to stand out like a petty picture against an immeasurable background." Sri Aurobindo, 1970, p. 17. But for the average person, in the absence of spiritual awakening, "**Life** passes away from him almost unseen, swift as a ray of light, and man falls engulfed and still absent from himself." Mouravieff, 1989, p. 3.

34. **Birthdeath:** Pure consciousness "shining, void and inseparable from the great body of radiance, has no birth, nor death." Leary, et al, p. 117. "As the flowing **rivers** disappear in the sea, losing their name and form, thus a wise man, freed from name and form, goes to the divine person who is beyond all." Radhakrishnan, Vol 1, p. 236.

35. **Cured of plurality:** "The perception of multiplicity, resulting from ignorance, is the cause of all suffering." Nikhilananda, Vol 1, p. 168. In meditation, "as we gain higher and higher spiritual altitude this world of diversity becomes for us more and more unified, integrated, and divine." Adiswarananda, 2003, p. xvii. **Die velt,** i.e, G. welt or the world. **Dasein:** for Heidegger, human existence or determinate being. The **Ancient of Days** is a Biblical title for God. **Same as it ever was:** "Once human beings have attained salvation (moksha)... the temporal world comes to an end, even though it was without a beginning." von Bruck, 1991, p. 55.

36. **Shabbat:** "If your intellect is freed from all its enemies and attains its sabbath rest, it lives in another age, an age in which it contemplates things new and undecaying." From the *Philokalia,* quoted in Smoley, 2002, p. 62.

ing, cloud-hidden, who-, what-, why- & whereabouts unknown, bathed in the white radiance of ecstasy central.[37] In the garden misty wet with rain, eight miles high, far from the twisted reach of yestermorrow.[38] Insinuate! Now put down the apple and back away slowly, and nobody dies! Here, prior to thought, by the headwaters of the eternal, the fountain of innocence, the mind shoreless vast and still, absolved & absorbed in what is always the case, face to face in a sacred space. Let's blake for a vision: ah, remama when she satya down in a crystal daze, grazing in the grass, toddling loose & lazy beneath a diamond sky with both hands waving free, rumblin', bumblin', stumblin', we Could... Go... All... The... Way![39] Into the blisstic mystic, no you or I, nor reason wise, a boundless sea of flaming light, bright blazing fire and ecstatic cinder, Shiva, me tinders, count the stars in your eyes.[40] Fulfilled,

---

37. **Riverman:** "And he showed me a pure river of water of life, clear as crystal, proceeding from the throne of God..." *Revelation* 22:1.

38. **Yestermorrow:** "There was never a time when I did not exist.... Nor is there any future in which we shall cease to be." Isherwood, 1987, p. 39

39. ***Satya*** is truth.

40. "The **blazing** fire turns wood to ashes: The fire of knowledge turns all karma to ashes." Isherwood, 1987, p. 63. "At length the whole combustible material is purged of its own nature, and passes into the similitude and property of fire... [which] having subdued all and brought all into its own likeness, composes itself to a high peace and silence..." Hugh of St. Victor, in Cutsinger, 2003, p. 20. "... we are swallowed up above reason and without reason in the deep quiet of the Godhead..." John of Ruysbrook, in Cutsinger, 2003, p. 230. ***Shiva:*** One of the gods of the Hindu trinity, he is "sometimes called Kala, and identified with time," but also worshipped "through the phallic symbol, or linga." Nikhilananda, 1964, p. 380

filledfull, what a shakti ma system![41]

A church bell in the distance, chimes of freedom flashing. Spiraling outside in, past the viaduct of dreams, the seventh trumpet dissolving in shee-its! of sound, One Living Being, Life of All, A Love Supreme, take the coltrain to the old grooveyard, return to forever and begin a new corea.[42] The key to your soul, ignited in wonder. Om, now I remurmur![43] Only the limitless Permanent is here. Nothing is real. NOTHING is realized. That's it in a knotshall.[44] The nature of reality, the rapture of nihility, a peace

41. ***Shakti*** is a name of the divine mother, the consort and creative power of brahman.

42. "John **Coltrane** almost forces one to believe in the existence of a higher power, by whatever name, in whatever form.... Clearly—or so it seems to me—John Coltrane broke through to the other side. He found The Light: and, for a time he became The Light." Carlos Santana with Hal Miller, liner notes to "Live Trane," Pablo Records. "[T]he simple truth seems to be that all things, including past and future, exist in the present. Present Time as a kind of forever..." Chick Corea, liner notes to "The Chick Corea New Trio," Stretch Records. "Eternity is another word for unity. In it, past and future are not apart; here is everywhere, and now goes on forever." Heschel, 1966, p. 112.

43. "God's transcendent presence leaves a **murmur** of sanctity in the universe." Gelernter, 2002, p. 45. "... our mind is like a fantastic sea shell" from which "we hear a perpetual murmur from the waves beyond the shore." ibid.

44. **Knotshall:** "It is necessary to renounce both sense and all workings of reason,... both that which is and all that is not, in order to be able to attain in perfect ignorance to union with Him who transcends all being and all knowledge." Lossky, 2002, p. 27. "Those who have known the inmost Reality know also the nature of is and is not." Bhagavad Gita. "Each existence is, as it were, a knot tied in an infinite rope, which knot is made at birth and untied at death." Woodroffe, in Adhiswarananda, 2003, p. 138.

magnificent, silent-still, crystal clear, outshining mystery, Truth of truth, spirit hovering over the serene depth of eternity, Divine spark, breath of life! Do the monkey bone, do the shingaling, get your slack back & take a trip, slip, lose your grip, & turn a backover flip and say: not the god of the philosophers, not the god of the scholars!

What you was trying to find, you done had it all the time, only God is left, now left behind: we swallow our tale and the Word is finished.[45] So much straw anyway.[46] Adameve, Christomega, lifedeath, sundown, Sonarise: Finn again, we rejoyce: salvolution, evelation, ululu-woo-hoo-aluation![47] Only the blissful wave of the

45. "... there is something even beyond this **Word**. It is the silent vastness out of which everything, even the Word, arises. It neither exists nor does not exist." Smoley, 2002, p. 103.

46. At the end of his life Aquinas was vouchsafed a mystical experience that caused him to remark that "all I have written seems to me like **so much straw** compared with what I have seen and what has been revealed to me."

47. "How fortunate *is he who has realized the unity of the present moment with the* ***alpha*** and ***omega*** of existence." Nasr, 1993, p. 39. "In the formula, 'I am the *Alpha* and the *Omega*, the first and the last,' *alpha* is the symbol of the divine man, or Divinity, before his fall into matter; and *omega* is the symbol of the perfected man, who has passed through the cycle of reincarnation and regained the spiritual consciousness." Pryse, 1965, p. 30. There is a "rounding out of the circle in which the beginning and end, the primal Origin of the creation and the ultimate Consummation of the creative process, meet and touch in Christ... " Pieper, 1989, p. 188. Or, from a Jewish perspective, "It is really only one circle.... religious ritual intends to sustain the circle of return. Just as religious myth means to remember it.... For even the end of time and beginning of time are in some sense identical with one another." Kushner, 1977, pp. 78, 81.

immortal now, rising forth from the effulgent sea of existence. Inhere in here. Nunc stans, everybody else siddhi.[48] Perfect equilibrium, symmetry, tranquility. What it's like to be dead, the Vertical Church of Perpetual Slack.[49] And you shall never grow so old again (or dopple, your monkey back).[50]

Cosmonight, cosmonaught (so be it). All-embracing secret center of depth, the meaning of Within, the realization of Being, O first and last truth of Self, knowing without knowledge all that can be unKnown: existence to the end of the beginning.[51] Rishi does it. Take your shoes off &

---

48. ***Nunc stans:*** the still point of the eternal now. ***Siddhi:*** spiritual powers on the vertical plane to which we have access through the *nunc stans.*

49. "… contemplation relates to the **vertical**…. There are, in fact two types of memory: 'horizontal memory,' which renders the past present, and 'vertical memory,' which renders that which is above as present below…" Powell, 2002, p. 44; Humans, of course, lost their slack with the fall, but slack retrieval is possible. "The principle of struggle or toil (effort) only came into play after the Fall… the Fall can be overcome and… the way of human evolution can return to that of mystical union instead of struggle…" Powell, 2002, p. 66.

50. "… for we have sinned and grown **old**, and our father is younger than we." Chesterton, 1995, p. 66. The material body is a lower-dimensional double or **dopple** of the immaterial soul. Being material, it is subject to aging and death. You have been warned, my primate friend.

51. **Meaning of within:** "… the mystery of the inner and the outer is perhaps the linchpin of the universe…" Smoley, 2002, p. 118. "… in ceasing thus to to see or to know we may learn to know that which is beyond all perception and understanding…" St. Dionysios the Areopagite, in Cutsinger, 2003, p.225.

set a spell.[52] Relux & call it a deity.[53] 'Disbeaware we disappear (who hesychasts is lost).[54] Signless, featureless, void of forms, night busted open, a blank pure consciousness obliterates the mind. A drop embraced by the sea held within the drop.[55] Unborn body of the bodiless one, dark rays shining from a midnight sun, your phase before you were bearthed & begaialed, empty tomb of a deathless child.[56]

Shut my mouth! Enough bull, it's ineffable. Stop prehending. The blankety-blank hole affear is over: not a thought but the absence of thought, luminous presence, all-negating Void Supreme, immobile, self-rapt, timeless, solitary, the El Supremo at the top of the stairs, a Starman waiting in the Sky, tip-toppermost of the poppermost

---

52. To paraphrase Ram Dass, "death is like taking off a tight pair of shoes."

53. "... we begin with leisure, the relaxing of the sense of time.... most of the spiritual life is really a matter of relaxing... of letting go, ceasing to cling, ceasing to insist on our way, ceasing to tense ourselves up for this or against that..." Bruteau, 1993, p. 24.

54. In Orthodox Christianity, a ***Hesychast*** (from the Greek for "hermit") is one who withdraws from the world in order to contemplate God in silence.

55. "Anyone can understand how the **drop** can blend with the ocean. But how the ocean can be contained within the drop is a very great mystery." Ginsburg, 2001, p. 78. "In other words, the wave is the sea, and the seabed, and the horizon... and the All..." Oakes, 1994, p. 195.

56. Buddha consciousness is "the Unbecome, the **Unborn**, the Unmade, the Unformed..." Leary, et al, p. 36. In Zen, it is sometimes referred to as "your face before you were born." "When the external world disappears and the mind itself ceases to function, as in the deepest contemplation of the mystics, Brahman shines directly, without the help of any medium." Nikhilananda, Vol 1, p. 294.

Man on a Flaming Pie. Unfearing, allahpeering darkness within darkness, benighting the way brightly. Wu, full frontal nullity![57] The body, an ephemeral harmelody of adams forged from within stars, our life, a fugitive dream within the deathless, sleeping what's-His-G-d-name.[58]

Mea kalpa, I'm a laya![59] Don't blame me if I shunya.[60] You're headed straight for the Orifice of the Divine Principle.[61] Know you're nought, you naughty boy. I am? That![62] O me ga! I can explain everything.[63] I know this place. Been here before. Where we started. No it

---

57. ***Wu*** is a Taoist concept meaning "emptiness" or "nothingness." "The nature of Being is said to be nothingness because Being is absolutely complete, in need of nothing, conscious of no wants." Damasene, 1999, p. 241. However, some interpret *wu* as the "minim point" or "hub of the universe," analogous to the smallest point where the spokes of a wheel converge at the center, the last "something" holding up the universe before there is "nothing." Fr. Seraphim Rose, in Damasene, p. 484.

58. "We are collectively one great being, the Son of God, which is known in its fallen state as Adam and in its unified state as Christ." Smoley, 2002, p. 96.

59. "This is, then, a story without beginning or end since the Self breathes out and in, loses itself and finds itself, for always and always, and these periods are sometimes known as its days and nights—each day and each night lasting for a ***kalpa***..." (Watts, 1968, p. 97). ***Laya:*** dissolution of the individual self into the infinite.

60. ***Shunya:*** " the void, the Nothing which is All." Dalal, p. 415.

61. "... the eternal **principle** of all Being lives whole and undivided in each one of us." Deussen, 1995, p. 152.

62. "The knower of Brahman becomes Brahman." Nikhilanda, Vol 1, p. 255.

63. "... when one knows Brahman one knows the universe." Nikhilanda, Vol 1, p. 287. "The initiate is not someone who knows **everything.** He is a person who bears the truth within a deeper level of his consciousness, not as an intellectual system, but rather as a level in his being... " Powell, 2002, p. 221.

this time.[64] A huge mythunderstanding. The word made fresh. Non-friction. Telos when it's over. Now. It is accomplished.[65] End of the piper trail. You're on your own. Above my head, beyond my ken. Thy wilber done. I'm unqualified.[66] Lost my aperture.[67] Just apophatic nonentity.[68] Cut me down to sighs. Too old, older than Abraham, too young, young as a babe's I AM.[69] Brahmasmi the Truth.[70] The whole Truth. Nothing but the Truth. So ham, me God.[71] We'll meet again. Up ahead, 'round the bend. The circle unbroken, by and by. A Divine child, a godsend, a touch of infanity, a bloomin' yes.

---

64. "And the end of all our exploring; Will be to arrive where we started; And know the place for the first time." T.S. Eliot, Little Gidding.

65. The last words of Jesus, **"It is accomplished,"** have an esoteric, teleological significance, conveying the idea that "He has initiated (perfected) himself," or achieved the end of the cosmic drama. Pryse, 1965, p. 57.

66. In non-dual, **"unqualified"** brahman, God and self are One, or "not-two," to be exact.

67. Your short life is like the **aperture** of a camera that quickly opens and closes shut. With the bit of light given to you, you must go into your darkroom and try to develop a pneumagraph of the Whole.

68. **Apophatic** or "negative theology" is theology by negations, or by unknowing.

69. Before **Abraham** was, I am." *John* 8:58. ***Aham asmi:*** I am. "There is only the eternal moment in which I AM. This name which Jesus applies to himself in St John is… the key to his mystery. And it is the discovery of this Name (in the depth of my own 'I AM') that is truly Salvation for each of us." Abhishiktananda, 1989, p. 342.

70. ***Aham brahmasmi:*** I am brahman.

71. ***So ham*** is sanskrit for "I am that," meaning that Atman (the individual self) is identical to Brahman (the cosmic self).

Words fall. But one clings. Still. You don't say. Emptiness! drowning the soul in its everlasting peace, an eternal zero, a spaceless and placeless infinite, supremely real and solely real, our common source without center or circumference, no place, no body, no thing, or not two things, anyway: blissfully floating before the fleeting flickering universe, stork naked in brahma daynight, worshiping in oneder in a weecosmic womb with a pew, it is finally...[72]

---

72. "[I}t is a **zero** which is All or an indefinable Infinite which appears to the mind a blank, because mind grasps only finite constructions..." Sri Aurobindo, 1970, p. 28. "[T]he 'I' that is the true Son of God, is totally free and unconditioned; it is not encumbered by being bound to a particular body in a particular time and place; it does not suffer the impediments of specificity." Smoley, 2002, p. 130. "The Thing-in-itself can be perceived—but only by one who, in himself, is **nothing**." Huxley, 1970, p. 224. "When, at the end of a time cycle, or kalpa, the universe is dissolved, it passes into a state of potentiality, a seed-state, and thus awaits its next creation.... The phase of expression is called by Sri Krishna, 'the day of Brahma,' and the phase of potentiality 'the night of Brahma.'" Isherwood, 1987, p. 169. **Finally:** " The whole universe shrivels into nothingness, though it has limitless possibilities which will be roused into activity by the divine overlord, the spirit of God floating on the waters." Radhakrishnan, 1939, p. 126. That is, "The world is not something which appears and is gone forever. It reappears eternally. It is not the first and only one produced, but merely one of a beginningless and endless series.... Here is the pulsing movement of the systole and diastole of the Cosmic Heart as Divine Power." Woodroffe, 2001, p. 49. "All comes from Nothing and returns to Nothing. But the *Nothing-Everything* is the Great Mystery, the Arcana of arcanas, before which reason confesses its impotence." Oswald Wirth, quoted in Waldo-Schwartz, 1975, p. 14. "One becomes conscious of a vast arc, curving from the divine source to oneself, which corresponds to the question, Where do I come from? while at the same time a line curving from oneself to Him corresponds to the question, Where am I going? And within this great circle... each person can discover the special lines of his own direction..." Steinsaltz, 1980, p. 148. "Thus the self is transformed from the 'substance' of ego to the Nothingness that preceeds all (new) creation and is intimately connected to the highest orders of the Holy One of Being, also called the Ayn Sof, the One of no end..." Kushner, 1990, p. 131.

# AUTOBIBLIOGRAPHY & SELF-REFERENCES

This book began with a vision of how the story of the cosmos might be told in one continuous narrative. Originally, it had the working title of "Singularities," the idea being that the sudden creation of the cosmos out of nothing—the big bang—was followed by several more, equally sudden ontological mutations, specifically, the appearances of Life, Mind, and spiritual Realization. Because the book began only as a "vision," I really had no idea whether or not I would be able to transpersonalate the vision onto paper. But at each step along the way I encountered the right thinker at the right time, to either reinforce my own ideas or help provide solutions to riddles I had been puzzling over, some of them for years.

While I have cited a great many references, it didn't start that way. Rather, I went to my personal library and pulled from the shelf every book, irrespective of the field or topic, that contained truths without which any vision of the whole of reality would be, in my view, incomplete. These included works by Alfred North Whitehead and Michael Polanyi (philosophy), Hans Jonas and later Robert Rosen (philosophy of biology), Weston LaBarre (psychoanalytic anthropology), W. R. Bion, R. D. Fairbairn and James Grotstein (psychoanalysis), Allan Schore and Daniel Siegal (attachment theory and developmental affective neuroscience), Gil Bailie (his Violence Unveiled), Sri Aurobindo, Sri Krishna Prem, and Franklin Merrell Wolff (neo-Vedantic philosophy), and Pierre Teilhard de Chardin (all-around utility man). I removed all of these (and a few other) books and placed them on the floor in no particular pattern, staring at them while waiting for them to tell me how they were connected to one another.

The problem was how to unify the "truths" from these seemingly unrelated fields into a more generalized "Truth" applying to all of them, without reducing one to the other. Surely there is great truth in modern cosmology, Darwinian evolution, and developmental neuroscience. However, at the same time, my years of practicing the yoga of Sri Aurobindo had revealed other truths that, outwardly at least, seemed to exist on another plane, separate from material, biological, or psychological truths.[1] In gazing at my books, it gradually occurred to me that they were obviously linked together by an evolutionary thread, in the sense that the cosmos was here prior to the biosphere, the biosphere prior to the emergence of self-aware minds, and minds prior to the discovery of non-dual awareness of mystical union. Indeed, this observation would qualify as a banality of the first order.

However, if my experiences with yoga revealed Truth—a point on which I increasingly had no doubt—then the question was not to explain how matter eventually came alive, started thinking, and realized its essential divinity. Rather, since I was convinced of the Truth of yogic realization, the central question became, what must the cosmos be like for such a transcendent experience to be possible? A related issue for me was the importance of envisioning the largest possible world consistent with spiritual reality, rather than artificially narrowing the world down in order to somehow wedge in a traditional notion of God. Frankly, I do not believe that religion will be able to survive (at least on a large scale) unless it is able to present a vision in which scientific discoveries and developments easily find their place. Religion must be able to "contain" science, not vice versa—God cannot be an afterthought, but the beforethought.

But I wasn't always so sure of the reality of Spirit, so the book reflects this. In fact, in a certain way, the book reflects the gradual awakening of someone pondering the cosmos, first trying to look for evidence of God outside, in physics and biology. This is what the "design theorists" do, and to a certain extent, their research is unassailable. Or, to be perfectly accurate, it is assailable, but not capable of being overturned except in the minds of people who already have an *a priori* commitment to a materialistic paradigm. But for the same reason, the design theorists' proof of a creator is generally only convincing to those who are already inclined to believe it. And even if you do believe it, you are not the least bit transformed by it. Rather, you are the same person you were prior to believing it, and still have to undertake some sort of spiritual practice in order to actually confirm what the "design" of the universe points toward. "Reading" the cosmic book is not the same as "understanding" it. Analogously, you could look at a musical score and be convinced that it demonstrated a high degree of order, but that is hardly the same as hearing music. Merely "proving" the existence of God is about as useful as proving the existence of Johnny Cash. It is one thing to say that Cash existed, another thing altogether to have had one's soul personally touched by his uncanny musical genius. As put by the great theologian Hans Urs von Balthasar, who felt that a well-developed aesthetic sense was the quickest route to actually perceiving the divine presence both in scripture and in the world,

> No explanations can help those who do not see beauty; no "proof of the existence of God" can help those who cannot see what is manifest in the world; no apologetic can be of any use to the one for whom the truth that radiates from the center of theology is not already evident.[2]

With regard to both art and nature, "Visible form not only 'points' to an invisible, unfathomable mystery; form is the apparition of this mystery…." [3]

So the book began in that manner, trying to use physics and Western philosophy to demonstrate the necessity of a cosmic intelligence of some sort behind the incredible order of the cosmos. But in doing this, I was gradually led to metaphysical conclusions that were more "general" and encompassing than physics. I was first alerted to the importance of part-and-whole in the works of Kafatos and Nadeau, especially *The Conscious Universe* and *The Non-local Universe.*[4] Upon reading these books, it dawned on me that the concept of "wholeness" was exactly what I was looking for in terms of a principle that allows spiritual experience to make sense. In other words, if spiritual realization discloses ultimate reality—which it does—then the universe *must* be a non-local whole.

Book Two was in many respects the most challenging to write, for the simple reason that there is so little literature that actually bears on the problem of Life, as opposed to biology. I was very much inspired by certain passages in Hans Jonas' *The Phenomenon of Life,* but beyond him and Bergson, I was initially unable to locate any other works that bore on the radical implications of the presence of life in the cosmos. A huge assist was provided by the brilliant Robert Rosen, whose *Life Itself* and *Essays on Life Itself* give scientific credence to the idea that physics cannot account for life because biology is more general than physics, because semantics cannot be reduced to syntax, and because to try to pull the subjective into the objective is to paint oneself into a metaphysical corner from which there is no escape.

Also very helpful in Book Two was Errol Harris, whose many works cohere around the idea that it is not possible to make a nontrivial statement about the universe without certain metaphysical assumptions, usually fallacious or self-refuting ones. If we take physics seriously, then the universe is indeed a whole governed by dialectical logic, not a bunch of separate, atomistic parts governed by formal logic. Harris' ideas provided further support for how and why life, mind, and spiritual experience are "built in" to our universe.

Being that I am a psychologist, Book Three was the easiest to write, even though it may contain some controversial ideas and conclusions. This is not because I am controversial, but because the truth is. Psychology, like most of the other humanities, has become highly politicized, vulnerable as it is to crass politicization and to the noxious practice of "deconstruction" by various interest groups often interested in normalizing abnormality. There is no question in my mind that the unification of, among other things, developmental psychoanalysis, attachment theory, and affective neuroscience (as in the cutting edge works of Allan Schore) represents the deepest and most fruitful approach we have ever had for the understanding of normal and abnormal human development. Applying these important ideas to history and prehistory is admittedly somewhat speculative, but I believe the evidence demands an explanation of just why human beings were (and are) so persistently irrational, self-defeating, narrow-minded, violent, and cruel. Those who posit that we are "fallen" beings are surely ahead of the historians and cultural relativists (at least in terms of wisdom), but I believe we need an explanatory mechanism that accounts for our "fall"—in other words, something that mediates between our divine and fallen states, and explains in scientific terms why humans are such persistent underachievers.

When I started this project, Book Four was the one I wasn't sure would be possible. The idea for a more flexible and universal religious language initially came to me many years ago, some time after absorbing the psychoanalytic writings of W. R. Bion. Bion is an interesting case, for even most psychoanalysts (who make up a small subset of psychologists and psychiatrists) frankly do not understand him, much less agree with him. However, those who do understand him tend to become "disciples," not only regarding him as perhaps the greatest psychologist, but a first rate philosopher and unorthodox mystic as well. In noting all of the diverse, seemingly contradictory theories that abound in psychology, one of the things Bion attempted to do was create an abstract, "unsaturated" language for the "communication and storage" of psychoanalytic observations and experiences. This gave me the idea that perhaps I could attempt the same thing with religion, since it too is a Tower of Babel riven by innumerable faiths, theories, rumors, wishes, experiences, and observations that cannot easily be reconciled.

One thing Bion always emphasized was that psychoanalytic theories could not be understood merely with the intellect, but had to be realized. This made his ideas very compatible with Eastern religious approaches (including Eastern Christianity), which teach one how to experience the truth of the doctrine, rather than how to merely know it with the intellect. Most academic theologians (and psychologists, for that matter) know what they are talking about, but have not necessarily experienced what they are talking about. On the other hand, many people have all kinds of spiritual experiences, but lack any way to clearly communicate them or to fit them into a more general framework. Unlike my competitors, my unsaturated spiritual language allows for a maximum of abstraction and realization.

Other material in Book Four was initially framed around personal experiences with the "integral yoga" of Sri Aurobindo. Later I was able to flesh this out with realizations from other traditions, but special mention should go to Richard Smoley's *Esoteric Christianity,* which jump-started an extremely fruitful strand that led to Robin Amis, Boris Mouravieff, and the incomparable Meditations on the Tarot. Other spiritual thinkers who were particularly helpful were Sri Krishna Prem, S. Radhakrishnan, Satprem, Cutsinger, Kushner, and von Bruck, whose *The Unity of Reality* provides such a well-lit path between Vedanta and esoteric Christianity.

One point about Ken Wilber, who is without question the most important theorist of transpersonal psychology and integral spirituality in general. His work was a tremendous influence on my earlier intellectual development, and to a large extent one leaves his imposing corpus asking the question, "What's left to say?" In order to have any thoughts of my own, I had to make him sort of an "unfluence," even though no human who deserves the name should be unfamiliar with his work. My only quibble with it is that my own experience has not been as neat and orderly as some of his models suggest, and I have tried to speak of spiritual matters almost exclusively from personal experience. Strange as it may seem, I do not like to speculate.

Now to the alpha and omega of the book, the Joycean prologue and epilogue. When I initially wrote the prologue, I thought that it was pretty much self-explanatory. Moreover, I didn't want to give away too much, for the same reason that a joke isn't funny if you have to explain it. However, the esteemed Dr. Ryan suggested that I include some footnotes in order to provide the flailing reader with a rudimentary linguistic life jacket. The footnotes are not meant to be exhaustive, and it is my hope that my creation myth will support other interpretations that I haven't thought of. It is obviously influenced by an esoteric reading of *Genesis* (both Christian and Kabbalistic), along with the Upanishads, Tao te Ching, Sri Aurobindo's epic cosmic poem, Savitri, and other scriptural flotsam and jetsam.

As is generally true of the prologue, the epilogue largely consists of, dare I say, "channeled" material, in the sense that many of these neologisms and homophones just popped into my head at odd moments once I set my mind to the task of trying to describe the indescribable in a Joycean, punning manner. However, not everything was entirely original. Having digested *Finnegans Wake* so many years ago, it is possible that some of these words were not so much plagiarized as cannibalized and rewordgitated. For example, I would be surprised if Joyce did not come up with "allegheirically," "deidreaming," "absurcular," or "laughty."[5] Also, being a baby-boomer who was once obsessed with the music of my youth, one of my ideas was to use that music as an initial "template" in order to "riff" off of. Much of the music of the 1960s was created in a spirit of conveying or celebrating non-ordinary experience (to put it euphemistically), so I thought that perhaps it might provide a sort of "familiar" language of transcendence, mainly in the epilogue. Here again, I don't know how much of this to "give away," because it may take the fun out of trying to decipher it. But if you must know some of the details, here's a footnote.[6]

I could not have committed this book without being aided and abetted by the above authors, thinkers, theographers and pneumatologists. I am particularly grateful to Sri Aurobindo and his spiritual collaborator known as "The Mother," who, although no longer technically living, are apparently able to… oh, never mind. That's a story for another book.

Special thanks also go to Dr. Raymond and Mrs. Jan Friedman, to Dr. Matthew Ryan, and to Gary Golter, Debbie Murray, and the rest of the staff at the Barrington Center, who have always provided the kind of genial and supportive work environment that makes my secret life possible. Special thanks as well to Dr. James Grotstein for many realizations in O, and to Richard Smoley for his valuable feedback.

I would also like to take the opportunity to thank my father and mother-in-law, Richard and Sue Morris, not only for their kindness and generosity, but for providing such wonderful role models for how to age without growing old, come what may. This book was written in the shadow of a great family tragedy, and for this reason is dedicated to the memory of my dear sister-in-law, KT, to my brother-in-law, Steve, and to my nephew, Aiden. And, of course, to Leslie, without whom. Period.

Finally, I owe a great debt of gratitude to my agent, John White, who was determined to publish this book even if he and I were the only ones who got the jokes.

# Endnotes

**Cosmonaught,** notes 1-46 as footnotes, pages 5-23

**Book 1,** pages 25-57

[1] Bear in mind, however, that if the universe has no purpose, then neither will anything you do instead of reading this book. Therefore, you might as well read the book.

[2] Descriptions I once heard in an Alan Watts lecture.

[3] Nerd alert: these numbers keep changing all the time, so please don't hold me to them. Unlike those ever-changing figures, I am trying to make a point that has no "expiration date."

[4] Molnar, 1996, p. 12.

[5] A phrase coined by W. R. Bion.

[6] Taylor, 1975, p. 68.

[7] Wright, 2000, p. 333.

[8] Einstein, 1931, p. 40.

[9] Sheldrake, in Abraham, et al., 1992, p. 4.

[10] W. Smith, 1984, pp. 14, 15.

[11] Jaki, 1999, p. 53.

[12] Overman, 1997, p. 192.

[13] Quoted in Davies, 1992, p. 152.

[14] Jonathan Lear, quoted in Denton, 1998, p. 260

[15] Harris, 2000, p. 159.

[16] Hawking, 1988, p. 291.

[17] Ward, 1996, p. 108.

[18] Ward, 1996, p. 18.

[19] Darling, 1993.

[20] Smolin, 1997, p. 37.

[21] Smolin, 1997, p. 45.

[22] Penrose, in Ward, 1996, p. 44.

[23] Ward, 1996, p. 113.

[24] Ward, 1996, p. 115.

[25] "The existence of God either has a probability of zero or of one (absolute certainty)…." Ward, 1996, p. 116.

[26] Compiled from various sources, including Overman (1997), Darling (1993), Ward (1996), and Smolin (1997).

[27] Smolin, 1997, p. 44.

[28] Quoted in Jammer, 1999, p. 48.

[29] Quoted in Darling, 1993, p, 123.

[30] Magee, 1999, p. 379.

[31] Quoted in Jammer, 1999, p. 264.

[32] Harris, 2000, p. 161.

[33] Whitehead, 1968, p. 138.

[34] Quoted in Barrow and Tipler, 1988, p. 472.

[35] Waldo-Schwartz, 1975, p. 34.

[36] Whitehead, 1967, p. 34.

[37] McKenna and McKenna, 1975, p. 32. Much of the analysis of Whitehead that follows relied upon some of the insights of McKenna and McKenna found in Chapter 3 of this book, "Organismic Thought."

[38] Whitehead, 1967, p. 35.

[39] Whitehead, 1968, p. 146.

[40] Whitehead, 1967, p. 58.

[41] Whitehead, 1967, p. 71.

[42] Whitehead, 1967, p. 91.

[43] Smolin, 1997, p. 57.

[44] McKenna, 1975, p. 32.

[45] Whitehead, 1968, p. 158.

[46] Zuckerkandl, 1969, p. 254.

[47] Rothstein, 1995.

[48] Rothstein, 1995, p. 109.

[49] Rothstein, 1995, pp. 125-126.

[50] Kafatos and Nadeau, 1990, p. 122.

[51] Zuckerkandl, 1969, p. 263.

[52] Kafatos and Nadeau, 1990, p. 175.

[53] Julian Huxley, Introduction to *The Phenomenon of Man,* Teilhard de Chardin, 1961, p. 13.

[54] Interestingly, this is similar to the Kabbalistic concept of time, whereby time is not seen as linear, but as "a process, in which past, present, and future are bound to each other, not only by cause and effect but also a harmonization of two motions: progress forward and a countermotion backward, encircling and returning. It is more like a spiral, or a helix, rising up from Creation…." Steinsaltz, 1980, p. 74. Thus, the past keeps coming back, so that it may even be modified in the present, a fact known to all psychoanalytically informed psychologists.

[55] Rosen, 1991.

[56] Rosen, 1991.

[57] Quoted in Barrow and Tipler, 1988, p. ix.

[58] To put it another way, *memory* is awareness of the internal relationship of time's flow (in contrast to *history,* which chronicles only the external relations of time).

[59] Harding, 1979, p. 60.

[60] Jonas, 1996, p. 169.

[61] Birch, in Russell et al., 1998, p. 236, emphasis mine.

[62] Smolin, 1997, pp. 251, 253.

[63] Bernard d'Espagnat, quoted in Kafatos & Nadeau, 1999, p. 78.

[64] Andrew Cochran, quoted in Murchie, 1978, p. 411.

[65] Loewenstein, 1999, p. 312.

[66] Loewenstein, 1999, p. 314,

[67] Smoley, 1997, p. 103.

[68] Rolston, 1999, p. xv.

[69] Birch, in Russell, et al., 1998, p. 240.

[70] Taylor, 1975, p. 144.

[71] Schopenhaur,1974, p. 50.

**Book 2,** pages 59-87

[1] Jonas, 1966, p. 3.

[2] Jonas, 1996, p. 180.

[3] Sri Aurobindo, 1994, p. 86.

[4] Lewontin, 2000b, p. 104.

[5] Jonas, 1996, p. 59.

[6] Ashish, 1970, p. 271.

[7] And here we are generously leaving aside the problem of Godel's theorem, which in any event mandates that it is impossible to formulate a nontrivial mathematical system without using assumptions that are not accounted for by the system.

[8] Harris, 1977, p. 55.

[9] Harris, 1965, p. 188.

[10] Harris, 1965, p. 196.

[11] Harding, 1979, p. 84.

[12] Rosen, 2000, p. 59.

[13] Teilhard de Chardin, 1965, p. 78.

[14] Loewenstein, 1999, p. xvi.

[15] Weaver, 1995, p. 139.

[16] Rosen, 2000, p. 36. This is one of the fundamental arguments that pervades Rosen's thinking.

[17] According to Jaki (2002), no amount of observations allows us to make the inductive leap to a "cosmos," that is, the strict totality of all materially interacting things.

[18] Another of Rosen's (1991) central arguments.

[19] W. Smith, 1984, p. 37. Rosen (1991) makes this point as well.

[20] Underhill, 1955, p. 30.

[21] Lewontin, 2000a, p. 4.

[22] Barfield, 1988, p. 39.

[23] Smith, 1984, p. 37.

[24] Martin Lings, quoted in Smith, 1984, p. 157.

[25] Hans Jonas, quoted in Weaver, 1995, p. 95.

[26] Rosen, 2000, p. 113.

[27] Rosen, 2000, p. 90.

[28] Harding, 1979, p. 111.

[29] Denton, 1998, p. 296.

[30] Polanyi, 1968, p. 229.

[31] Polanyi, 1968.

[32] Maritain, 1998, p. 29.

[33] Denton, 1998, p. 213.

[34] I believe this is found in Ward, 1996.

[35] Kurt Godel, quoted in Berlinski, 1998, p. 402.

[36] Jaki, 1999, p. 82.

[37] Barfield, 1965, p. 64.

[38] Attributed to the German biologist E. von Brucke, quoted in Jaki, 1999, p. 88.

[39] Morowitz, 1992, p. 4.

[40] Morowitz, 1992, p. 32.

[41] Crick, 1981, p. 88.

[42] Actually, *much* worse odds, if we accept the calculations of Stanley Jaki (1999), who has noted the central importance of the moon to the development of life, and just how unlikely were the events that gave us our "governess of floods" (Shakespeare) to create tide pools where life first left the oceans.

[43] Although Robert Wright (2000) argues strongly in his *Nonzero* that the evolution of conscious, intelligent life was inevitable, based on game theory.

[44] Whitehead, 1958.

[45] Rosen, 2000, p. 107.

[46] Another of Rosen's main arguments.

[47] Wilber, 1999, p. 22.

[48] Denton, 1998, p. 340.

[49] Charles Birch, in Russell, et al., 1998, p. 238.

[50] Harris, 2000, p. 123.

[51] Rosen, 2000, p. 124.

[52] Jaki, 2000, p. 10.

[53] Murchie, 1978, p. 412.

[54] Polanyi, 1967, p. 44.

[55] Weaver, 1995, p. 150.

[56] Jaki, 1999, p. 85.

[57] Interestingly, I find that those who most vocally accuse religionists of being literal-minded fundamentalists are every bit as literal about religion as those they criticize. No remotely sophisticated notion of Spirit could be so easily lampooned and dismissed.

[58] Harris, 1987, p. 30.

[59] Harris, 1993, p. 453.

[60] Harris, 1977, p. 69.

[61] Harris, 1958, p. 93.

[62] Weaver, 1995, p. 18.

[63] Harris, 1977, p. 69.

[64] Weaver, 1948, p. 51,

[65] Smith, 1984, p. 90.

[66] Sri Aurobindo, 1993, p. 137.

[67] Molnar, 1996, p. 117.

[68] This section is very much influenced by Hans Jonas, 1966.

**Book 3,** pages 89-184

[1] A phrase coined by Robert Anton Wilson.

[2] Blake, 1941, pp. 989, 1023.

[3] "The formative power in the universe is the power of imagination.... the fact that ordinary men are able to make no effective use of this means of knowing is because, as with any other faculty that is insufficiently used and trained, their imagining power remains in a childish and practically useless state.... Unable to be used as an instrument of knowing, for most people it is wasted in idle day-dreaming." Sri Krishna Prem, 1969, p. 87. Properly understood, imagination is a "transformer" or "mode of sensitivity" that serves as a "living membrane between the unknown and known...." Thompson, p. 96.

[4] Becker, 1997, p. 87.

[5] Mithen, p. 116.

[6] Klein & Edgar, 2002, p. 99.

[7] Dates have been assembled from various sources. Again, please don't hold me to them, otherwise you will miss the timeless forest for the date trees.

[8] Ridley, 2003, p. 35.

[9] But as recently as just 500–300,000 years ago, according to Klein and Edgar, 2002, p. 157.

[10] Klein & Edgar, 2002, p. 155.

[11] While there is some suggestion that our Neanderthal cousins might have been up to something perhaps 100,000 years ago, for example, occasionally burying their dead with tools, the evidence is "fragmentary and open to a number of conflicting interpretations" (Pfeiffer, 1982, p. 11).

[12] Teilhard de Chardin,1965, p. 165.

[13] Pfeiffer, 1982, p. 11.

[14] Jaynes, 1976, p. 9.

[15] McCrone, 1991, p. 13.

[16] Koestler, 1978, p. 275.

[17] Miller, 2000, p. 17-18.

[18] Ridley, 2003, p. 224.

[19] Ridley, 2003, p. 20.

[20] Pfeiffer, 1982, p. 9.

[21] Tomberg, 1992, p. 221.

[22] Quoted in Pinker, 2002, p. 296.

[23] Not to say that group cohesion through collective self-delusion has not been (and does not continue to be) an important factor in human adaptation, just not in the way most anthropologists and historians understand it. See chapter 3.4.

[24] Miller, 2000.

[25] Sri Aurobindo, 1962, p. 133.

[26] Sullivan,1960, p. 5.

[27] *Philosophy of Religion,* vol., ii, 1994, p. 8.

[28] Balthasar quoted in Oakes, 1994, p. 190.

[29] Quoted in Barfield, 1988, p. 128.

[30] Cutsinger, 1997, pp. 125, 128, 123.

[31] Schuon, quoted in Cutsinger, 1997, p. 111.

[32] Cutsinger, 1997, p. 129.

[33] Pfeiffer, 1982, p. 5.

[34] Campbell, 1983, p. 63.

[35] Campbell, 1983, p. 64.

[36] Joyce, *Finnegans Wake.*

[37] Jaynes, 1976, p. 9.

[38] Magee, 1998, p. 144.

[39] Magee, 1997, p. 266.

[40] Satprem, 1984, p. 200.

[41] McKenna, in Abraham, Mckenna & Sheldrake, 1992, p. 50.

[42] Sri Aurobindo, 1962, p. 134.

[43] Merrell-Wolff, 1994, p. 42.

[44] Wolfgang Smith, 1984, p. 146.

[45] Wolfgang Smith, 1984, p. 146.

[46] Heschel, 1996, p. 4.

[47] Quoted in Young, 2002, p. 112.

[48] Miller, 2000, p. 370.

[49] Jaki, 2002, p. 8.

[50] Taylor, 1975, p. 19.

[51] "Cosmion" is one of the many neologisms coined by Eric Voegelin.

[52] Sri Aurobindo, 1972, p. 88.

[53] Pierre-Joseph Bonnaterre, quoted in Shattuck, 1980, p. 18.

[54] Schore, 2003b, p. 3.

[55] Schore, 2003b, p. 4.

[56] Schore, 2003b, p. 13.

[57] Schore, 2003b, p. 41.

[58] A term coined by Colin Wilson, but which I will be using in a more specific sense, discussed at length below.

[59] Francine Prose quoting Watson in a review of "Raising America" by Ann Hulbert, in the *Los Angeles Times Book Review,* April 20, 2003.

[60] D. W. Winnicott, quoted in Schore, 2003a, p. 221.

[61] Pierre Janet, quoted in Schore, 2003a, p. 187.

[62] Pinker, 2002, p. 62.

[63] Schore, 2003a, p. 33.

[64] Schore, 2003a, p. 72.

[65] Schore, 2003a, p. 271.

[66] This is such a rich subject, that I could not possibly do justice to it in the context of this book, and have necessarily simplified it to the bare minimum. For further

study, recommended books include any by Allan Schore, *Becoming Attached,* by Robert Karen, and *The Developing Mind,* by Daniel Siegel.

[67] Karen, 1994, p. 374.

[68] Karen, 1994, p. 396.

[69] Karen, 1994, p. 396.

[70] The term "object" is an unfortunate and misleading holdover from Freud's obsolete metapsychology, which conceptualized the earliest relationships as taking place between an *instinct* and its *object.* Modern "object relations" psychoanalysis focuses on the internalized relationship between *two subjects,* but confusingly retains the old nomenclature.

[71] Grotstein, 2000, p. 154.

[72] Grotstein, 2000, p. 158.

[73] In Schore, 1994, p. xxv.

[74] Schore, 1994, p. 62.

[75] Grotstein, 2000, p. 446.

[76] Horner, in Schore, 1994, p. 446.

[77] Schore, 1994, p. 446.

[78] Pinker, 2002, p. 392. Of course, Pinker does not believe that this implies an immaterial soul, but that our genes are somehow fully responsible for our personality. Such a metaphysically challenged view makes reincarnation appear plausible by comparison.

[79] Powell, 2002, p. 62.

[80] John Bowlby, quoted in Karen, 1994, p. 65.

[81] Here again, these dates and events were compiled from various, sometimes conflicting sources, and are subject to constant revision.

[82] For a more detailed explanation, see Stanley's (1996) *Children of the Ice Age,* which I have largely relied upon here.

[83] LaBarre, 1970, p. 86.

[84] Mithen, 1996, p. 209.

[85] Klein & Edgar, 2002, p. 272.

[86] LaBarre, 1991, p. 23.

[87] LaBarre, 1991, p. 34. I hear a cacophony of voices in my head complaining about my "stereotypical" characterization of female nurturing. First, I have no interest in mixing perennial psychology and contemporary politics, but more importantly, our primary concern here is the evolution of the helpless baby, so settle down.

[88] The idea of the child-as-savior is clearly recognized in world mythologies, for example, in the baby Jesus of Christianity. An infant in particular is seen as the innocent redeemer of a weary and guilt-stained humanity, a fresh start with open-ended potential, free of the accumulated psychological "toxins" of the world.

[89] LaBarre, 1991, p. 38.

[90] Schore, 2003a, p. 80, emphasis mine.

[91] Morgan, 1995, p. 171.

[92] Miller, 2000, p. 86.

[93] Miller, 2000, p. 95.

[94] Miller, 2000, p. 95.

[95] "Marriage Lowers Testosterone," Cromie, *AOL Gazette,* September 29, 2002.

[96] Powell, 2002, p. 549.

[97] Tomberg, 1997, p. 83.

[98] Kingsland, 1958, p. 208.

[99] Powell, 2002, p. 576.

[100] Tomberg, 1992, p. 104.

[101] McKenna, 1991, p. 100.

[102] Tomberg, 1992, p. 122.

[103] Voegelin, in Federici, 2002, p. 90.

[104] Perhaps I should emphasize that mind parasites are ultimately ephemeral human creations that operate "horizontally" as long as there are human minds to host them. This is in stark contrast to spiritual entities, which operate *vertically* (from a higher realm into our own) and preexist the human beings that may open themselves to their influence.

[105] Grotstein, 2000, p. 152.

[106] McKenna, in Abraham, et al.,1992, p. 92.

[107] LaBarre, 1954, p. 270.

[108] Bion, 1967, p. 112.

[109] Sagan, 1974, p. xv.

[110] Ortega Y Gassett, 1957, pp. 156-157.

[111] Bion, 1967, p. 114.

[112] Becker, 1997, p. 190. Importantly, this is not to say that good and evil do not exist, only that mind parasites cause psychological splitting, so that good is just as likely to be called evil, and evil good. It is not morality that motivates such individuals, but aggression toward what has been externalized.

[113] Godwin, 1994, pp. 17–39.

[114] McLeod, 2001, p. 211.

[115] Murray, 2003, p. 87.

[116] LaBarre, 1954, p. 248.

[117] LaBarre, 1954, p. 226.

[118] LaBarre, 1954, p, 234.

[119] Harris, 2004, pp. 8, 9.

[120] Sagan, 1988, p. 52.

[121] LaBarre, 1970, p. 22.

[122] Mouravieff, 1989, p. 99.

[123] Mill, 1859, p. 86.

[124] Murray, 2003, p. 161.

[125] Schoeck, 1966, p. 9.

[126] Jonas, 1966, p. 7.

[127] Elgin, 1993, pp. 34-35.

[128] deMause, 2002, p. 251.

[129] deMause, 2002, p. 254.

[130] LeBlanc, 2003, p. xi.

[131] LeBlanc, 2003, p. 8.

[132] LeBlanc, 2003, p. 95.

[133] Edgerton, 1992, p. 1.

[134] Edgerton, 1992, p. 15.

[135] Edgerton, 1992, p. 140.

[136] Sandall, 2001, p. 101.

[137] R. Hotz, *Deciphering the Miracles of the Mind,* Los Angeles Times, p. A1.

[138] Becker, 1997, p. 149.

[139] Ehrenreich, 1997, p. 61.

[140] Burkert, 1983, pp. 2, 13.

[141] Burkert, 1983, p. xii.

[142] Bailie, 1997, p. 16.

[143] Edgerton, 1992, p. 92.

[144] Rascovsky, 1995, p. 22.

[145] Grotstein, 2000, p. 176.

[146] Rascovsky, 1995, p. 107.

[147] Grotstein, 2000, pp. 247, 242.

[148] Neumann, 1970, p. 40.

[149] Bailie, 1997, p. 13.

[150] Bailie, 1997, p. 28.

[151] Bailie, 1997, p. 127.

[152] Keeley, 1996, pp. 37, 39.

[153] Keeley, 1996, p. 67.

[154] Keeley, 1996, p. 93.

[155] Dodds, 1951, p. 41.

[156] Dodds, 1951, p. 41.

[157] Gress, 1998, p. 60.

[158] deMause, 2002, p. 258.

[159] Breiner, 1990, p. 48.

[160] Gress, 1998, p. 79.

[161] Mouravieff, 1989, p. xxv.

[162] Breiner, 1990, pp. 29, 30.

[163] Neumann, 1970, p. 272.

[164] Neumann, 1970, p 79.

[165] Neumann, 1970, p. 350.

[166] Quoted in Postman, 1994, p. 8.

[167] Breiner, 1990, pp. 50, 51.

[168] Harris, 2004, p. 80.

[169] Harris, 2004, p. 123.

[170] Elias, "The Civilizing of Parents," in Goudsblom & Mennell, 1998, p. 192.

[171] Gress, 1998, p. 80.

[172] Gress, 1998, p. 195.

[173] Manchester, 1992, p. 3.

[174] Neumann, 1970, p. 271.

[175] Manchester, 1992, pp 21-27.

[176] Barzun, 2000, p. 24.

[177] Barzun, 2000, p. 25.

[178] Tuchmen, 1978, p. 34,.

[179] Tuchman, 1978, pp. 49, 52.

[180] Huizinga, 1996, p. 17.

[181] Huizinga, 1996, pp. 20-21.

[182] Huizinga, 1996, pp. 282-284.

[183] Huizinga, 1996, p. 29.

[184] Huizinga, 1996, p. 27.

[185] Stone, 1977, p. 77.

[186] Stone, 1977 p. 78.

[187] Stone, 1977, p, 80.

[188] Cleaver and Dod, quoted in Postman, 1994, p. 47.

[189] Stone, 1977, p. 80.

[190] La Barre, 1970, p. 18.

[191] Stein, 1987.

[192] Weaver, 1995, p. 93.

[193] Sandall, 2001, p. 12,

[194] Keen, quoted in Sandall, 2001, p. 13.

[195] *Popper,* 1971.

[196] Weaver, 1995, p. 76.

[197] *Newsweek,* April 19, 1999. "Children of the Ice," by Sharon Begley. By no means is this an aberration. In an article by P. Vesilind in the October 2003 issue of *National Geographic,* anthropologist Alejandro Terrazas tells us that "When a Maya priest made a sacrifice, he was operating in his special universe—helping that universe continue. Good or bad aren't factors. I don't want to make moral determinations; I want to understand." The point is that it is not possible to understand a "special universe" that feeds on human blood from *within* that universe, because sacred violence is its very foundation. To question it is to awaken from the cultural nightmare that sanctifies and legitimizes these sadistic impulses.

[198] Sandall, 2001, p. 37.

[199] Pinker, 2002, pp. 66, 67.

[200] Thomas Sowell, quoted in Pinker, 2002, p. 67.

[201] Etounga-Manguelle, in Harrison & Huntington, 2000, pp. 70-71.

[202] Etounga-Manguelle, in Harrison & Huntington, 2000, p. 73.

[203] Atlantic Monthly, Oct. 2002. "The Next Christianity," by Philip Jenkins, p. 60.

[204] Sandall, 2001, p. 36.

[205] Sandall, 2001, p. 116.

[206] Popper, quoted in Sandall, 2001, p. 118.

[207] *Los Angeles Times,* August 16, 1998. "Africa's Silent Shame," by Dean Murphy, p. A1.

[208] deMause, 2002, p. 40.

[209] *Los Angeles Times,* September 17, 2002, p. A1.

[210] Psychiatrist Irwin Savodnik, reviewing "Honor Lost," Norma Khouri, in *The Weekly Standard,* June 16, 2003.

[211] Psychiatrist Irwin Savodnik, reviewing "Honor Lost," Norma Khouri, in *The Weekly Standard,* June 16, 2003.

[212] From the website *www.memri.org,* which provides direct translations of Arab media.

[213] *Los Angeles Times,* May 19, 1996. "Tales of Bloodthirsty Beast Terrifying Mexico," Mark Fineman, p. A1, 6.

[214] *Los Angeles Times,* May 3, 1997. "Egyptian Women Scarred by Hate," John Daniszewski, p. A1.

[215] Taylor, 1989, pp. 185-186, emphasis mine.

[216] Muller, 2002, p. 169.

[217] Taylor, 1989, p. 188.

[218] Faivre & Needleman, 1995, p. 26

[219] Schuon, in Cutsinger, 1997, p. 50.

[220] LaBarre, 1954, p. 237.

[221] *Los Angeles Times,* July 4, 2003, "The Powerful Pull of Freedom," Dinesh S'Souza, (emphasis mine).

[222] Taylor, 1975, p. 10.

[223] Wilson, 1977, pp. 77, 24.

[224] Erdmann & Stover, 1991, p. 96.

[225] LaBarre, 1970, p. xv.

[226] Book Four explains how.

[227] Rudhyar, 1983, pp. 13, 14.

[228] Rudhyar, 1983, p. 22.

[229] The Mother, 1977, CW vol. 9, p. 46.

[230] Sagan, quoted in LaBarre, 1991, p. 39.

[231] LaBarre, 1954, p. 244.

[232] Pieper, 1989, p. 59.

[233] Another word from *Finnegans Wake.*

[234] This sounds like Jonas again (1966), to whom I am more than happy to give credit. I have read his brief introduction to *The Phenomenon of Life* so many times that it has become part of me, and for a long time served almost as a "koan" as I puzzled over the question of what Life could *be.*

[235] Becker, *The Heavenly City of Eighteenth-Century Philosophers,* quoted in Jaki, 2000, p. 69-70.

[236] Oakes, 1994, p. 37.

[237] Reich, 1953, p. 3-4.

**Book 4,** pages 430-575

[1] Powell, 2002, p. 243.

[2] Federici, 2002, p. xxi.

[3] Mouravieff, 1989, p. 70.

[4] Smoley, 2002, p. 52.

[5] Schuon, in Cutsinger, 1997, p. 51; Cutsinger, p. 51.

[6] Pryse, 1910, p. 8.

[7] "[T]here is a universal tradition about moments in which men have slipped out of time into eternity.... It is as if one were to find a keyhole through which one may pass into a world...." Watts, 1994, pp. 79, 80. "Entrances to holiness are everywhere.... Culture and organized religion conspire to trick us into believing that [they] are only at predictable times and prearranged places." Kushner, 1977, pp. 48, 56.

[8] Sri Aurobindo Birth Centenary Library, 1972, vol. 16, pp. 291-292.

[9] *All India Magazine*, August 2002, Sri Aurobindo, p. 14.

[10] Heschel, 1966, p. 231.

[11] Sullivan, 1960, p. 10.

[12] Magee (1997) uses the light analogy, although to illustrate something else.

[13] Damascene, 1999, p. 24.

[14] *Sri Aurobindo Birth Centenary Library*, 1972, vol. 22, pp 189-90.

[15] *Sri Aurobindo Birth Centenary Library*, 1972, vol. 22, pp 189-90.

[16] Heschel, 1966, p. 99.

[17] Smoley, 2002, pp. 2, 6.

[18] Kingsland, 1958, p. 49.

[19] von Bruck, 1991, p. 59.

[20] Markides, 2001, p. 48.

[21] Heschel, 1966, p. 168.

[22] Radhakrishnan, 1923, Vol 2, p. 516.

[23] Plotinus, 1964, p. 78.

[24] Radhakrishnan, 1923, Vol 2, pp. 515, 518.

[25] Nikhilananda, 1946, p. 17.

[26] Words, according to Bion, are "containers" of meaning. He coined the term "saturated" to describe a word that was so filled with preconceived meaning that it was no longer free to accumulate meaning based on experience, and to therefore *evolve.*

[27] Heschel, 1966, p. 11.

[28] Funk, 1998, pp. 9, 24.

[29] McLeod, 2001, p. 9.

[30] Huxley, 1992, p. 13.

[31] Huxley, 1992, p. 13.

[32] Federici, 2002, p. 224.

[33] Federici, 2002, p. 224.

[34] Dawson, 2002, p. xxxix.

[35] Merrell-Wolff, 1994, p. x.

[36] Pearce, 2002, p. 1.

[37] Merrell-Wolff, 1994, p. 24.

[38] Or, let us say that Christianity hasn't been able to unify science and revelation since Aquinas, and that perhaps it is time for an update.

[39] Pryse, 1910, p. 2.

[40] Schuon, in Nasr, 1986, p. 69.

[41] Ashish, in Ginsburg, 2001, p. 87.

[42] Magee, 1999, p. 371.

[43] Reddy, 1984, p. 132.

[44] Young, 2002, p. 91.

[45] Harris, 1977, p. 89.

[46] Young, 2002, p. 103,

[47] Harris, 2004, pp. 137-141.

[48] Cutsinger makes the important point that the logos "did not become *a* man, as one too often hears. He became man, with the result that our human nature as such has been infused… with the very nature of God." 2003, p. xviii.

[49] Magee, 1997, p. 6.

[50] Harris, 2004, p. 148.

[51] Harris, 2004, p. 151.

[52] Schuon, in Nasr, 1986, p. 71.

[53] Radhakrishnan, Vol 2, p. 512 [emphasis mine].

[54] Schuon, in Cutsinger, 1997, p. 89.

[55] Oakes, 1994, p. 67.

[56] "Science cannot be established in terms of art nor art in terms of science. Why, then, should faith depend for its validity upon justification by science?" Heschel, p. 171.

[57] Heschel, 1966, p. 30.

[58] Smith, in Borella, 2001, p. xii.

[59] Kass, 2003, p. 54 (emphasis mine). Kass' book is mainly a philosophical and anthropological reading that reveals eternal wisdom about such things as male-female relations, parenting, brotherhood, education, justice, and morality. As such, Kass discovers in the Torah a universality with regard to leading a good life in this

world, but he does not touch on a universal esoteric spirituality, as the present book attempts.

[60] Mouravieff, 1992, p. xviii (emphasis mine).

[61] Needleman, in Faivre & Needleman, 1995, p. xxiv.

[62] What follows (and parts of what preceded), it should be acknowledged, was very much inspired, if not purloined, from W. R. Bion, who recognized the identical problems afflicting psychoanalysis. In a series of classic works in the 1960s, he endeavored to create an "unsaturated" language for psychoanalytic observation and communication, in large measure because of the great number of competing, overly abstract or concrete psychoanalytic theories. For the record, he also used the symbol "O" to represent the ultimate unknowable reality, but as it applied to the evolving experience between analyst and patient.

[63] "Faith is relation to God; belief a relation to an idea or a dogma." "Reason seeks to integrate the unknown with the known; faith seeks to integrate the unknown with the divine." Heschel, 1966, pp. 166, 171. To put it another way, conventional education is an assimilation of the known, whereas spiritual education involves a conquest of the unknown.

[64] Mouravieff, 1989, p. 3.

[65] Pearce, 2002, p. 201.

[66] Wilber, 2000, p. 12.

[67] Ashish, in Ginsburg, 2001, p. 61.

[68] Pieper, 1999, p. 87.

[69] Sri Aurobindo, 1976, p. 66.

[70] Sri Aurobindo, 1970, p. 47.

[71] Smoley, 2002, p. 75.

[72] Smoley, 2002, p. 160.

[73] Smoley, 2002, p. 180.

[74] McDermott, in Faivre & Needleman [eds], 1995, p, 290.

[75] Sri Krishna Prem, 1969, p. 18. The "back yard" analogy was used by Wilson (1967).

[76] Evidently, we play host to about four thousand distinct thoughts in a typical day, one hundred million in an average lifetime. Markides, 2001, p. 119. Now we know

how many thoughts it takes to fill the average soul (I'd love to turn them off).

[77] Sri Aurobindo, On Himself, p. 83.

[78] McLeod, 2001, pp. 74, 212.

[79] McLeod, 2001, p. 209.

[80] Sri Aurobindo in *All India Magazine,* "Yoga: Its Meaning and Objects," August 2002, p. 36.

[81] Sri Aurobindo in *All India Magazine,* "Yoga: Its Meaning and Objects," August 2002, p. 36.

[82] Michael Holdrege, quoted in Steiner, 1994a, p. xvii.

[83] Schuon, in Nasr, p. 68.

[84] Bruteau, 1993, p. 27.

[85] Powell, 2002, p. 71.

[86] Smoley, 2002, p. 185.

[87] Powell, 2002, p. 79.

[88] von Bruck, 1991, p. 192.

[89] Amis, 1995, p. 175.

[90] Steinsaltz, 1980, p. 128,

[91] Easwaran, 1987, p. 87.

[92] Powell, 2002, p. 11.

[93] Sri Aurobindo, 1972, vol. 22, p. 475.

[94] White, 1990, p. 14.

[95] Smoley, 2002, p. 97.

[96] von Bruck, 1991, p. 110.

[97] Smoley, 2002, p. 244.

[98] Harris, 1993, p. 110.

[99] In Cutsinger, 1997, p. 182.

[100] Damascene, 1999, p. 287.

[101] Sri Aurobindo, quoted in Satprem, 1984, p. 256.

[102] Kingsland, 1958, p. 36.

[103] Adiswarananda, 2003, p. 318.

[104] Damascene, 2003, p. 311.

[105] Smoley & Kinney,1999, p. 62.

[106] von Bruck, 1991, p. 245.

[107] Oakes, 1994, p. 196.

[108] Merrell-Wolff, 1994, p. 84.

[109] Merrell-Wolff, 1994, p. 85

[110] *Romans* 12:1.

[111] Nasr, 1993, p. 131.

[112] Heschel, 1966, p. 58.

[113] von Bruck, 1991, p. 110.

[114] Choudhary, 1981, p. 221.

[115] Merrell-Wolff, 1994, p. 20.

[116] Bruteau, 1993, p. 19.

[117] Tomberg, 1992, p. 130.

[118] Upanishad translations are by Prabhavananda & Manchester, unless otherwise noted.

[119] Kushner, 1998, p. 51.

[120] Tomberg, 1992, p. 146.

[121] Tomberg, 1992, p. 146.

[122] Markides, 2001, p. 119.

[123] That is, while we call God "God," God calls himself "I AM," just as you do not refer to yourself in the third person (unless you are a self-absorbed professional athlete).

[124] Easwaran, 1987, p. 141.

[125] Powell, 2002, p. 298.

[126] Bollas, 1995, pp. 189, 193.

[127] Tomberg, p. 198.

[128] Easwaran, 1987, p. 209.

[129] *Purusha* is the absolute soul or conscious principle of the cosmos, *maya* the phenomenal world of nature.

[130] Mouravieff, 1989, p. 163, paraphrasing Talleyrand.

[131] Space doesn't permit a full explication of just what this means, but it is the essence of modern psychoanalytic thought. Books I would recommend include *The Matrix of the Mind* by Thomas Ogden, *The Shadow of the Object* by Christopher Bollas, *The Developing Mind* by Daniel Siegal, and *Who is the Dreamer Who Dreams the Dream* by James Grotstein.

[132] Easwaran, 1987, p. 209.

[133] Michael Nagler, in Easwaran, 1987, p. 290.

[134] Strong, 1948, p. 118.

[135] Heschel, 1966, p. 182.

[136] Merrell-Wolff, 1994, p. 40; Mouravieff, 1989, p. 44.

[137] von Bruck, 1991, p. 17.

[138] Griffiths, 1980, p. 187.

[139] von Bruck, 1991, p. 20.

[140] The Mother (Mirra Richard),1984, p. 124.

[141] In Cutsinger, 2003, p. 216.

[142] Teilard quoted in King, 1999, p. 39. Kushner, 1977, pp. 144, 149.

[143] Borella, in Cutsinger, 2003, p. 46.

[144] Of course, the Book of Genesis tells us that the Tree of Life is guarded by sword-wielding cherubim. But this "defense is not absolute and general; it is *specific*." That is, it is a defense against the will-to-power and domination that typifies the attitude of scientific materialism, "which is prevented by the flaming sword of the Garden of Eden from repeating the act committed with respect to the Tree of Good and Evil.... Instead of putting forward his hand to *take*, the human being opens his mind, his heart and his will to *receive* that which will be graciously bestowed upon him...." Powell, 2002, p. 68. In other words, the flaming sword "invites, encourages and directs all those who are worthy, and all that which is worthy in each person, to the benefits of the Tree of Life; and forbids, discourages and sends

away all those who are unworthy...." Powell, 2002, p. 69.

**Cosmobliteration,** notes 576-643 as footnotes, pages 246-262

**Autobibliography and Self References,** pages 271-278

[1] Although a sadhak of Sri Aurobindo's yoga, I am happy to be inclusively described as a Judeo-Vedantic esoteric Christian taoist yogic hermeticist.

[2] Quoted in Oakes, 1994, p, 174.

[3] Balthasar, in Oakes, 1994, p. 148.

[4] Perhaps I should say "re-alerted," for my doctoral dissertation (later published in 1991) was on the holistic physics of David Bohm and how it related to modern psychoanalytic metapsychology.

[5] Among words that may be found in *Finnegans Wake* are jewsus, notshall, and remurmur. For that matter, I recently discovered that Blake used "nobodaddy" in one of his poems.

[6] In those few pages you will find allusions to Van Morrison's "Astral Weeks," "Higher Than the World," "In the Garden," and "Into the Mystic"; George Harrison's "I Me Mine"; Bob Dylan's "Mr. Tambourine Man" and "Chimes of Freedom"; the Beatles' "Tomorrow Never Knows" and "She Said She Said"; The Byrds' "Eight Miles High" and "The Ballad of Easy Rider"; Frank Sinatra's "Come Fly with Me"; Nick Drake's "River Man"; the Beach Boys' "Feel Flows"; John Coltrane's "A Love Supreme"; Chick Corea's "Return to Forever"; Steely Dan's "Show Biz Kids"; David Bowie's "Starman"; the Talking Heads' "Once In a Lifetime"; The Friends of Distinction's "Grazing in the Grass"; Linda Lyndell's "What a Man"; and Echo & the Bunnymen's "Crystal Days"; not to mention passages inspired by ESPN's Chris Berman, The Beverly Hillbillies, Bruce Springsteen, Pascal, Ken Wilber, The Church of the Subgenius (PO Box 140306, Dallas, TX), T. S. Eliot, Homer Simpson, Molly Bloom, John Cleese's "Fawlty Towers," and John Lennon's account of how the Beatles were given their name by a man on a flaming pie.

# Bibliography

Abhishiktananda, S. (1989). *His Life Told Through His Letters.* Delhi, India: ISPCK.

Abraham, R., McKenna, T., Sheldrake, R. (1992). *Trialogues on the Edge of the West.* Santa Fe, NM: Bear & Co.

Adiswarananda, S. (2003). *Meditation and Its Practices.* Woodstock, VT: Skylight Paths.

Amis, R. (1995). *A Different Christianity.* Albany, NY: State University of New York Press.

Anonymous [Tr. Robert Powell]. (2002). *Meditations on the Tarot.* New York: Jeremy Tarcher.

Ashish, S. (1970). *Man, Son of Man.* Wheaton, IL: The Theosophical Publishing House.

Aurobindo, Sri. (1962). *The Human Cycle, The Ideal of Human Unity, War and Self-Determination.* Pondicherry: Sri Aurobindo Ashram Trust.

———. (1970). *The Life Divine.* Pondicherry: Sri Aurobindo Ashram Trust.

———. (1972). *On Himself.* Pondicherry: Sri Aurobindo Ashram Trust.

———. (1976). *The Synthesis of Yoga.* Pondicherry: Sri Aurobindo Ashram Trust.

———. (1993). *Savitri.* Pondicherry: Sri Aurobindo Ashram Trust.

———. (1993). *The Hour of God* (pamphlet). Pondicherry: Sri Aurobindo Ashram Trust.

———. (1994). *The Upanishads.* Pondicherry: Sri Aurobindo Ashram Trust.

———. (1972). Sri Aurobindo Birth Centenary Library. Pondicherry: Sri Aurobindo Ashram Trust.

———. (2002). "Life and Yoga." *All India Magazine.* August.

Bailie, G. (1997). *Violence Unveiled.* New York: Crossroad.

Balthasar, H. (1982). *The Glory of the Lord: A Theological Aesthetics Vol 1.* San Francisco: Ignatius Press.

Baron-Cohen, S. (1997). *Mindblindness: An Essay on Autism and Theory of Mind.* Cambridge, MA: MIT Press.

Barfield, O. (1988). *Saving the Appearances.* Hanover, NH: Wesleyan.

Barrow, J., & Tipler, F. (1988). *The Anthropic Cosmological Principle.* Oxford: Oxford University Press.

Barzun, J. (2000). *From Dawn to Decadence: 1500 to the Present.* New York: Harper Collins.

Becker, E. (1997). *The Denial of Death.* New York: The Free Press.

Berger, P. (1990). *A Rumor of Angels.* New York: Anchor.

Berlinski, D. (1998). "Godel's Question." In Dembski, ed., 1998.

Bion, W. (1967). *Second Thoughts.* New York: Jason Aronson.

Birch, C. (1998). "Neo-Darwinism, Self-Organization, and Divine Action." In Russell, et al, [eds], *Evolutionary and Molecular Biology.*

Bishop, J. (1986). *Joyce's Book of the Dark.* Madison, WI: The University of Wisconsin Press.

Blake, W. (1941). *The Complete Poetry of William Blake.* New York: Modern Library.

Boaz, N. (1997). *Eco Homo.* New York: Basic.

Bollas, C. (1995). *Cracking Up: The Work of Unconscious Experience.* New York: Hill and Wang.

Borella, J. (2001). *The Secret of the Christian Way.* Albany, NY: State University of New York Press.

Breiner, S. (1990). *Slaughter of the Innocents: Child Abuse Through the Ages and Today.* New York: Plenum.

Brockman, J. (1995). *The Third Culture.* New York: Touchstone: Harper & Row

Bruteau, B. (1993). *Radical Optimism.* New York: Crossroad.

———. (1997). *God's Ecstasy: The Creation of a Self-Creating World.* New York: Crossroad.

Burkert, W. (1983). *Homo Necans: The Anthropology of Ancient Greek Sacrificial Ritual and Myth.* Berkeley, CA: University of California Press.

Campbell, J. (1974). *The Mythic Image.* Princeton, NJ: Princeton University Press.

———. (1983). *The Way of the Animal Powers,* Vol. 1, Historical Atlas of World Mythology. London: Alfred van der Marck Editions.

Campbell, J., and Robinson, H. (1980). *A Skeleton Key to Finnegans Wake.* New York: Penguin.

Chariton, I. (1966). *The Art of Prayer: An Orthodox Anthology.* London: Faber and Faber Limited.

Chesterton, G. (1995). *Orthodoxy.* San Francisco, CA: Ignatius.

Choudhary, K. (1981). *Modern Indian Mysticism.* Delhi: Motilal Banarsidass.

Clement, O. (1993). *The Roots of Christian Mysticism.* Hyde Park, NY: New City.

Crick, F. (1988). *Life Itself.* New York: Simon & Schuster.

Cutsinger, J. (1987). *The Form of Transformed Vision.* Macon, GA: Mercer University.

———. (1997). *Advice to the Serious Seeker.* Albany, NY: State University of New York Press.

——-. (2003), *Not of This World: A Treasury of Christian Mysticism.* Bloomington, IN: World Wisdom.

Dalal, A., ed. (2001). *A Greater Psychology: An Introduction to the Psychological Thought of Sri Aurobindo.* New York: Jeremy Tarcher.

Damascene, H. (1999). *Christ the Eternal Tao.* Platina, CA: Valaam.

Darling, D. (1993). *Equations of Eternity.* New York: Hyperion.

Davies, P. (1992). *The Mind of God.* New York: Simon and Schuster.

Dembski, W. [ed]. (1998). *Mere Creation.* Downers Grove, IL: InterVarsity.

Dawson, C. (2002). *Dynamics of World History.* Wilmington, DE: ISI.

Denton, M. (1998). *Nature's Destiny.* New York: Free Press.

Deussen, P. (1995). *The System of the Vedanta.* Delhi: D. K. Publishers.

Deutsch, E. 1973). *Advaita Vedanta.* Honolulu, HI: University of Hawaii Press.

Dodds, E. (1951). *The Greeks and the Irrational.* Berkeley, CA: University of California Press.

Dowman. K. (1980). *The Divine Madman.* Clearlake, CA: Dawn Horse Press.

Easwaran, E. (1987). *The Upanishads.* Tomales, CA: Nilgiri Press.

Eccles, J. (1984). *The Human Mystery.* London: RKP.

Edgerton, R. (1992). *Sick Societies.* New York: Free Press.

Ehrenreich, B. (1997). *Blood Rites: Origins and History of the Passions of War.* New York: Henry Holt and Company.

Einstein, A. (1931). *Ideas and Opinions—The World as I See It.* New York: Random House/Modern Library.

Elgin, D. (1993). *Awakening Earth.* New York: William Morrow and Company.

Erdmann, E. & Stover, D. (1991). *Beyond a World Divided.* Boston: Shambhala.

Faivre, A., & Needleman, J. [eds]. (1995). *Modern Esoteric Spirituality.* New York: Crossroad.

Federici, M. (2002). *Eric Voegelin.* Wilmington, DE: ISI.

Ferguson, K. (1994). *The Fire in the Equations.* London: Bantam.

Fox, M. (1982). *Meditations with Meister Eckhart.* Santa Fe, NM: Bear & Co.

Frankl, G. (1990). *Archaeology of the Mind.* London: Open Gate.

Funk, M. (1998). *Thoughts Matter: The Practice of Spiritual Life.* New York: Continuum.

Gelernter, D. (2002). "Judaism Beyond Words." *Commentary,* Vol. 114, No 2, pp. 39-45.

Ginsburg, S. (2001). *In Search of the Unitive Vision.* Boca Raton, FL: New Paradigm.

Godwin, R. (1991). Wilfred Bion and David Bohm. "Toward a Quantum Metapsychology." *Psychoanalysis and Contemporary Thought,* Vol. 14, No 4.

———. (1994). "Psychoanalysis, Chaos and Complexity: The Evolving Mind as a Dissipative Structure." *Journal of Melanie Klein and Object Relations,* Vol. 12, No. 2.

Goodwin, B. (1994). *How the Leopard Changed Its Spots: The Evolution of Complexity.* New York: Scribner.

Goudsblom, J., and Mennell, S. [eds]. (1998). *The Norbert Elias Reader.* Oxford: Blackwell.

Gress, D. (1998). *From Plato to NATO.* New York: Free Press.

Griffiths, B. (1980). *The Golden String.* Springfield, IL: Templegate.

Grotstein, J. (2000). *Who Is the Dreamer Who Dreams the Dream?* Hillsdale, NJ: Analytic Press.

Guenon, R. (1981). *Man and His Becoming.* New Delhi: Oriental Book Reprint Corporation.

———. (1984). *The Multiple States of Being.* Burdett, NY: Larson Publications.

Hall, M. (1988). *The Secret Teachings of All Ages.* Los Angeles: Philosophical Research Society.

Harding, D. (1979). *The Hierarchy of Heaven and Earth.* Gainesville, FL: University Press of Florida.

Harris, E. (1958). *Revelation Through Reason.* New Haven, CT: Yale University Press.

———. (1965). *The Foundations of Metaphysics in Science.* London: Allen and Unwin.

———. (1977). *Atheism and Theism.* Atlantic Highlands, NJ Humanities Press International.

———. (1987). *Formal, Transcendental, and Dialectical Thinking.* New York: State University of New York Press.

———. (1988). *The Reality of Time.* Albany, NY: State University of New York Press.

———. (1993). *The Spirit of Hegel.* Atlantic Highlands, NJ: Humanities Press International.

———. (2000). *The Restitution of Metaphysics.* Amherst, NY: Humanity.

Harris, L. (2004). *Civilization and its Enemies: The Next Stage of History.* New York: Free Press.

Harrison, L., and Huntington, S., [eds]. (2000). *Culture Matters: How Values Shape Human Progress.* New York: Basic Books.

Haught, J. (2000). *God After Darwin.* Boulder, CO: Westview.

Hawking, S. (1988). *A Brief History of Time.* New York: Bantam.

Heschel, A. (1966). *Man is Not Alone.* New York: Harper & Row.

Hiley, B., & Peat, D. [eds]. (1987). *Quantum Implications.* New York: RKP.

Hotz, R. "Deciphering the Miracles of the Mind." *Los Angeles Times,* October 16, 1996, p. A1.

Huizinga, J. (1996). *The Autumn of the Middle Ages.* Chicago: University of Chicago Press.

Huxley, A. (1970). *The Perennial Philosophy.* New York: Harper Colophon.

———-. (1992). *Huxley and God.* New York: Harper Collins.

Isherwood, C., and Prabhavananda, S. (1987, 1944). *Bhagavad Gita.* Hollywood: Vedanta Society of Southern California.

Jacobs, M. (2000). *Illusion: A Psychodynamic Interpretation of Thinking and Belief.* London: Whurr.

Jaki, S. (1999). *Means to Message.* Grand Rapids, MI: Wm B. Eerdmans.

———-. (2000). *The Limits of a Limitless Science.* Wilmington, DE: ISI Books.

———-. (2002). A Mind's Matter. Grand Rapids, MI: Wm. B. Eerdmans.

Jammer, M. (1999). *Einstein and Religion.* Princeton, NJ: Princeton University Press.

Jastrow, R. (1979). *God and the Astronomers.* New York: Harper & Row.

Jaynes, J. (1976). *The Origin of Consciousness in the Breakdown of the Bicameral Mind.* Boston: Houghton Mifflin.

Jonas, H. (1966). *The Phenomenon of Life: Toward a Philosophical Biology.* Chicago: University of Chicago Press.

———-. (1996). *Mortality and Morality: A Search for the Good After Auschwitz.* Evanston, IL: Northwestern University Press.

Joyce, J. (1959, 1939). *Finnegans Wake.* New York: Viking.

Kafatos, M., and Kafatos, T. (1991). *Looking In Seeing Out: Consciousness and Cosmos.* Wheaton, IL: Theosophical Publishing House.

Kafatos, M., and Nadeau, R. (1990). *The Conscious Universe.* New York: Springer.

———-. (1999). *The Non-Local Universe.* New York: Oxford University Press.

Kapleau, P. (1980). *Zen: Dawn in the West.* New York: Anchor/Doubleday.

Karen, R. (1994). *Becoming Attached: First Relationships and How They Shape Our Capacity to Love.* New York: Oxford University Press.

Kass, L. (2003). *The Beginning of Wisdom.* New York: Free Press.

Keeley, L. (1996). *War Before Civilization.* New York: Oxford University Press.

King, U., [ed]. (1999). *Pierre Teilhard de Chardin.* Maryknoll, NY: Orbis.

Kingsland, W. (1958). *The Gnosis or Ancient Wisdom in the Christian Scriptures.* London: George Allen & Unwin.

Klein, R., and Edgar, B. (2002). *The Dawn of Culture.* New York: John Wiley & Sons.

Koestler, A. (1972). *The Roots of Coincidence.* London: Hutchinson.

——-. (1978). Janus: A Summing Up.

Krishna Prem, Sri, and Madhava Ashish, Sri. (1969). *Man, The Measure of All Things.* Wheaton, IL: Theosophical Publishing House.

Kushner, L. (1977). *Honey from the Rock.* Woodstock, VT: Jewish Lights.

——-. (1981). *The River of Light.* Woodstock, VT: Jewish Lights.

——-. (1998). *Eyes Remade for Wonder.* Woodstock, VT: Jewish Lights.

——-. (2001). *The Way Into the Jewish Mystical Tradition.* Woodstock, VT: Jewish Lights.

LaBarre, W. (1954). *The Human Animal.* Chicago, IL: University of Chicago Press.

——-. (1970). *The Ghost Dance: The Origins of Religion.* Garden City, NY: Doubleday & Company.

——-. (1991). *Shadow of Childhood.* Norman, OK: University of Oklahoma Press.

Leary, T., Metzner, R., Alpert, R. (1964). *The Psychedelic Experience.* Seacaucus, NJ: Citadel.

LeBlanc, S. (2003). *Constant Battles: The Myth of the Peaceful,* Noble Savage. New York: St. Martin's Press.

Lewontin, R. (2000a). *The Triple Helix.* Cambridge, MA: Harvard University Press.

——-. (2000b). "It Ain't Necessarily So: The Dream of the Human Genome and Other Illusions." *New York Review of Books.*

Lipsey, R. (1988). *An Art of Our Own: The Spiritual in Twentieth Century Art.* Boston: Shambhala.

Loewenstein, W. (1999). *The Touchstone of Life.* New York: Oxford University Press.

Lossky, V. (2002). *The Mystical Theology of the Eastern Church.* Crestwood, NY: St. Vladimir's Seminary Press.

MacFarlane, A. (2000). *The Riddle of the Modern World.* New York: Palgrave.

Magee, B. (1997). *The Philosophy of Schopenhaur.* New York: Oxford University Press.

——-. (1998). *The Story of Thought.* London: Dorling Kindersley.

——-. (1999). *Confessions of a Philosopher.* New York: Modern Library.

Manchester, W. (1992). *A World Lit Only by Fire.* Boston: Little, Brown.

Markides, K. (2001). *The Mountain of Silence.* New York: Doubleday.

McCrone, J. (1991). *The Ape That Spoke.* New York: Avon.

McKenna, T. (1991). *The Archaic Revival.* New York: HarperCollins.

McKenna, T., and McKenna, D. (1975). *The Invisible Landscape.* New York: Seabury.

McLeod, K. (2001). *Waking Up to Your Life.* New York: HarperCollins.

Merrell-Wolff, F. (1994). *Experience and Philosophy.* Albany: State University of New York Press.

Mill, J. S. (1956, 1859). *On Liberty.* New York:Liberal Arts.

Miller, G. (2000). *The Mating Mind.* New York: Doubleday.

Mitchell, S. [tr]. (1988). *Tao Te Ching.* New York: Harper & Row.

Mithen, S. (1996). *The Prehistory of the Mind.* New York: Thames and Hudson.

Muller, J. (2002). *The Mind and the Market.* New York: Knopf.

Murray, C. (2003). *Human Accomplishment.* New York: HarperCollins.

Molnar, T. (1996). *Archetypes of Thought.* New Brunswick, NJ: Transaction.

Morgan, E. (1995). *The Descent of the Child.* New York: Oxford University Press.

Morowitz, H. (1992). *Beginnings of Cellular Life: Metabolism Recapitulates Biogenesis.* New Haven, CT: Yale University Press.

Mother, The (Mirra Richards). (1977). *Collected Works.* Pondicherry: Sri Aurobindo Ashram Trust.

———. (1984). *On Thoughts and Aphorisms.* Pondicherry: Sri Aurobindo Ashram Trust.

Mouravieff, B. (1989). *Gnosis, Book One: The Exoteric Cycle.* East Sussex, Great Britain: Agora Books.

———. (1992). *Gnosis, Book Two: The Mesoteric Cycle.* Exeter, Great Britain: BPCC Wheatons.

———. (1993). *Gnosis, Book Three: The Esoteric Cycle.* Exeter, Great Britain: BPCC Wheatons.

Muggeridge, M. (2002). *A Third Testament.* Farmington, PA: Plough.

Munitz, M. (1986). *Cosmic Understanding.* Princeton, NJ: Princeton University Press.

Murchie, G. (1978). *The Seven Mysteries of Life.* Boston: Houghton Mifflin.

Nasr, S. (1986). *The Essential Writings of Fritjof Schuon.* Rockport, MA: Element.

———. (1993). *The Need for a Sacred Science.* Albany, NY: State University of New York Press.

Neville, R. (1993). *Eternity and Time's Flow.* Albany, NY: State University of New York Press.

Neumann, E. (1970). *The Origins and History of Consciousness.* Princeton, NJ: Bollingen.

Nikhilananda. (1946). *Self-Knowledge.* New York: Ramakrishna-Vivekananda Center.

———. (1949). *The Upanishads, Volume One.* New York: Ramakrishna-Vivekananda Center.

———. (1952). *The Upanishads, Volume Two.* New York: Ramakrishna-Vivekananda Center.

——. (1956). *The Upanishads, Volume Three.* New York: Ramakrishna-Vivekananda Center.

——. (1959). *The Upanishads, Volume Four.* New York: Ramakrishna-Vivekananda Center.

——. (1963). *The Upanishads* (one volume abridgment). New York: Harper & Row.

Oakes, E. (1994). *Pattern of Redemption: The Theology of Hans Urs von Balthasar.* New York: Continuum.

Ortega y Gassett (1957) *The Revolt of the Masses,* New York: Norton.

Overman, D. (1997). *A Case Against Accident and Self-Organization.* New York: Rowman & Littlefield.

Pagels, E. (1981). *The Gnostic Gospels.* New York: Vintage.

Peacocke, A. (1993). *Theology for a Scientific Age.* Minneapolis, MN: Fortress.

Pearce, J. (2002). *The Biology of Transcendence.* Rochester, VT: Park Street.

Pfeiffer, J. (1982). *The Creative Explosion.* New York: Harper & Row.

Pieper, J. (1989). *An Anthology.* San Francisco: Ignatius.

——. (1999a). *Leisure the Basis of Culture.* Indianapolis, IN: Liberty Fund.

——. (1999b). *The End of Time.* San Francisco: Ignatius.

Pinker, S. (2002). *The Blank Slate.* New York: Viking.

Plotinus. (1964). *The Essential Plotinus,* translation by E. O'Brien. Indianapolis, IN: Hackett.

Polanyi, M. (1967). *The Tacit Dimension.* New York: Anchor Books.

——. (1968). *Knowing and Being.* Chicago: University of Chicago Press.

Polanyi, M., and Prosch, H. (1975). *Meaning.* Chicago: University of Chicago Press.

Popper, K. (1977). *The Open Society and Its Enemies.* Princeton, NJ: Princeton University Press.

Postman, N. (1994). *The Disappearance of Childhood.* New York: Vintage.

Powell, R. [tr]. (2002). *Meditations on the Tarot.* New York: Jeremy Tarcher.

Pryse, J. (1965, 1910). *The Apocalypse Unsealed.* Pomeroy, WA: Health Research.

Radhakrishnan, S. (1923). *Indian Philosophy,* Volumes One & Two. New York: Oxford University Press.

——. (1939). *Eastern Religions & Western Thought.* New York: Oxford University Press.

Rascovsky, A. (1995). *Filicide: The Murder, Humiliation, Mutilation, Denigration. and Abandonment of Children by Parents.* Northvale, NJ: Jason Aronson.

Reddy, V. (1984). *Metahistory.* Pondicherry, India: Aurodarshan Trust.

Reich, W. (1953). *The Murder of Christ.* New York: Simon & Schuster.

Ridley, M. (2003). *Nature via Nurture.* New York: HarperCollins.

Rolston, H. (1999). *Genes, Genesis and God.* Cambridge University Press.

Rosen, R. (1991). *Life Itself.* New York: Columbia University Press.

———. (2000). *Essays on Life Itself.* New York: Columbia University Press.

Rothstein, E. (1995). *Emblems of Mind: The Inner Life of Music and Mathematics.* New York: Avon.

Rudhyar, D. (1983). *Rhythm of Wholeness.* Wheaton, IL: Theosophical Publishing House.

Russell, J., Stoeger, W., & Ayala, F., [eds]. (1998). *Evolutionary and Molecular Biology: Scientific Perspectives on Divine Action.* Notre Dame, IN: University of Notre Dame Press.

Sagan, E. (1988). *Freud, Women and Morality: The Psychology of Good and Evil.* New York: Basic.

Sandall, R. (2001). *The Culture Cult.* Boulder, CO: Westview.

Satprem. (1984). *Sri Aurobindo or The Adventure of Consciousness.* New York: Institute for Evolutionary Research.

Schoeck, H. (1966). *Envy: A Theory of Social Behavior.* Indianapolis, IN: Liberty Fund.

Schopenhaur, A. (1966). *The World as Will and Representation.* New York: Dover.

———. (1974). *The Fourfold Root of the Principle of Sufficient Reason.* La Salle, IL: Open Court.

Schore, A. (1994). *Affect Regulation and the Origin of the Self.* Hillsdale, NJ: Lawrence Erlbaum Associates.

———. (2003a). *Affect Dysregulation and Disorders of the Self.* New York: W. W. Norton & Company,

———. (2003b). *Affect Regulation and the Repair of the Self.* New York: W. W. Norton & Company.

Schumacher, E. (1977). *A Guide for the Perplexed.* New York: Harper & Row.

Shankara (1947). *Crest-Jewel of Discrimination.* Hollywood, CA: Vedanta Press.

Shattuck, R. (1980). *The Forbidden Experiment.* New York: Farrar Straus Giroux.

Siegel, D. (1999). *The Developing Mind.* New York: Guilford

Smith, H. (1965). *The Religions of Man.* New York: Harper & Row.

Smith, W. (1984). *Cosmos & Transcendence.* Peru, IL: Sherwood Sugden & Company, Publishers.

———. (1995). *The Quantum Enigma.* Peru, IL: Sherwood Sugden & Company.

Smoley, R. (2002). *Inner Christianity.* Boston: Shambhala.

Smoley, R., and Kinney, J. [eds.] (1999). *Hidden Wisdom,* New York: Penguin/Arkana.

Smolin, L. (1997). *The Life of the Cosmos.* New York: Oxford University Press.

Spencer-Brown, G. (1973). *Laws of Form.* New York: E.P. Dutton.

Spilsbury, R. (1974). *Providence Lost: A Critique of Darwinism.* London: Oxford University Press.

Stanley, S. (1996). *Children of the Ice Age.* New York: Harmony.

Stein, H. (1987). *Developmental Time, Cultural Space.* Norman, OK: University of Oklahoma Press.

Steiner, R. (1994a). *Theosophy.* Hudson, New York: Anthroposophic Press.

——-. (1994). *How to Know Higher Worlds.* New York: Anthroposophic Press.

Steinsaltz, A. (1980). *The Thirteen Petalled Rose.* New York: Basic.

Stone, L. (1977). *The Family, Sex and Marriage in England 1500-1800.* New York: Harper Torchbooks.

Strong, M. (1948). *Letters of the Scattered Brotherhood.* New York: HarperCollins.

Sullivan, J. (1960). *Beethoven: His Spiritual Development.* New York: Vintage.

Taylor, C. (1975). *Hegel.* New York: Cambridge University Press.

——-. (1989). *Sources of the Self.* Cambridge: Harvard University Press.

Teilhard de Chardin, P. (1965). *The Phenomenon of Man.* New York: Harper & Row.

Thompson, W. (1989). *Imaginary Landscape.* New York: St. Martin's .

Tomberg, V. (1992). *Covenant of the Heart.* Rockport, MA: Element.

Tuchman, B. (1978). *A Distant Mirror: the Calamitous 14th Century.* New York: Alfred A. Knopf.

Underhill, E. (1955). *Mysticism.* Cleveland, OH: Meridian Books.

von Bruck, M. (1991). *The Unity of Reality,* New York: Paulist Press.

Ward, K. (1996). *God, Chance & Necessity.* Rockport, MA: Oneworld Publications.

Waldo-Schwartz, P. (1975). *Art and the Occult.* New York: George Braziller.

Warr, K. (1979). *The Orthodox Way.* Crestwood, NY: St. Vladimir's Press.

Watts, A. (1957). *The Way of Zen.* New York: Vintage.

——-. (1958). *Nature, Man and Woman.* London: Thames and Hudson.

——-. (1968). *Does It Matter?* New York: Vintage.

——-. (1994). *Talking Zen.* New York: Weatherhill.

Weaver, R. (1948). *Ideas Have Consequences.* Chicago: University of Chicago Press.

——-. (1995). *Visions of Order.* Wilmington, DE: ISI.

White, J. (1990). *The Meeting of Science and Spirit.* New York: Paragon House.

Whitehead, A. N. (1967). *Science and the Modern World.* New York: Free Press.

——-. (1958). *Introduction to Mathematics.* Oxford: Oxford University Press

——-. (1960). *Religion in the Making.* New York: Meridian.

——-. (1968). *Modes of Thought.* New York: Free Press.

Wilber, K. (2000). *Integral Psychology.* Boston: Shambhala.

——-. (1995). *Sex, Ecology, Spirituality.* Boston: Shambhala.

——-. (1999). *One Taste.* Boston: Shambhala.

Wilson, C. (1967). *The Mind Parasites.* Berkeley, CA: Oneiric.

——-. (1985). *Rudolf Steiner: The Man and His Vision.* Wellingborough, Northamptonshire: Aquarian.

Winnicott, D. (1965). *The Maturational Processes and the Facilitating Environment.* New York: International Universities Press.

Woodroffe, J. (2001). *The World as Power.* Madras, India: Ganesh & Company.

Wright, R. (2000). *Nonzero.* New York: Pantheon.

Young, F. (2002). *Virtuoso Theology.* Eugene, OR: Wipf and Stock Publishers.

Zuckerkandl, V. (1969). *Sound and Symbol: Music and the External World.* Princeton: Bollingen.

# Index